A Partisan Church

TODD SCRIBNER

A Partisan CHURCH

American
Catholicism
and the Rise of
Neoconservative
Catholics

THE CATHOLIC UNIVERSITY OF AMERICA PRESS
Washington, D.C.

Text design by Kachergis Book Design, Pittsboro, NC

Library of Congress Cataloging-in-Publication Data
Scribner, Todd.
A partisan church : American Catholicism and the rise of
neoconservative Catholics / Todd Scribner.
pages cm
Includes bibliographical references and index.
ISBN 978-0-8132-2729-0 (pbk. : alk. paper) 1. Catholic Church—
United States—History—20th century. 2. Catholic Church—
United States—History—21st century. 3. Conservatism—United
States—History—20th century. 4. Conservatism—United States—
History—21st century. 5. Conservatism—Religious aspects—
Catholic Church—History—20th century. 6. Conservatism—
Religious aspects—Catholic Church—History—21st century.
I. Title.
BX1406.3.S37 2015
282'.7309045—dc23
2014039457

CONTENTS

PREFACE

IN HIS BOOK *The Restructuring of American Religion* Robert Wuthnow highlighted some of the fundamental shifts that occurred in American religion during the second half of the twentieth century. Preeminent among them was the decline of denominational affiliation as a defining marker of religious identity and, in its stead, the increasing importance of political ideology. As political orientation became increasingly salient as a marker of religious identity, long-standing animosities between competing denominational identities—Catholic and Protestant in particular—declined. As a consequence, adherents of traditionally competing denominations began to work more closely together in the public sphere. Likewise, those of the same tradition were often pitted against one another as liberal and conservative factions within the tradition struggled to achieve competing ends. Conflict within long-standing denominational structures became more pointed and the continuity that existed within these structures began to fragment.

In the early stages of research for this book, I was intrigued by Wuthnow's proposition and interested in exploring how this trend contributed to American Catholic identity in the post–World War II period. I narrowed my focus to a small but influential band of intellectuals that emerged in the mid-seventies: the neoconservative

The opinions expressed in this book are those of the author and do not necessarily represent the policies or positions of the United States Conference of Catholic Bishops.

Catholics. Originally composed of Richard John Neuhaus, Michael Novak, and George Weigel, they were active in the public sphere, vied for policies that lined up with their political worldview, and were often critical of religious contemporaries who disagreed with them.

A longtime Lutheran pastor, Richard John Neuhaus served for seventeen years at a predominately black Lutheran church in Brooklyn, New York.[1] During this period, the heyday of which occurred during the sixties, he became intimately involved in both the civil rights and antiwar movements. Working alongside other prominent religious figures, including Daniel Berrigan and Rabbi Abraham Joshua Heschel, Neuhaus was active in the antiwar movement and critical of the use of American power overseas. By the early seventies he had grown estranged from the liberal, Democratic worldview that he had once embraced and within a few years broke away from many of the contemporaries with whom he once associated, as his own views began shifting to the right and many of his former allies continued on a leftward path. Although a supporter of Jimmy Carter during the 1976 election, he soon grew disenchanted with what Carter had to offer and within a few short years expressed, even if only privately at first, sympathy for a Reagan-style Republicanism.[2]

Coming to prominence in the 1960s, Michael Novak had spent an extended period in the seminary, beginning in the late forties and extending throughout most of the next decade. After abandoning his studies for the priesthood he began graduate studies at Harvard, garnered a reputation as a left-wing Catholic intellectual, and published a series of high-profile books on issues related to the church and American political life.[3] After leaving Harvard, Novak

1. More will be said below on the logic of including Richard John Neuhaus, a Lutheran at the time, in the same category as the neoconservative Catholics.

2. For some biographical insights, see John Allen, "Fr. Richard John Neuhaus, Dead at Age 72," *National Catholic Reporter,* January 8, 2009, http://ncronline.org/news/people/fr-richard-john-neuhaus-dead-age-72 (accessed March 2, 2013); Damon Linker, *The Theocons: Secular America under Siege* (New York: Doubleday, 2006). In Linker's book, see in particular ch. 1.

3. Some of Novak's more important early works that often define his left-wing period

took a teaching position at Stanford and, in 1968, transferred to the State University of New York at Old Westbury. It was during his teaching stint at Old Westbury, along with his ongoing involvement with the antiwar movement, that he too began to grow alienated from the far-left-wing politics with which he had been associated for at least the previous decade. By the mid-seventies Novak, like Neuhaus, began to shift rightward on the political spectrum. By 1980 he had abandoned support of socialism, embraced democratic capitalism, and eventually accepted the designation of neoconservative.[4]

George Weigel provides a slightly different portrait than either Neuhaus or Novak. Growing up in 1960s Baltimore, Weigel was a generation younger than both of them. A theology student in both college and graduate school during the late sixties and early seventies, Weigel did not become an active participant in the antiwar movement. He was not directly engaged in the theological disputes that raged in the years immediately following the Second Vatican Council, although his theological studies during this period certainly made him aware of the general tenor of the debate. After leaving a teaching position at a seminary in Washington State, he worked at the World without War Council, an institute headed by the pacifist antiwar activist Robert Pickus. Weigel's early writings focused extensively on issues related to war and peace and, while he never embraced pacifism, the influence of Pickus was undeniable. As with his counterparts, Weigel eventually embraced the neocon-

---

include *The Open Church: Vatican II, Act II* (New York, Macmillan, 1964); *Belief and Unbelief: A Study of Self Knowledge* (Macmillan, 1965); *Theology for Radical Politics* (New York: Herder and Herder, 1969).

4. For more autobiographical information on Novak, see *Confession of a Catholic* (San Francisco: Harper and Row, 1983); "Controversial Engagements," *First Things* (April 1999), http://www.firstthings.com/article.php3?id_article=3136&var_recherche=controversial+engagements (accessed March 2, 2013); "Errand into the Wilderness," *On Cultivating Liberty: Reflections on Moral Ecology* (Lanham, Md.: Rowman and Littlefield, 1999), 259–304. For a critical, yet generally fair account of Novak's thought and development during this period and afterward, see Gary Dorrien, *The Neoconservative Mind* (Philadelphia: Temple University Press, 1993). Novak's most comprehensive autobiographical publication is his memoir: see *Writing from Left to Right: My Journey from Liberal to Conservative* (New York: Crown, 2013).

servative designation. That said, given the generational differences, his transition from liberal to neoconservative was not as publicly controversial as it was for Neuhaus or Novak nor is it accessible via his public writings.[5]

Their mutual shift from liberal to conservative allied the three with like-minded conservative intellectuals who were suspicious of the growing welfare state and supportive of the "Reagan revolution." Politics was an important component of their religious identity, in part because of their efforts to reconcile their political and religious worldview. Sometimes it is difficult to determine which of these two elements was preeminent. Nevertheless, as my research progressed it also became clear that there is a specifically religious component to their thought that is not reducible to the purely political. Following the Second Vatican Council the fragmentation that was already occurring due to political differences within the church was exacerbated as competing interpretations related to the meaning of Vatican II proliferated throughout the American Catholic community. Debates within the church not only took place along political lines but also focused on fundamental questions regarding what it means to be Catholic.

One of the central lines along which differences emerged and on which the neoconservative Catholics focused related to ecclesiology. This emphasis has been generally overlooked in the secondary literature written on the neoconservative Catholics. I thought it important to rectify this oversight and, in addition to their specifically political interests, highlight those areas where ecclesiological questions were important. Not to include a focus on the latter elements of their thought has the unfortunate tendency to distort their thinking. Consequently, the central task of this book is to clarify their political perspective and understand it in light of their broader religious self-understanding, all the while emphasizing the ecclesiological underpinnings of their worldview.

5. For a semi-autobiographical account of Weigel, see *Letters to a Young Catholic* (New York: Basic Books, 2004).

To do this, and with respect to the use of sources, I focused on their published material with a particular emphasis on resources published before the end of the Cold War. I chose the period roughly associated with the fall of the Soviet Union as the end point in my study because with its end the lines that defined political debate in American life changed significantly. Following the Cold War, debates tended to focus on the role of American power in a post-Soviet world and on domestic, culture-war phenomena, both of which came into the ascendant. To trace out the thought of the neoconservative Catholics on this new array of issues in addition to their Cold War thinking would quickly become unwieldy. Their post-Cold War thought is deserving of a separate study.

The astute reader will notice that the total number of publications of Michael Novak's cited surpass that of Richard John Neuhaus and George Weigel, thus possibly giving the impression that the analysis provided herein is skewed toward Novak's worldview to the detriment of the other two. This is not the case. Given that George Weigel is a generation younger than both Novak and Neuhaus he did not begin to publish material regularly until the late seventies. By virtue of the fact that this book ends with the close of the Cold War there is a limited number of publications of Weigel from which to draw, but certainly plenty to define his thinking as it was during that period. On the other hand, Richard John Neuhaus is a contemporary of Novak and was prolific as a writer from the 1960s onward, thus giving the impression that there would be a roughly equivalent number of sources to use from each thinker. This is probably true; nevertheless, I found that during this period Neuhaus tended to focus on a somewhat more narrow range of issues than did Novak. Citing the works of Neuhaus simply to achieve an equal number of citations ran the risk of redundancy. I am confident that what I included of his accurately reflects his thought during this period. I leave it to others to decide whether this is so.

❖ INTRODUCTION

THE YEARS FOLLOWING the Second Vatican Council signified a period of rupture and turmoil in the American Catholic Church. If the problem was not with the council's actual teachings, as it was for some, the reception of those teachings often caused a sense of disorientation, as Catholics of every stripe sought to reconfigure the boundaries of what it meant to be a Catholic in the modern world. One area particularly affected was Catholic intellectual life. Writing shortly after the council closed and reflecting on some of the disruptions that were already being felt, Philip Gleason noted that "Catholic intellectual positions that once seemed permanently established dissolved, leaving even Catholic philosophers, theologians, and moralists feeling as though they have nothing distinctive to say as Catholics."[1]

More than two decades later, Patrick Allitt echoed Gleason's sentiment, arguing that the church's once distinctive and widely shared intellectual worldview had undergone a period of "gradual erosion." These differences were evident on issues of theological importance. This erosion was also of consequence on a range of political and cultural questions. Liberal Catholics, conservative Catholics, neoconservative Catholics, traditionalist Catholics, and others began to compete with one another to define what constituted a Catholic

1. Philip Gleason, "Catholicism and Cultural Change in the 1960s," *The Review of Politics* 34, no. 4, (October 1972), 96.

worldview, thus making it nearly impossible to pinpoint a "Catholic position" on any given topic that would be satisfactory to everyone involved.[2]

Accompanying the fragmentation of American Catholic intellectual life, secular politics was undergoing its own disruptions. Political conservatism, which had been bubbling under the surface of American life since the mid-fifties, surged during the seventies. This was accompanied by the rise of a religiously based political conservatism, perhaps most clearly typified by Jerry Falwell, Pat Robertson, and the Moral Majority. Having broken off from their liberal counterparts during that same period, the political neoconservatives became a prominent fixture in American politics for the next three decades. Their emergence signified the contentious character of Democratic politics following the nomination of George McGovern in 1972. The new left, feminism, various liberation movements, and other related political movements further differentiated the political scene. Foreign policy questions related to the Cold War and U.S. intervention overseas, on the one hand, and domestic issues related to abortion, race, and the economy on the other contributed to an increasingly partisan political tone in the following decades. By the early eighties conservative thought had become increasingly polarized, with the emergent conservative movement becoming primarily ensconced within the ranks of the Republican Party and political liberalism within the Democratic one.

The seventies and eighties also marked a period in which many Americans were concerned about the possibility of American decline: a failed war in Vietnam, a faltering economy, insecurity in relation to the Soviet Union, and a sense of cultural dissolution. The concern over political and cultural decline reflected a broader national public mood, which expressed "a much deeper pessimism about the state of America and its future, and a growing rejection of

2. Patrick Allitt, *Catholic Intellectuals and Conservative Politics in America, 1950–1985* (Ithaca, N.Y.: Cornell University Press, 1993), 1–15.

recent liberal orthodoxies."[3] Was America in a position from which it could continue to lead the free world or had its glory days come and gone? Reflecting a pessimistic sentiment, one essay written in *Newsweek* responded in the early seventies to this hypothetical, declaring that "we have arrived at a plateau in our history, the years of middle and decline."[4] Responding to these challenges and to questions fundamental to American identity were a backdrop to many of the debates that were occurring during this period.

The polarization that was occurring in secular political life had important implications for American religion. In the decades following World War II religious identity in the United States was marked by a decline in the importance of denominationalism and the ascendance of political ideology as an increasingly significant marker in the public religion. Given the state of relations between Catholics and Protestants as late as mid-century, this shift was as unexpected as it was important. Throughout the 1940s and into the following decade, Protestant animosity toward Catholics was pointed, with the National Association of Evangelicals at one point passing a resolution that the Catholic Church upheld "Satanic ideologies," the Presbyterian Church adopting a statement at its annual meeting condemning the worship of Mary among Catholics, and the Episcopal Church warning against marriage to Catholics.[5]

As Catholics began to enter into the mainstream by mid-century, such overt forms of animosity began to wane. In part due to the GI Bill and other government-funded programs, education levels among Catholics increased significantly, which in turn enhanced social mobility from blue- to white-collar professions.[6] These developments contributed to a much wider geographical displacement of Catho-

---

3. Philip Jenkins, *Decade of Nightmares: The End of the Sixties and the Making of Eighties America* (New York: Oxford University Press, 2006), 4.

4. Quoted in Bruce Schulman, *The Seventies: The Great Shift in American Culture, Society, and Politics* (Cambridge, Mass.: Da Capo Press, 2002), 49.

5. Robert Wuthnow, *The Restructuring of American Religion* (Princeton, N.J.: Princeton University Press, 1990), 74.

6. Ibid, 74–86.

lics and greatly enhanced their interaction with non-Catholics, thus further diminishing anti-Catholic sentiment. Within a few decades, Catholics were no longer the "outsiders" within the American community that they had once been; the long-standing religious tensions that had once functioned as the primary point of division between Catholics and their non-Catholic religious contemporaries had begun to wane. This was indicative of a much broader trend. In the post-war world, the denominational structure that had functioned as the primary marker of religious identity and belonging became "less significant as a basis for social and cultural tensions and divisions."[7] In its place, political affiliation became a more important factor that determined who cooperated with whom and on what issues.

Robert Wuthnow highlighted the importance of this shift toward political identity and away from denominational identity when he noted that "the division between religious liberals and conservatives is one that cuts across denominational lines, rather than pitting one set of denominations against another." Consequently, "conservative Baptists and conservative Catholics may share more in common than conservative Baptists do with liberal Baptists. And liberal Methodists may have greater empathy for liberal Baptists than they do for conservatives in their own denomination."[8] The same sort of logic applied to adherents of the Catholic tradition; as fault lines began to develop between politically liberal and conservative Catholics, their political activities began to correlate more closely with politically like-minded but religiously different individuals and groups.

While it would be an error to exaggerate the monolithic character of American Catholicism in either the period preceding the "decline of denominationalism" or in the pre-Vatican II world, the disruptions that occurred in Catholic intellectual life in the second half of the twentieth century shattered any sort of continuity that existed at an earlier age. Battle lines were quickly drawn between competing camps within American Catholicism on a wide range

7. Ibid, 94.
8. Ibid, 219–21.

of issues that often paralleled those occurring in secular political circles. Ecclesiological concerns also came to the forefront, as Catholics debated the proper locus of power within the church, the role of the laity vis-à-vis the clergy, and the church's relationship to the world.

This book will examine the outline of these disruptions and explore the way in which one group of intellectuals—the neoconservative Catholics—sought to reestablish a coherent and unified Catholic identity through the end of the Cold War. It will focus in particular on the writings of Richard John Neuhaus, Michael Novak, and George Weigel. These three are generally considered among the first wave of neoconservative Catholics that emerged in the late seventies and early eighties. While both Novak and Weigel are clearly identifiable as Catholic throughout the period under discussion and thus deserve inclusion here, given Neuhaus's Protestant identification until the early nineties, why include him among the neoconservative Catholics prior to his conversion? A number of factors feed into the inclusion of Neuhaus in this study.

First, the decrease in the salience of denominational identity played an important role in the formation of this alliance. The Lutheran and Catholic divide that separated Neuhaus from the other two and which, in an earlier day and age, would have effectively prohibited political cooperation, ceased to be a significant barrier in the decades following the Second World War. Second, many of the pieces in his intellectual life were well in place by the mid-eighties and thus continuity exists in his thinking from his pre- to post-religious conversion experience. His publication of *The Catholic Moment* and the ideas expressed therein evidenced a growing sympathy toward the Catholic Church before his actual conversion and, in hindsight, anticipated it. Fourth, while he often focused on the failures of mainline Protestantism in his earlier, pre-Catholic days, the worldview that he espoused was generally consistent with that of both Novak and Weigel. Finally, and perhaps most telling, Weigel himself has identified their writings as traditionally having "been the focus of analysis and critique precisely as 'neoconservative.'"[9] While Neuhaus did not convert until 1991, referring to the three of them as neoconservative Catholics is a useful shorthand, both because it has become an established marker to refer to their worldview and because the shared "family resemblances" that ground their thought are conducive to a corporate analysis.

To understand how the neoconservative Catholics addressed the fragmentation in the Catholic Church it is important to develop a conceptual framework that guided their thought. Chapter 1 will begin to flesh out the theoretical frameworks that informed the neoconservative Catholics' religious and political worldview and in doing so highlight some of the similarities and differences in their writings that allow for their distinctive worldviews to take shape. Neuhaus, Novak, and Weigel affirmed many of the same philosophical commitments, but each constructed a different intellectual framework that they argued could function as a springboard for the renewal of American political and religious life. Grounding these frameworks in a historical narrative helped to give their arguments a greater degree of credibility by decreasing their abstract character and linking them to a specific understanding of the American and Catholic experience. Through this narrative they sought to show that American political life and the Catholic social teaching tradition are compatible and even complementary. The development of these narratives and how they ground their respective intellectual frameworks will be the focus of the second chapter.

The next four chapters will turn to some of the contentious political debates that wracked both the church and secular society during the late seventies and eighties. These chapters will highlight the interplay between Catholic political thought and secular political life on debates that occurred on a wide array of issues and in particular highlight the way in which the neoconservative Catholics navigated

---

9. George Weigel, "The Neoconservative Difference: A Proposal for the Renewal of Church and Society," in *Being Right: Conservative Catholics in America*, ed. Mary Jo Weaver and R. Scott Appleby, 139 (Bloomington: Indiana University Press, 1995).

these issues. Given the intensity of the abortion debate, no analysis of Catholic life would be complete without looking at the manner in which this issue played itself out. What may be surprising is the rather nuanced approach that the neoconservative Catholics took with respect to this issue during the seventies; they did not align themselves with the militant pro-life movement that emerged after *Roe v. Wade*. This will be the subject of chapter 3. Given the time period under discussion Novak and Neuhaus will receive most of the attention while Weigel will be generally overlooked.

While abortion was an issue of importance within Catholic life in the years following the *Roe* decision, the Cold War loomed much larger in neoconservative Catholic thought during this period. Chapter 4 will look at the way in which the neoconservative Catholics engaged the communist threat within a more secular context, while chapter 5 will examine some of the debates that occurred within the church. Chapter 6 will move from the general to the specific and will examine the way the neoconservative Catholics understood the political and social turmoil at work in much of Latin America as a product of Soviet interference. The bulk of this chapter will analyze the way in which the neoconservative Catholics conceptualized the communist threat in the region, their critique of the American bishops' analysis of the Latin American conflicts, and the emergence of liberation theology. The debates that ensued on these issues often broke down along politically "conservative" and "liberal" lines.

The neoconservative Catholics hewed to a more politically conservative agenda, promoted the benefits of democratic capitalism, and affirmed its usefulness in diminishing existing inequities. Both during the Cold War and afterward, they looked to the United States as being in the best position to advance the values and institutional structures consistent with this vision. In contrast, liberal Catholic intellectuals were often skeptical of American power and continually called its leadership to task for failing to advance democratic norms and provide economic opportunity to underrepresented and overlooked populations.[10] These concerns extended beyond a failure of leadership to the validity of the institutional structures that shaped the economic, political, and social relationships internationally. Consequently, it was not unusual to find them supporting liberation movements in Latin America, Africa, and elsewhere, and opposing American efforts overseas, which they believed only served to support American self-interest at the expense of the poor, the downtrodden, and the marginalized of the developing world.[11]

Most disconcerting for the neoconservative Catholics was their perception that liberal factions had succeeded in securing prominent positions of power within the church and, in doing so, were positioned to institutionalize their political vision as though it corresponded to official church teaching. This was evident not only among Catholic social justice activist leadership but among many of the bishops who had, it was argued by the neoconservative Catholics, capitulated to a secular, left-wing political worldview that was inconsistent with a proper understanding of Catholic social teaching. At one point Weigel remarked that following Vatican II "the liberal mainstream seemed to have effectively shut off critical debate within many of the key organizational structures of American Catholicism, imposing its own 'correct' positions with a vigor, indeed ruthlessness."[12]

The distorted vision promoted within these circles found expression in many of the bishops' official teachings, perhaps most notably in their policy proposals related to nuclear weapons, the Cold War, and the economy. By the mid-eighties the left-wing drift of the bishops had become so pronounced on these issues that both Neuhaus and Novak were comfortable in declaring that the National Conference of Catholic Bishops (NCCB) had become "the Democratic

---

10. R. Scott Appleby, "The Triumph of Americanism: Common Ground for U.S. Catholics in the Twentieth Century," in *Being Right,* ed. Weaver and Appleby, 49–50.

11. David O'Brien, "What Happened to the Catholic Left," in *What's Left? Liberal American Catholics,* ed. Mary Jo Weaver et al., 270–72 (Bloomington: Indiana University Press, 1999).

12. Weigel, "The Neoconservative Difference," 145.

Party at prayer."[13] Only decades later, with the election of Cardinal Timothy Dolan of the Archdiocese of New York to the presidency of the United States Conference of Catholic Bishops (USCCB), the most recent iteration of the NCCB, and the informal death of the "Bernardin machine" that followed in its wake, could the neoconservative Catholics breathe a sigh of relief that this liberal Catholic experiment was finally coming to an end.[14]

The neoconservative Catholic critique of the American bishops' political and policy positions is an important theme that runs throughout this book. For some time they were deeply concerned that large swaths of the American Catholic hierarchy had veered far to the left in their political analysis. Given their leadership and teaching role in the church the bishops play an indispensable role in the transmission of the faith to future generations. Failing to properly conceptualize the manner in which the moral and political tradition of the church coincides with the "signs of the times" and the political realities currently at play run the risk of providing a distorted understanding of the faith and its application to "real world" problems.

That said, policy disagreements were not the only, or even the most important, source of division. The fact that the bishops were spending so much effort addressing technical policy questions pointed to a deeper, more troubling problem for the neoconservative Catholics: the growing conviction that the American hierarchy had embraced a deficient and misguided ecclesiology. This point became explicit in their thought some years later when Weigel noted that "the American Catholic neoconservative perspective emerged in the late 1970s and early 1980s out of religious, indeed theological, and specifically ecclesiological concerns."[15] It was their contention that

13. Richard John Neuhaus, "Letter to the Editor," *New York Times,* February 12, 1979, A16; Novak, "A Closed Church, Again," *Commonweal,* February 5, 1982, 113.

14. George Weigel, "The End of the Bernardin Era," *First Things* (February 2011), available at http://www.firstthings.com/article/2011/01/the-end-of-the-bernardin-era (accessed February 16, 2013).

15. Weigel, "The Neoconservative Difference," 138.

the hierarchy's embrace of a faulty ecclesiology distorted their engagement with political affairs because it misconstrued the proper relationship between the church's mission and political life. An in-depth exploration of the neoconservative Catholic ecclesiological critique of the American hierarchy and, more broadly, liberal Catholic leadership will be the focus of the final chapter.

1 ❖ BOTH AMERICAN AND CATHOLIC

ONE OF THE CENTRAL FEATURES of neoconservative Catholic thought consists in the conviction that the American political tradition is compatible with, if not an outgrowth of, the Christian political tradition; support for one reinforces one's support for the other. Such a perspective draws on what David O'Brien has referred to as "republican Catholicism."[1] The republican Catholic worldview expresses a sense of optimism with respect to the "American experiment in ordered liberty" and is generally supportive of appeals to religious liberty and related political values expressed at the founding of the United States. The church historian R. Scott Appleby used O'Brien's terminology to argue that the neoconservative Catholics represent a resurgent republican-style Catholicism that "embraces American ideals unapologetically if not uncritically" and that "defines itself through an interior, privatized piety, on the one hand, and a mutually correcting, public dialogue with non-Catholic Americans, on the other."[2]

The neoconservative Catholics affirmed American ideals through the use of the more neutral, nonsectarian language of the natural

---

1. David O'Brien, *Public Catholicism* (New York: Orbis Books, 1989).
2. Appleby, "The Triumph of Americanism," in *Being Right,* ed. Appleby and Weaver, 40–41.

law. They often engaged non-Catholic, yet like-minded, Christians and other religious bodies as a way to help achieve their political and cultural objectives. Their faith is not, contrary to Appleby's claims, expressive of an "interiorized, privatized piety." Nor does it promote a gauzy and vague Christian foundation for the American republic. George Weigel, for example, held firmly to the position that the American constitutional system is rooted in the scholastic, Catholic thought of the thirteenth century. It is hard to imagine that someone like Bishop John Carroll of Baltimore would ever dare, at least publicly, to make a similar claim. Their Catholic identity is an integral part of their political thought both in its formation and in its expression. If Appleby errs in his analysis, it is in his underestimation of the public importance of their Catholicism.

Opposite the danger of underestimating the public importance of their Catholicism is the danger of overestimating it. Damon Linker, the author of one of only a few books that provides a historical analysis of the three neoconservative Catholics, falls prey to this temptation.[3] His basic premise is that the neoconservative Catholics want to create a Republican party that is rooted in a Catholic Christian worldview and that expresses this worldview through the implementation of policies consistent with it. In his book *The Theocons* he "tells the story of how a small group of 'theoconservative' intellectuals has decisively contributed to the unprecedented rise of public religiosity in our time.... The story ends with an examination of the theocons' deeply troubling vision of the nation's future—a future in which the country is thoroughly permeated by orthodox Christian piety, and secular politics are driven out in favor of an explicitly theological approach to ordering the nation's public life."[4]

The primary sin of the neoconservative Catholics, argued Linker, is in their rejection of the "liberal bargain," which he believed is central to the American founders' understanding of the relationship

3. Damon Linker, *The Theocons: Secular America under Siege* (New York: Doubleday, 2006).
4. Ibid., xiii.

between church and state. As a way to avoid religious conflict and maintain public order, Linker argued, the founders established a system in which "believers are expected only to give up the ambition to political rule in *the name of their faith*—that is, the ambition to bring the whole of social life into conformity with their own inevitably partial and sectarian theological convictions."[5] In this understanding of American political life, religion is and ought to remain a largely private phenomenon, in which people can worship God as they see fit without the danger of state interference.

In contrast to Appleby, who argued that the republican style of the neoconservative Catholics downplays a clearly Catholic, theological identity in favor of affirming the American republican tradition, Linker claims that their exaggerated Catholic public presence results in the abandonment of the American republican tradition. Consequently, for Linker, the neoconservative Catholics are not, to use O'Brien's terminology, republican Catholics. Their rejection of the liberal bargain signifies a rejection of one of the fundamental bases of the American political system. Throughout the rest of this study it will be important to keep in mind how closely, and in what fashion, the neoconservative Catholics link their religious worldview to their political one. Given that many of their political arguments are grounded on a Catholic and, more broadly, Christian ethic, analyzing their political worldview absent consideration of their religious one provides a truncated understanding of their thought. That the neoconservative Catholics affirm the complementarity of the Catholic social teaching tradition and the American political tradition is widely accepted in the scholarly literature. What is often overlooked in this same literature is any recognition of the different ways in which Neuhaus, Novak, and Weigel conceptualized the relationship between Catholic social teaching and developments in American political life.

Although they share a number of intellectual commitments, there

5. Ibid., 224.

are important differences as well, both in terms of how they understand the relationship between Catholic social teaching and American political traditions and in terms of their specific intellectual
interests. These differences make it difficult to lump them together
in some sort of shared school of thought. Tracing out their public
identity will thus consist in highlighting shared commitments and
pointing out how they take advantage of these commitments to argue against opposing points of view, all the while keeping in mind
how they differ from each other. In short, Michael Novak focused
on developing the idea of democratic capitalism, Richard Neuhaus
began a thorough examination of the relationship between religion
and public life, and George Weigel took up the cause of the "John
Courtney Murray project."

Although each took on different "projects" during this period,
they share a number of common characteristics. Any attempt to
understand the neoconservative Catholics requires that one pay attention to the important differences in their thought, while at the
same time recognizing the "family resemblances" that function as
a shared intellectual framework. Contrary to commentators who
argue otherwise, the neoconservative Catholics do not represent a
movement or shared project as such, even though they agree on important fundamentals that give rise to their distinctive perspectives.
One of the most outspoken proponents of the idea that they embrace a shared ideological worldview is Damon Linker, who claimed
that Neuhaus is the "founder of the theocon movement" and has
long served as its "de facto leader and inspiration."[6] He is not; the
three of them have very distinct interests. He further argued that
Neuhaus's *Naked Public Square* functions as a "manifesto" for the
theoconservatives.[7] It does not; although Novak and Weigel were
sympathetic with much of what Neuhaus wrote in this book, they
are far more diverse in their thinking than Linker allows. Weigel
more accurately portrayed the relationship that exists between the

6. Ibid., 7.
7. Ibid., 46.

three when he noted that neoconservative Catholicism is "less a 'movement' than an ongoing community of intellectual conversation and cooperation."[8] Exploring the intellectual worldviews of each will help to demonstrate why this is so.

One of the shared fundamentals that the neoconservative Catholics affirmed was the importance of institutional pluralism, which is itself rooted in the distinction between state and society. Throughout their writings they voiced support for and adherence to the virtues of a democratic, pluralistic society, and resistance to the ever-present danger of decline into an authoritarian, monistic state. The state/society distinction is a characteristic of influential segments of Catholic thought and thus connected their thinking to a much broader intellectual tradition that they drew on for support.

While it has taken on greater importance with the rise of the modern, bureaucratic state, the state/society distinction has roots that extend to the early days of Christianity.[9] Early Christian political thought anticipated it in its conviction that the church is an autonomous "society" in the face of the ruling secular authorities. It presupposed that there are, as the Catholic sociologist John Coleman put it, "free spaces" in society that remain independent of state power. These would typically include institutions like unions, universities, and other voluntary associations.[10] With the rise of the modern bureaucratic state and the apparent threat that it poses to free institutions, this distinction found a home in influential strains of modern Catholic political thought. John Courtney Murray, for example, argued that one of the fundamental principles underlying the American political tradition was the idea that "the state is distinct from society and limited in its offices toward society."[11] A contemporary of Murray, Jacques Maritain also emphasized this

8. Weigel, "The Neoconservative Difference," 139.

9. John A. Coleman, SJ, "A Limited State and a Vibrant Society," in *Christian Political Ethics,* ed. John A Coleman, 25–26 (Princeton, N.J.: Princeton University Press, 2008).

10. Ibid., 23–27.

11. John Courtney Murray, *We Hold These Truths: Catholic Reflections on the American Proposition* (Lanham, Md.: Rowan and Littlefield, 2005), 49.

distinction and developed what was perhaps its clearest formulation in modern times by a Catholic thinker.[12]

Maritain criticized the general failure of modern political thought to distinguish the role of the state from that of the "body politic," or its conceptual equivalent, civil society.[13] It is in the latter that distinct, relatively autonomous institutions related to the family, education, economics, politics, and religious life flourish. In pre-modern political thought the power of the state was, at least in theory if not always in practice, carefully delimited and was concerned primarily with "the maintenance of law, the promotion of the common welfare and public order, and the administration of public affairs."[14] One of the fundamental problems with modern political thought, according to Maritain, is in its tendency to exaggerate the importance of the state and watch idly as it began to co-opt responsibilities that once belonged to the various organs of civil society.[15]

The neoconservative Catholics expressed concerns similar to those of Maritain and supported a clear delineation of responsibilities between the state and civil society. As early as the mid-sixties Novak argued in favor of the separation of civil society and the state and emphasized the importance of maintaining clear boundaries between the two entities as a way to limit the state, which is always seeking further expansion of its power.[16] Neuhaus lamented the insidious tendency of modern man to equate the notion of state and society. What particularly concerned him was the tendency of many intellectuals, political leaders, and even everyday people to support the expansion of state power into spheres in which it once dared not tread.[17] Finally, Weigel at one point asserted that "society, the

12. Coleman, "A Limited State and a Vibrant Society," 37.

13. D. Q. McInerny, "The Social Thought of Jacques Maritain," *The Catholic Social Science Review* 12 (2007): 157.

14. Jacques Maritain, *Man and the State* (Washington, D.C.: The Catholic University of America Press, 2004), 12.

15. Ibid., 21.

16. Michael Novak, "Moral Society and Immoral Man," *A Time To Build* (New York: Macmillan, 1964), 354–69.

17. Richard John Neuhaus, *The Naked Public Square* (Grand Rapids, Mich.: Eerdmans, 1984), ix.

natural human habitat, exists prior to the state. The state is at the service of society and not vice versa."[18]

This distinction provides the basis for their support of institutional pluralism. In a widely read and influential essay titled "To Empower People," Richard Neuhaus and his coauthor Peter Berger expressed concern over the current direction of American political life and its tendency to centralize power in the state. In reaction, they called for a reaffirmation of "mediating institutions," defined as "those institutions standing between the individual in his private life and the large institutions of public life."[19] Such institutions would help to devolve power from the federal to the local level and in doing so empower people to make the decisions that will define their community and their lives. In a reflection published some years later, Novak commented on the importance of Neuhaus and Berger's essay and argued that it signified an important shift in political discourse. He wrote that "until the appearance of the term (mediating institutions), public policy discourse in the United States tended to be pulled toward one of two polar notions: the *individual* or *the state*."[20] Confronting this dichotomy and taking advantage of alternative terminology gave Berger and Neuhaus an opportunity to move beyond the conservative and liberal mindset that dominated American political discourse.

Novak's praise of the essay's seminal influence is a bit misguided given that the central theme promoted in the essay is an extension of similar ideas found in the political theorist Robert Nisbet's book *Community and Power*. Nisbet argued that modern man finds himself living in a kind of halfway house. Throughout much of history, humans were immersed in their local communities and established identities in relation to the array of organizations that made up

18. Weigel, *Tranquillitas Ordinis: The Present Failure and Future Promise of American Catholic Thought on War and Peace* (Oxford: Oxford University Press, 1987), 115.

19. Peter L. Berger and Richard John Neuhaus, "To Empower People," in *To Empower People: From State to Civil Society,* 2nd ed., ed. Michael Novak, 158 (Washington, D.C.: The American Enterprise Institute Press, 1996).

20. Michael Novak, "Introduction," in *To Empower People,* ed. Novak, 3.

these communities. With the growth of the modern state, intermediate institutions like the family, interest associations, the church, and professional organizations have begun to decline in relevance. This is due to the tendency of the modern state to usurp the responsibilities and role-defining capacity that these intermediate institutions once exercised.[21]

Tracing the developmental arc of modern political thought through Bodin, Hobbes, Rousseau, and then Marx, Nisbet argued that this trend has, in its most extreme manifestation, culminated in the "absolute state." He wrote that "in this type of State, the basic needs for education, recreation, welfare, economic production, distribution and consumption, health, spiritual and physical, and all other services of society are made aspects of the administrative structure of political government."[22] The absolute state seeks to obliterate "all the intermediate layers of value and association that commonly nourish personality and serve to protect it from external power and caprice.... The political enslavement of man requires the emancipation of man from all authorities and memberships that serve, in one degree or another, to insulate the individual from external political power."[23]

The most obvious examples of the absolute state in the modern world are the Soviet Union and Germany under Hitler's fascist rule. But even where the absolute state has not yet become a reality, as in Western Europe or the United States, there are tendencies in that direction.[24] Following the breakdown of intermediate institutions, it is in the state that people have begun to feel their most basic sense of membership and belonging.[25] Nisbet argued that this tendency contributed to the rise of nationalistic movements in many parts of the world. It is also out of this context that an Ayn Rand–style libertarianism can be argued to have emerged. Averse to the ever-

21. Robert Nisbet, *Community and Power* (New York: Oxford University Press, 1962).
22. Ibid., 282. See ch. 6 in Nisbet's book in particular.
23. Ibid., 202.   24. Ibid., 70–74.
25. Ibid., 201–7.

growing power of the state and yet with increasingly fewer intermediate institutions to turn to for protection, more emphasis is placed
on the individual and the need to protect her from the intrusion of
state power.

Like Nisbet, Neuhaus and Berger were wary of the modern state
and its tendency toward a more totalistic approach to modern life.
Also following the lead of Nisbet, they argued that it is important to reenergize mediating institutions since they "are the value-
generating and value-maintaining agencies in society" that will help
to alleviate the "anomic precariousness of individual existence in isolation from society and the threat of alienation to the public order."[26]

The emphasis on mediating institutions in neoconservative
Catholic thought sheds light on important themes that repeatedly
emerge in their writings. First is the encroachment of the modern
bureaucratic state in every area of life. This encroachment is exacerbated by the breakdown of civil society and the institutional pluralism that traditionally comprised it. Mediating institutions provide
an attempt to reassert the importance of the institutional pluralism
that, according to the neoconservative Catholics, underlies healthy
forms of community. While sharing an appreciation for institutional pluralism in Western political life, they developed different, albeit often complementary, lines of thought.

Novak's most significant contribution during this period re-
sides in his macro-level studies related to democratic capitalism and
his attempt to provide a theoretical foundation for this economic
and political system. His book *The Spirit of Democratic Capitalism*
provided a moral and intellectual vision that sought to defend the
relationship between capitalism, political democracy, and a moral
culture.[27] In contrast to the more macro-level perspective taken by
Novak, Neuhaus's writings during the eighties tended to focus on
the micro level. In particular, he examined the central role of one

26. Berger and Neuhaus, "To Empower People," 159–63.
27. Michael Novak, *The Spirit of Democratic Capitalism,* 2nd ed. (New York: Madison
Books, 1991), 19–28.

mediating institution in particular: religious institutions. Throughout American history, Neuhaus argued, the Christian churches had played an indispensable role legitimating belief in the American political system. In post-Vietnam America many of the same churches that once defended the American political tradition now turned on it with a vengeance. Religious rhetoric less often functioned as a support for this tradition and in many instances actively sought to undermine it. Finally, George Weigel's intellectual vision shares much in common with both Neuhaus and Novak. As Novak does, Weigel tends to look at the big picture rather than isolating a specific mediating institution. But, like Neuhaus, Weigel is very much interested in the role that religion plays in political society, an interest that became particularly pronounced in his work related to the thought of John Courtney Murray. The remainder of this chapter will examine each thinker individually and examine how both their shared and individual interests played out in their thought.

Michael Novak and Democratic Capitalism

The American Enterprise Institute (AEI), which originally published "To Empower People," followed it with a series of summer institutes that touched on many of the same themes. The papers presented at these institutes were subsequently published and the volumes titled, in consecutive order: *Capitalism and Socialism: A Theological Inquiry; Democracy and Mediating Structures: A Theological Inquiry;* and *The Corporation: A Theological Inquiry.* In all three the idea of mediating institutions functioned as a backdrop and in each Michael Novak contributed an essay.

The first institute was held in the summer of 1978, just one year after Berger and Neuhaus's essay on mediating institutions. Contributors focused on the moral and spiritual underpinnings of capitalist and socialist economic systems, while pointing out strengths and weaknesses in each. Novak picked up on a theme that he continued to focus on in the later symposiums, namely, the cultural underpinnings of institutions in a democratic capitalist society. Rather than examining specific institutions in detail, he used broad brush strokes to argue that the cultural character of democratic capitalism is the most underanalyzed of elements in the Western capitalist system. Democratic capitalism, properly understood, was not merely an economic system but embraced a moral vision that had to be embraced and lived out for it to work properly. While a great deal of attention has been given to the moral vision of socialism, the same cannot be said of the moral vision of capitalism.[28] His essay written for the following year's institute developed this vision further.

Democracy and Mediating Institutions: A Theological Inquiry focused on the cultural, religious, and moral characteristics of the institutions that comprise a democratic capitalist perspective. Assigned the task of summarizing the major themes presented at the institute, Novak repeatedly highlighted the point that economic institutions cannot be understood simply from a dollars-and-cents perspective. Properly understood, democratic capitalism is embedded in a much larger context than one that relies on a disembodied economic analysis. One of the deficiencies in many of the writings on capitalism is the failure to recognize that "capitalism can work morally only so long as it has implicit moral capital on which to draw, so long as it can assume that people will practice stewardship, honesty fidelity, and similar restraints on their behavior. Its cultural system is as important as its economic system."[29]

Economic theories and the institutional structures that embody them are fundamentally about culture and thus every economic system relies on a public ethic. Here he attributed the rise of the political neoconservatives at least partly to their recognition that the ethic then dominant in major sectors of American society was undermining the values that make the American system work: the

28. Michael Novak, "Seven Theological Facts," in *Capitalism and Socialism: A Theological Inquiry,* ed. Michael Novak, 109–23 (Washington, D.C.: The American Enterprise Institute for Public Policy Research, 1979).

29. Michael Novak, "Changing the Paradigms: The Cultural Deficiencies of Capitalism," in *Democracy and Mediating Structures: A Theological Inquiry,* ed. Michael Novak, 192 (Washington, D.C.: American Enterprise Institute for Public Policy Research, 1980).

bourgeois ethic. The elites of American society had begun to "attack the bourgeois virtues of fidelity, hard work, loyalty," and had thus begun to undermine the fundamental values that had made America (and the West more generally) productive and vibrant.[30]

The third institute focused specifically on the corporation as a mediating institution. With presentations such as "The Development of the Corporation," "Western Guilt and Third World Poverty," and "The Social Critique of the Corporation," the institute aimed at exploring the historical, economic, and even theological significance of this type of structure. In his contribution Novak took the strange step of comparing the corporation, "a much despised incarnation of God's presence in the world," to the figure in Isaiah 53:2–3, a passage that is generally referenced in relation to Christ: "He is despised and rejected of men; a man of sorrows, and acquainted with grief; he was despised and we esteemed him not."[31] With such an auspicious beginning, it should not come as much of a surprise that throughout the rest of the essay he provides a fairly glowing account of the multinational corporation, the specific corporate entity under discussion, and highlights seven signs of grace, "a suitably sacramental number," that can be found in the multinational corporation. These include creativity, liberty, and the inherent social motive of the multinational to seek the wealth of all humanity.[32] In one of the final sections he defends the multinational against various criticisms and dismisses them as inherently problematic when understood within the right context.

This tendency to whitewash the drawbacks of the multinational corporation highlights one of the problems in this essay: Novak's marked tendency to downplay any political and social dangers that accompany the corporate model. Intent as he is on providing a defense of the corporation, particularly against those who criticize its

30. Ibid., 188–91.

31. Michael Novak, "A Theology of the Corporation," in *The Corporation: A Theological Inquiry,* ed. Michael Novak, 203 (Washington, D.C.: American Enterprise Institute for Public Policy Research, 1981).

32. Ibid., 207–13.

"bigness" and the concentration of power in such institutions, Novak remains largely unmoved. Although he acknowledged these concerns he quickly shifted to the argument that the concentration of power and size in multinational corporations is quite possibly, in practice, a benefit.[33] This is somewhat surprising given that one of the underlying themes in this essay is an emphasis on the importance of mediating institutions. He does not address how a huge multinational corporation can express anything other than an impersonal character matched perhaps only by the state. His failure to address this issue reflected a bias that both Berger and Neuhaus point to in their original text, "To Empower People." Here they wrote critically of certain tendencies in modern conservative thought including their concern that "today's conservatism typically exhibits the weakness of the left in reverse: it is highly sensitive to the alienations of big government, but blind to the analogous effects of big business. Such one-sidedness, whether of left or right, is not helpful."[34]

Although each of Novak's essays discussed above focus on a different aspect of economic life in modern life, one of the shared themes was Novak's emphasis on the importance of the idea of democratic capitalism. It is in this shift to the idea of democratic capitalism that Novak focused most of his intellectual energy in the following years. Less interested in specific types of mediating institutions, he is instead intent on developing a larger theory about society, within which various mediating institutions from different spheres relate. Traditionally, one of the key arguments made by the defenders of capitalism was its practical successes. What had been given less attention is the theoretical defense of democratic capitalism. To counteract socialist movements that have not demonstrated many practical successes but have provided a powerful moral appeal, democratic capitalism needed to provide a moral vision that could counter the criticisms of its detractors.[35]

33. Ibid., 215.

34. Berger and Neuhaus, "To Empower People," 162.

35. See in particular the introduction of Novak, *The Spirit of Democratic Capitalism*, 13–28.

Fundamental to the democratic capitalist system is a vision of society that emphasizes "pluralism in pluralism." At the broadest level, it affirms three general divisions in society: the political, the economic, and the moral/cultural spheres. Novak admitted to borrowing this model from Daniel Bell, who had promoted this idea a few years earlier in his writings.[36] While conceptually distinct from one another, these spheres regularly interact with one another, creating pressures and counter-pressures that balance off concentrations of power in any particular sphere. This is not to say that they do not have a shaping influence on each other at various junctures. He wrote that "each of these systems has its own special institutions and methods, disciplines and standards, purposes and limits, attractions and repulsions. Each has its own ethos. Each also creates problems for the other two. These tensions are desirable; a pluralist system is designed to foment them."[37] It is through this creative tension that progress is constantly pushed forward.

Further, each of these spheres is pluralistic. The moral/cultural sphere is comprised of a wide range of churches, synagogues, mosques, and even secular institutions, each of which is trying to spread its message to others. The economic sphere has unions, corporations, investors, and others, who each struggle to establish themselves financially. In the political sphere interest groups struggle to pass legislation conducive to their interests and politicians act according to interests of their own. The various spheres of government in the American systems function as a check on each other. While never perfect, the pluralism present on multiple levels helps to maintain a balance of power among and within these different areas of life.[38]

The pluralism inherent in the democratic capitalist model is not, argues Novak, something that can be taken for granted; contrary

36. Novak, "Seven Theological Principles," 112; Daniel Bell, *The Cultural Contradictions of Capitalism* (New York: Basic Books, 1976).

37. Novak, *The Spirit of Democratic Capitalism*, 170.

38. Ibid., 172–86.

visions constantly threaten it. It is under threat, on the one hand, by a traditionalist vision of society and, from the opposite direction, a socialist one. Rather than supporting pluralism, both promote a unitary order that concentrates power in the hands of a few. Socialist forms of unitary order seek to subjugate the economic sphere to the political one. The fundamental source of injustice from this perspective is economic inequality, and the inevitable consequence, class conflict.[39] The most obvious manifestation of a socialist form of unitary order in the modern world is communism. On the other hand, traditionalist forms of unitary order are often religious in nature; they are, writes Novak, typically "preoccupied by problems of order and stability.... Sins against order are regarded as sins against God."[40] Societies defined by a traditionalist vision often flirt with some form of theocracy: representative of such a worldview would be certain regions during the Middle Ages when Christendom was at its peak or in certain parts of the modern-day Middle East.

In both cases, whether socialist or traditionalist, one sphere of life co-opts the authority and responsibilities of one or both of the other spheres. Democratic capitalism, in contrast to these alternative visions, differs insofar as it posits tyranny as its primary enemy. Systems of checks and balances and of multiple concentrations of power counter attempts at consolidating power in one person or institution.[41] Within a modern American context the decentralization of power raised questions concerning the proper relationship that religious institutions and leaders ought to have in relation to political life.

On the one hand, Novak recognized the importance of religious institutions in the formation and continuing credibility of social systems. Such institutions have an important legitimating function in life. In a speech given at the Ethics and Public Policy Center in September 1980, he specifically repudiated the position that religion has had no role in the emergence of Western political life and admitted

39. Ibid., 83.   40. Ibid.
41. Ibid., 84.

that democracy owed many of its basic moral energies to the Christian and Jewish traditions.[42] Nevertheless, he was nervous about attributing an irrevocable connection between the two, out of the fear that such a move would push the West toward a political monism that would not benefit democracy in the long run. His hesitancy on this question highlights a fairly important divide within the neoconservative Catholic camp that was made evident through a public disagreement between Michael Novak and Richard Neuhaus.

Taking pluralism as the indispensable starting point in his political thought, Novak shied away from any attempt to assert a religious belief system that is indispensable to an understanding of American political life. While admitting that Christianity has helped to shape democratic capitalism, he wrote that "in a generally pluralistic society, there is no one sacred canopy. By *intention* there is not. At its spiritual core, there is an empty shrine."[43] He further argued that Christians err when they assert that America is at its core a Christian nation. Americans are free to affirm whatever faith they might hold and take advantage of that faith in the public square, but no religious system can command the political system. It is the role of the state to protect a public forum that allows for vigorous debate among competing religious viewpoints, but without ever allowing a particular religious institution to impose a totalistic vision on the rest of society.[44]

Neuhaus contended that Michael Novak's "empty shrine" flirted with, if not embraced, the naked public square, which "is the result of a political doctrine and practice that would exclude religion and religiously grounded values from the conduct of public business. The doctrine is that America is a secular society."[45] Contrary to Novak,

---

42. The speech from which this argument was taken was eventually published in a book: Michael Novak, "Democracy Takes Sin Seriously," in *Solzhenitsyn and American Democracy*, ed. Michael Novak and George Will, 9–15 (Washington, D.C.: Ethics and Public Policy Center, 1981), 9–15.

43. Novak, *The Spirit of Democratic Capitalism*, 53.

44. Ibid., 67–70.

45. Neuhaus, *The Naked Public Square*, ix.

Neuhaus argued that the empty shrine is a direct threat to pluralism and the American way of life insofar as it removes the legitimating ground from the American way of life. Not only is the ground of the American political tradition religious, but it is specifically Judeo-Christian.[46]

In response, Novak flatly denied this accusation, claiming that "the 'empty shrine' does not entail a 'naked public square.'"[47] He argued that the Founding Fathers intentionally decided against creating a Constitution that explicitly upheld one religion over another so as to curtail the power of the state and to provide a forum in which rigorous debate can commence on important public issues. They intentionally kept alive a kind of "openness" to the transcendent, one in which anyone can express their own understanding of that term. By not filling in its details, they avoided the dangers of creating an idolatry of the state, lest it impose an image of the transcendent that happens to affirm its own self-image.[48]

This disagreement provides a springboard into the thought of Richard Neuhaus. Part of the difference between Novak and Neuhaus is rooted in their different points of focus. Novak was intent on avoiding unitary orders that threaten institutional pluralism. Relating religious systems too closely to political ones carries with it the risk of blurring the difference between the religious and political sphere. Taken to an extreme, one runs the risk of identifying the two spheres and making an idol out of the latter. Neuhaus, on the other hand, argued that the very possibility of pluralism in a social and political sense is at risk if one does not recognize the close affinity between religion, politics, and culture.

Richard Neuhaus, Religion, and the State

If only one theme clearly emerged in Neuhaus's writings throughout the seventies and eighties, it is that religious ideas and institu-

---

46. Ibid., 121–22.
47. Michael Novak, "Three Porcupines of Pluralism," *This World,* no. 19 (1987): 37.
48. Ibid., 37–38.

tions play a definitive role in the health and well-being of any society. This assertion becomes clear in his stated conviction that "religion is the heart of culture and culture is the form of religion. On this view, then, politics is a function of culture and culture, in turn, is reflective (if not a function) of religion."[49] There is a line that can be drawn from religious ideas and sentiments to the form that culture takes and the political ideas and structures to which it gives rise. For Neuhaus, in any given society religion is the most fundamental expression of how a people organize their life together. To marginalize the public presence of religious institutions and ideas risks severing people from one of the central legitimating forces of their political life. It is the marginalization of religion from its public role and, worse still, the denial by some that it should have a public role at all that Neuhaus termed the rise of the naked public square.

While the idea of the "naked public square" acquired cultural capital with the publication of his book of the same name, the seeds of this idea can be found almost a decade earlier in his book *Time Toward Home*. Here Neuhaus already began expressing concerns about the slow disappearance of religious belief as a legitimating force in American life. Given his emphasis on the indispensable function of religion in any culture, he further argued that secularists who thought they were pushing religion out of the public square were mistaken. The loss of a Christian defense of the American democratic experiment would not lead to the removal of religion from the public square, but only its replacement with something else, and perhaps something more sinister. On this point he remarked that "in the absence of the Absolute point of reference that we speak of as God, some lesser and finally dehumanizing myth will be enlisted to serve the needs of communal identity and cohesiveness which will not go unserved for very long."[50] By the time he and

---

49. For example, he refers to this notion in Richard John Neuhaus, "The Post-Secular Task of the Church," in *Christianity and Politics: Catholic and Protestant Perspectives*, ed. Carol Friedley Griffith, 1 (Washington, D.C.: Ethics and Public Policy Center, 1981), and then again in his *The Naked Public Square*, 132.

50. Neuhaus, *Time Toward Home* (New York: Seabury Press, 1975), 249.

Peter Berger wrote about religion as a mediating institution just a few years later, they could write that "public policy is presently biased toward what might be called the symbolic nakedness of the public square."[51] From this vantage point, to argue that religion has no place in public life overlooks the fact that something will function as religion and, in doing so, create something resembling a God against which political and social behavior will be defined.

The implications for both the American experiment and American Christianity were significant. Without the legitimating force of the Christian tradition behind it, the American experiment in democracy was faced with the threat of dissolution, as the moral and religious foundations on which that experiment rested was no longer vital. While addressing this theme in many of his writings, Neuhaus made his most systematic attempt at spelling out this dilemma in his book *The Naked Public Square*. Here he argued that the past century has witnessed the marginalization of religion and religious institutions in the public sphere. This has happened to such an extent that in the post–World War II period religion has been effectively banished from the activities surrounding political life. Much of this was a direct result of Supreme Court decisions and complementary legislative action that affirmed a privatized view of religion and effectively excluded religious belief systems from shaping policy. This had the unfortunate effect of disconnecting legislation from the moral traditions that provide it legitimacy. On this point, he writes that if we continue down this road "there is nothing in store but a continuing and deepening crisis of legitimacy if courts persist in systematically ruling out of order the moral traditions in which Western law has developed and which bear, for the overwhelming majority of the American people, a living sense of right and wrong. The result, quite literally, is the *outlawing of the basis of law*."[52] If moral traditions that are rooted in religious traditions cannot play a role in the process of public discourse then legislation loses its

51. Berger and Neuhaus, "To Empower People," 192.
52. Neuhaus, *The Naked Public Square*, 259.

coherence in the eyes of large swathes of the population. The delegit-imation of law through the marginalization of religiously grounded moral traditions has a further consequence: the normative founda-tion of our very democracy comes into question.[53]

The fundamental premise at work here is that every society needs some religious foundation to ground its moral claims and, conse-quently, its laws. In terms of Western society, the foundations in-clude a Judeo-Christian worldview. Remove religion from its proper place in relation to political society and that society is left with a void. Such a situation is untenable. The naked square cannot remain naked. Reiterating something he had written a decade earlier, Neu-haus wrote that "religious evacuation of the public square cannot be sustained, either in concept or in practice.... When recognizable religion is excluded, the vacuum will be filled ersatz by religion, by religion bootlegged into public space under other names."[54]

Such a perspective has roots that sink deeply into a more secular sociological tradition. In particular, Emile Durkheim develops the relationship between religion, morality, and society in such a way that it helps to clarify Neuhaus's own thinking. The importance of "moral consensus" to every society was developed by Durkheim in his classic, *The Elementary Forms of Religious Life*.[55] In this pi-oneering book, Durkheim sought to understand the fundamental characteristics of religion in society. He isolated what he and oth-ers at the time thought was the most primitive form of religious life, that of the aboriginal inhabitants of Australia. This case study provided, Durkheim believed, access to the basic characteristics of religious life that were common to all religions yet most evident in the simplest examples.[56] Dismissing a variety of definitions pertain-

---

53. George Weigel, "Public Nudity?" review of *The Naked Public Square*, by Richard John Neuhaus, *This World* 9 (1984): 117.

54. Neuhaus, *The Naked Public Square*, 80.

55. Emile Durkheim, *The Elementary Forms of Religious Life*, trans. Karen E. Fields (New York: The Free Press, 1995).

56. Robert Nisbet, *The Sociology of Emile Durkheim* (New York: Oxford University Press, 1974), 166–67.

ing to religion, Durkheim argued that one of its most fundamental features centers on the idea of the sacred, which stand in contrast to things profane. In contrast to the profane, which represents the regular and the banal, the sacred is set apart, superior and distinct from things of everyday life.[57]

Examining the sacred in primitive societies, Durkheim focused on what he refers to as the totemic principle, which is "simultaneously the symbol of both the god and the clan, because both the god and the clan are really the same thing."[58] The totemic principle provides a source of common identity and meaning; it binds a given people together in community. While more "advanced" religions express a greater level of complexity, the same general principles apply. At all times and places, religious rituals and beliefs express a social content—the needs, the desires, and the values of a given people.[59] For this reason, Durkheim defined religion as a "unified system of beliefs and practices relative to sacred things, that is to say, things set apart and forbidden—beliefs and practices which unite into one single moral community called a church, all those who adhere to them."[60]

In his book *The Naked Public Square* Neuhaus made the assertion that what Durkheim found to be true of all societies is most certainly true of America, that a moral consensus of some form or another is required in every viable society; "there must be some ultimate value or truth which lays upon individuals and communities a claim that gives meaning to duty."[61] For Neuhaus, and in an American context, this moral consensus to which Durkheim refers is most clearly represented by a religious system of thought, Protestant Christianity. While not committing to the idea that religious belief can be reduced to society, as Durkheim did,

57. Durkheim, *The Elementary Forms of Religious Life*, 37–38.
58. Daniel Pals, *Seven Theories of Religion* (New York: Oxford University Press, 1996), 104.
59. Ibid., 105–6.
60. Durkheim, *The Elementary Forms of Religious Life*, 44.
61. Neuhaus, *The Naked Public Square*, 204.

Neuhaus did agree with Durkheim that moral consensus provides the substructure that gives rise to political and cultural belief systems.[62] To undermine and banish the given belief system on which a given society is built will inevitably lead to the disruption of the political and cultural ideas that give shape to that society.

Like other mediating institutions, Neuhaus noted, religious structures have become increasingly marginalized in the face of the bureaucratic state. What emerges is an inherent tension. The absence of a vibrant religious presence in the public sphere does not mean that moral values are no longer needed. A people's search for social and political coherence continues. With the decline of mediating institutions, the state takes on the responsibility of providing publicly accessible forms of meaning in the public square. He contended that "when the value-bearing institutions of religion and culture are excluded, the value-laden concerns of human life flow back into the square under the banner of politics.... If the state ordering of society is to exclude those institutions that generate and bear values, then the state must be prepared to assume the burden of meeting the human yearning for life that is not value-less. The totalitarian, whether Fascist or Communist, welcomes that burden."[63]

As dangerous as the Soviet Union might be, for Neuhaus the primary threat to American-style liberalism is not external but internal. The evacuation of religion from the public square sets the conditions for the emergence of totalitarianism, or at least something approximating it. This is because religion is the only institution that can keep the state in check by placing it under transcendent judgment and, in doing so, relativize its authority.[64] The idea that religion has functioned as an important check on state power is a theme that Weigel examines, particularly as seen through his work related to John Courtney Murray.

62. Pals, *Seven Theories of Religion*, 117–18.
63. Neuhaus, *The Naked Public Square*, 157.
64. Ibid, 118.

George Weigel and the American Proposition

While writing throughout the forties on issues related to inter-credal relations, John Courtney Murray is most widely remembered for his work on "church/state" relations in the fifties and, eventually, for his book *We Hold These Truths*. One of his major intellectual efforts consisted in his attempt to provide a rationale that would help to reconcile the American separation of church and state in light of Catholic teaching, which had for a long time been opposed to such an institutional framework. One step in this process consisted in his attempt to historicize the thought of Pope Leo XIII by arguing that his criticisms of church/state separation were applicable to a European context, but not an American one.[65] This was due primarily to the different social and political conditions of each. In continental Europe, "while technically church-state doctrine was one of 'separation,' the effect of the doctrine was social monism, because Continental Liberalism banished religion to the realm of the private, leaving the state as the only social actor."[66] Fallout from the French Revolution had tainted the relationship between state and church from a Vatican perspective. The total separation of these institutions in a European context hindered the freedom of the church, Murray argued, but the relationship between church and state in the United States was different and should be treated as such. In the United States religious institutions, while technically separate, have a vital role in the shaping of society; they are not banished to the margins. While initially controversial, Murray's rationale was eventually vindicated by the Second Vatican Council and the publication of *Dignitatis Humanae*.[67]

---

65. Todd David Whitmore, "The Growing End: John Courtney Murray and the Shape of Murray Studies," in *John Courtney Murray and the Growth of Tradition*, ed. J. Leon Hooper et al., vii–x (Kansas City, Kan.: Sheed and Ward, 1996). For a more in-depth analysis of John Courtney Murray's views on church/state issues and religious freedom than in Whitmore's essay see William R. Luckey, "The Contribution of John Courtney Murray, S.J.: A Catholic Perspective," in *John Courtney Murray and the American Civil Conversation*, ed. Robert P. Hunt et al. (Grand Rapids, Mich.: Eerdmans, 1992).

66. Whitmore, "The Growing End," ix.

67. Ibid., x.

Murray's ideas relating to the American proposition were of lasting influence on George Weigel. It was largely through his thought that Weigel made sense of the American political tradition and the relationship of that tradition to Catholic thought. At one point he went so far as to declare that "John Courtney Murray stands as the great theological synthesis of the American Catholic experience."[68] The fruits of this engagement are often referred to as the "John Courtney Murray project."

One of the goals in his early writings was to further this project, arguing that "it is time to take up the task outlined, but never completed, in John Courtney Murray's grand project: the articulation of a moral rationale for and defense of the American democratic experiment."[69] Weigel's effort to develop Murray's thought followed shortly after David Hollenbach recognized in Murray's writings an important resource for public life. In a 1976 essay for the journal *Theological Studies,* Hollenbach argued that "the entire Murray project ... is based upon the hope that there is enough life in the American public philosophy effectively to establish justice, promote the general welfare, and secure the blessings of liberty for all."[70]

The idea of a "public philosophy" is a key term here. It also embodied one side of an important historical debate in post-World War II America. In his book, *Believing Skeptics,* Robert Booth Fowler argued that from 1945 through the early 1960s an influential group of political thinkers were skeptical of political ideology and any argument that based political perspectives on absolute truth claims. Sydney Hook, Arthur Schlesinger, and Daniel Bell, among others, remained deeply suspicious of ideological outlooks, all of which were thought to be inherently dangerous.[71] They worried that

68. Weigel, *Tranquillitas Ordinis,* 110.

69. Ibid., 387.

70. David Hollenbach, "Public Theology in America: Some Questions for Catholicism after John Courtney Murray," *Theological Studies* 37 (1976): 297.

71. Robert Booth Fowler, *Believing Skeptics: American Political Intellectuals, 1945–1964* (Westport, Conn.: Greenwood Press, 1978), 3–8; for a brief overview of these contrasting perspectives see also Robert F. Cuervo, "John Courtney Murray and the Public Philosophy,"

ideology, tied as it often was to moral absolutism, would be accompanied by political absolutism; in an age in which totalitarianism had ravaged the world, the threat of absolutism of any sort was an objectionable phenomenon.[72]

In contrast, Fowler also addressed a second class of intellectuals who focused on the importance of public philosophy and natural law as the necessary precursor to political thought. Such a perspective took for granted that the world is rooted in a normative reality that had to be taken into consideration as prior to politics. Proponents of such a vision "contended that the crisis of political justification could be resolved by recognizing that there was, in fact, no crisis, that all along there continued to exist natural standards for life and politics rooted in the eternities of the universe."[73] Fowler focused primarily on the example of Walter Lippmann, who repeatedly emphasized the importance of natural law and public philosophy as a framework for political decision-making. Also mentioned in the same vein are Reinhold Niebuhr, Jacques Maritain, and Eric Voegelin.[74] Not mentioned, although certainly at home in this perspective, was John Courtney Murray, who pushed the idea of public philosophy in his major work *We Hold These Truths*. Murray held the idea of public philosophy to be important because "its teachings are principles of the right order of a democratic society, principles self-evident to the reason of those trained in the study of the common good."[75] At the core of the public philosophy for Murray was his idea of the American consensus.

The American consensus presupposes a common set of principles through which the public philosophy finds expression in the life of the people. The essential contents of the consensus include:

---

in *John Courtney Murray and the American Civil Conversation*, ed. Robert P. Hunt et al., 67–88 (Grand Rapids, Mich.: Eerdmans, 1992), 67–88.

72. Fowler, *Believing Skeptics*, see in particular ch. 4 and 5.

73. Ibid., 71–89.

74. Ibid., 73–76.

75. Cuervo, "John Courtney Murray and the Public Philosophy," 75.

- the idea that there is a sovereign God that stands in judgment over all nations;
- the notion that there are truths that are publicly accessible through the natural law;
- an affirmation of the consent of the governed;
- the recognition that a free government depends on virtuous people who are inwardly governed by the moral law; and
- an acknowledgment that human rights are inalienable and inherent and precede any act of government.[76]

Unfortunately, Murray argued, the American consensus had lost traction within the popular American mind, not to mention influential intellectual circles, in recent decades and it was unclear as to whether or not it could much longer endure. Noting the tendency within contemporary political philosophies to reject any normative moral truth claims and instead appeal to positivism and pragmatism, he worried that the American people may soon follow suit. This would result in the dismantling of the multistoried mansion of democracy and replace it with a flat majoritarianism that would prove incapable of validating human rights and other fundamental moral principles on an objective and lasting standard. If this was to be avoided, and the American experiment in democracy was to be saved, this consensus would have to be revitalized by the one segment of the American population that still took it seriously: American Catholicism.[77]

It is in the context of the American proposition, the centrality of Catholic tradition, and the importance of its revitalization that Weigel developed his own thought. He argued that "what America lacks today, in our view and in Murray's, is a religiously grounded public philosophy capable of informing and disciplining the public moral argument that is the lifeblood of democracy."[78] Such a phi-

---

76. John Courtney Murray, *We Hold These Truths: Catholic Reflections on the American Proposition* (New York: Rowman and Littlefield, 2005), 44–53.

77. Ibid., 53–57.

78. Weigel, "The Neoconservative Difference," 155.

losophy is rooted in a particular understanding of the relationship between religion and political life. At its core was the notion that religious freedom as established in the Constitution, but not as understood by modern secularists bent on stripping it from the public square, respects the consciences of individual believers and restricts the power of the state over them.

Leaders within the Catholic Church were long skeptical of religious freedom, partly due to the fear that it represented an indifferentism that would damage the church's ability to boldly express the faith. The Second Vatican Council changed all this with the declaration on religious liberty, which for all intents and purposes legitimated the American experiment in religious liberty.[79] As important a shift as it represented in church teaching, it also had important political implications. Built on the idea that people have the inherent right to freedom of conscience, the church's declaration on religious liberty is an inherently anti-totalitarian document. As such, Weigel contended that it "can be taken as a tacit, but critical, affirmation of democracy and democratic pluralism. Not only was the confessional state envisioned by apologetic Catholicism abandoned; the declaration clearly implied that democratic pluralism, under the conditions of the modern world, was the most appropriate embodiment of Catholic social theory."[80]

In the face of anti-Catholic secularist voices of post–World War II America Murray sought to demonstrate that Catholic thought was compatible with, and perhaps even essential to, the American proposition. At the time, Murray argued that American constitutionalism was rooted in the natural law tradition.[81] On this point Weigel concurred, but followed this agreement by lamenting the fact that after Vatican II the church herself began to abandon the moral tradition that underlies the American experiment. Weigel

79. Joseph Komonchak, "Catholic Principle and the American Experiment: The Silencing of John Courtney Murray," *U.S. Catholic Historian* 17, no. 1 (Winter 1999): 41.

80. Weigel, *Tranquillitas Ordinis*, 106.

81. Murray, *We Hold These Truths*, 53.

wrote that "the Church in the United States has not only failed to develop its heritage of thought over the past generation; the Church's most influential teaching centers have, in the main, largely abandoned their heritage."[82] The tendency to do so was worrying because, as with Murray, Weigel believed that the Catholic community has an important role to play in the revitalization of the American consensus. It is an error to assume, he argued, that the American experiment is the product of Enlightenment rationalism. Rather, it has its deepest taproots in Catholic medieval thought.[83] Reconnecting the Catholic tradition to the principles established in America's founding documents is thus an important step in the revitalization of the American consensus. Failing to do so ran the risk of undercutting the intellectual foundations that provided the American experiment in democracy legitimacy.

Weigel's appeal to the "heritage" of the Catholic faith, which he believed large segments of the Catholic elite and hierarchy had abandoned, opened the door to a historical element to his thought. It is inadequate to understand George Weigel's reliance on Murray and his particular understanding of the American consensus as merely a conceptual schema. The intellectual framework that Weigel used is embedded in a historical narrative that further fleshed out his philosophical, political, and religious worldview. Weigel is not alone in this. Both Novak and Neuhaus also ground their respective intellectual worldviews in a broader historical narrative. The next chapter will explore the specific narratives that each of them used and the resulting implications. Through these historical narratives, the neoconservative Catholics sought to demonstrate that the Catholic social theological tradition, and particularly its social teaching tradition, is compatible with American liberal thought.

82. Weigel, *Tranquillitas Ordinis,* ix.

83. Weigel, "The Future of the John Courtney Murray Project," in *John Courtney Murray and the American Civil Conversation,* ed. Robert P Hunt et al. (Grand Rapids, Mich.: Eerdmans, 1992), 282.

2 ❖ THE NARRATED LIFE

IN HIS BOOK *After Virtue* Alasdair MacIntyre argued that modernity was in a state of moral crisis, with debates between competing parties an often fruitless exercise that resolved little. What was the reason for this? In the contemporary Western world all that is left are disconnected, key expressions and bits and pieces of conceptual schemes, but no comprehensive paradigm that can be appealed to as a way to judge the legitimacy of moral claims. Gone are any objective and widely accepted criteria that could function as the basis for a shared moral or political discourse. In its place are subjective standards that are used by different people at different times and for different purposes.[1] The loss of a reliable moral framework brings into the question modernity's ability to rationally secure moral agreement in our culture. Lacking an objective framework to weigh moral claims, MacIntyre argues that we are left with emotivism, "the doctrine that all evaluative judgments and more specifically all moral judgments are nothing but expressions of preference, expressions of attitude or feeling, insofar as they are emotive or evaluative in character."[2]

One of the key purposes of his book is to determine how modernity can move beyond emotivism and reestablish a reliable moral tradition that can be used to help ground moral debate. He argues

1. Alasdair MacIntyre, *After Virtue: A Study in Moral Theory* (Notre Dame, Ind.: University of Notre Dame Press, 1984), 191–94.
2. Ibid., 11–12.

that identity emerges only within the context of historically situated experiences and practices that are lived out in the pursuit of specific ends. We conceive of our lives in the context of stories, because "man is in his actions and practice, as well as in his fictions, a story-telling animal.... Deprive children of stories and you leave them unscripted, anxious stutterers in their actions as in their words."[3] While the primary focus of his book was the reconstruction of our moral sensibilities, the themes that he espouses have clear and unmistakable implications in other spheres of life.

MacIntyre's emphasis on the importance of narrative and the use of narrative as a primary mechanism to construct our own identities and the communities within which we live is pertinent to our discussion of the Catholic neoconservatives. In an age in which the political narrative that once tied the American experience into a unified and coherent whole collapsed, what could be more important than the formation of a new narrative that can make sense of an American political identity? With the fracturing of Catholic identity following Vatican II and the loss of a clear sense of what it meant to be a Catholic, is it surprising that attempts were made to reconstruct a commonly, if only broadly, accepted identity? In a review of MacIntyre's book, Michael Novak argued that the "proper mainstream of ethical discourse is the narrative or story that a culture and its participants make exemplary. Rules make sense, he shows, only within stories. These stories are both cultural and inherited by individuals. They are given original and distinctive shape by each individual, and yet belong to all."[4]

Throughout the seventies and eighties, the neoconservative Catholics argued about specific points related to specific issues that ranged from Latin America and liberation theology to the economy, the Cold War, and nuclear weapons. While these are all important topics for discussion, an equally crucial component in their thought

3. Ibid., 216.
4. Michael Novak, "Alasdair MacIntyre Takes Flight," *National Review,* November 13, 1981, 1349.

consisted in the attempt to reconstruct a narrative that connects their religious identity with their political one. This task is important for both personal and public reasons. Each of the neoconservative Catholics, either through a self-revelation, as was the case with Weigel, or a publicly identifiable shift, as with Neuhaus and Novak, grew alienated from a liberal political worldview and more amenable to American conservative thought. Each of them also experienced a religious transition alongside their political one. As both their political and religious identities shifted in the seventies and eighties, the stories that had once grounded their lives were no longer adequate. Psychologically it was critical to reconstruct these narratives so as to take into account the disruptions that occurred following their respective political and religious conversions. An analysis focusing on how their stories became upended during their political conversion and reconstructed in its aftermath is a potentially interesting angle from which to examine the neoconservative Catholics. That is not the project here, at least not directly.

More important for our purposes is the way in which the neoconservative Catholics constructed a political and religious narrative that provides an apologetic for their respective worldviews. During the eighties each of the neoconservative Catholics developed an increasingly politically conservative narrative that was paired with a distinctive understanding of the Catholic moral and theological tradition. These discrete narratives, when merged, reinforced each other. What results is a master, historical narrative that provided credibility to their political and religious agenda. Simultaneously, it created a publicly accessible schema that invited others to adopt their narrative as a basis for their own worldview. Whether consciously or not, they are in effect trying to create a narrative that could function as a new legitimating force in American Catholic life. Such a narrative would simultaneously undermine the political and religious agendas of those who provide a competing historical narrative. Each of the neoconservative Catholics participated in this intellectual endeavor but each does so from a slightly different perspective.

Neuhaus spent a great deal of energy studying the relationship between religion and politics and strenuously argued against any attempt to strip religion from the public sphere. He tried to make the case that Christianity was central to the American experiment in democracy and called the churches to reaffirm this connection. Weigel turned to John Courtney Murray, whom he believed offered the intellectual resources necessary to rejuvenate the American experiment. Finally, Novak sought to develop the idea of democratic capitalism, both as a counterpoint to socialist and traditionalist worldviews and as a way to win over skeptical Catholics to the market system. While different, there are overlapping interests that guide the distinct projects of each of the neoconservative Catholics. Each sought to contribute to the renewal of the American political tradition in an age in which the legitimacy of this tradition had come into question. In doing so the neoconservative Catholics sought to demonstrate that American political thought is consistent or at least compatible with the Catholic social teaching tradition. This "reconciliationist" approach marked an important theme in their writings that put them at the heart of the republican Catholic tradition.

Neuhaus's conceptualization of the relationship between religion, political life, and society, Weigel's embrace and development of the John Courtney Murray project, and Novak's exploration of democratic capitalism provided the foundation on which each attempted to build his historical narrative. Exploring the ways in which each of their historical narratives functions as a backdrop to their particular conceptual schemas will elucidate an aspect of their thinking that is often overlooked. Given the differences between the neoconservative Catholics in this effort, addressing each one of them largely independently from the other is unavoidable.

Richard Neuhaus and the American Experiment

To understand Richard Neuhaus's thought during the eighties it is important to recall the relationship that he understood religion to have with a society's cultural and political institutions. A quote taken from an essay he titled "The Post-Secular Task of the Churches" neatly summarizes it. Here he wrote that "religion is the heart of culture, culture is the form of religion, and politics is a function of culture. That way of putting things is reminiscent of Paul Tillich, but the assumptions behind the bias could as well be attributed to Durkheim or Hegel or even to the philosophers of antiquity. Religion, the binding beliefs of a people, is, generally speaking, the dominant factor in how they [a people] order their life together."[5] Religious ideas and, more broadly, a shared moral consensus, are integral factors in the rise of political values in a given society. The historical narrative that emerged in his writings reflects the importance of this dynamic in an American context.

The relationship, as he understood it, between religion, culture, and politics is a dynamic phenomenon. As religious institutions and ideas rise and fall or change in relation to the society around them, they can become alienated from the political ideas that they once supported, thus leading to a crisis of legitimacy. Two general consequences can follow. First, a new set of institutional structures can fill the newly emergent void and in doing so provide a defense of these ideas. Or, the political and social system under question can undergo an upheaval and experience a significant amount of change and perhaps dissolution.

In the context of American political culture, Neuhaus emphasized the important role that Christianity played in the development of an American-style liberal democracy. As far back as the seventeenth century the earliest settlers often expounded on the exceptional place and character of this new land. References to the "New Jerusalem" or to the New World as "a city on the hill" helped to shape the early American experience. Neuhaus maintained that these expressions alluded to the conviction of the early settlers that "God had a hand in America's beginnings and was guiding it to the fulfillment

5. Neuhaus, "The Post-Secular Task of the Churches," 1.

of his appointed purpose."[6] Echoing this sentiment on more than one occasion, he claimed at one point that the American experiment in democracy "participates, albeit partially, in that new community to which the Christian Gospel points in the coming of the Kingdom of God."[7] To be fair, Neuhaus never absolutized the idea of America's exceptional character; the "chosen" quality of the American experiment and the values that this experiment affirmed was never a given. Both its long-term value and its durability could be judged only in retrospect. There is no reason to assume that America today could not turn out to be a modern-day Babylon tomorrow. Nor, even if it is of value in the overall sweep of history, political, social, economic, and religious changes could eventually undermine the strength and stability of the experiment.

Over the course of about fifteen years, from the mid-seventies to late eighties, Neuhaus became more confident with the idea that the American experiment was, if not directly under siege, undergoing a slow decay. This process had a long back story, one that Neuhaus was interested in exploring. To understand the current conditions of American political life in the late twentieth century, he thought it important to step back and understand the role that Protestantism had in this process, the changes that Protestantism underwent over the past century, and the consequences of its decline.

Neuhaus's take on the relationship between American religion and American political life become apparent in a series of essays he wrote over a period from the mid-seventies to the late eighties: *Time Toward Home*, "The Post-Secular Task of the Churches," *The Naked Public Square*, and *The Catholic Moment*. At the center of this story is the rise and fall of the mainline Protestant churches, which had "for two centuries provided a transcendent vision of the American possibility; in the social gospel movement it proposed wedding that vision to a very immanent program of social reform; in New Deal liberalism that marriage was consummated; amid the departure of

---

6. Neuhaus, *The Naked Public Square*, 208.
7. Neuhaus, "The Democratic Prospect," *Worldview* 19 (July/August 1976): 14.

New Deal confidence and the arrival of assassinations, Vietnam, and riotous discontent, the marriage was terminated."[8]

Recalling the works of European visitors to America during the nineteenth century, Neuhaus argued that there was a sense among scholars of the day that the Christian ethos was central to American culture and her political experiment in democracy. For better or worse the Christian sensibility of the American people shaped the American political vision well into the twentieth century.[9] It was an impression that Neuhaus shared.[10] While accurate insofar as he goes, there is another angle to this story that requires comment.

The historian of religion Mark Noll noted that many laymen and leaders alike in the Christian churches were in fact hostile to the republican political tradition well into the eighteenth century. Nevertheless, by the American Revolution many theologically conservative Christians had grown to embrace and even champion many of liberalism's major tenets. The merging of a republican and Christian worldview was largely the result of efforts by leading Christian intellectuals to fold these political ideas into a religious worldview.[11] By the time of the Revolution, and certainly in the decades following, "religion was so deeply intertwined with revolutionary political ideology that it seems virtually impossible to distinguish between them."[12]

The fusion between republican and Christian worldviews makes Neuhaus's argument more complex and highlights some potential weaknesses in his analysis. First, Neuhaus was certainly not naïve about the powerful influence that non-religious factors can have on a religious tradition. Nevertheless, throughout his writings his em-

---

8. Neuhaus, "The Post-Secular Task of the Churches," 14.

9. Neuhaus, *The Naked Public Square*, 202–3.

10. Ibid., 209.

11. Mark Noll, *America's God: From Jonathan Edwards to Abraham Lincoln* (New York: Oxford University Press, 2002), 55–75.

12. Ruth Bloch, "Religion and Ideological Change in the American Revolution," in *Religion and American Politics: From the Colonial Period to the Present*, 2nd ed., ed. Mark A. Noll et al., 53 (New York: Oxford University Press, 2007).

phasis tended to focus on the foundational role that Christianity had in the emergence of culture and the American political worldview. Reading Neuhaus one is often left with the sense that while other elements may have contributed to the formation of the American political system, Christianity was the necessary condition in the process. But scholars such as Noll have pointed out that there was for some time a certain separation, if not a chasm, between the two traditions under discussion. Throughout his writings during this period Neuhaus did not make much of an effort to analyze the roots of liberalism independent of the Christian worldview that he argued underlay it.

Further, he does not directly wrestle with the significant ways in which "secular" culture helped to shape Protestantism in the eighteenth and early nineteenth centuries. The historian Nathan Hatch has argued in a similar fashion to Mark Noll, asserting the central importance of Christianity in the early American republic was in its support for political idioms is consistent with the republican tradition. Yet it was a very American form of Christianity, distinct from its European counterparts, which came to support this political tradition. Through its development on American soil, large swaths of Protestant Christianity became "democratized" and, in the process, participated in the democratization of American culture in the decades following the Revolution.[13] In other words, Christianity was not merely a carrier of republican values that gained its full expression in the aftermath of the American Revolution but slowly became imbued by those values during its American experience.

Although Neuhaus unfortunately missed, overlooked, or ignored this more complex interaction, he accurately noted that American Christianity did play an important role in providing a rationale for republican virtues in the decades following the American Revolu-

13. Nathan Hatch, "The Democraticization of Christianity and the Character of American Politics," in *Religion and American Politics,* ed. Noll et al., 102–4; a more extended version of this article can be found at Nathan Hatch, *Democratization of American Christianity* (New Haven, Conn.: Yale University Press, 1989).

tion. As time passed the legitimating function fulfilled by the nine-teenth-century churches shifted to their twentieth-century progeny, "who are today described as the mainline, liberal, or ecumenical Protestant denominations."[14] The fundamental problem that Neu-haus highlighted in this shift was that by the mid-twentieth century the influence of the mainline churches had begun to wane, to lose adherents, and diminish in its political clout, thus leaving a void that needed to be filled. The decline in the influence of the main-line churches and the vacuum that remained constitutes the second major step in his historical narrative.

Recently scholars in the sociology of religion have reaffirmed the slow decline of mainline Protestant churches over the past centu-ry. The reasons for this decline relate directly to their inability to maintain a healthy tension with the surrounding culture. Failure to remain distinct from the wider culture lessens the value that any religion holds for prospective members and thus diminishes the likelihood that it will attract new followers.[15] Roger Finke and Rod-ney Starke, both of whom who have championed this perspective, argue that "people tend to value religion on the basis of how costly it is to belong—the more one must sacrifice in order to be in good standing, the more valuable the religion ... the more 'mainline' the church (in the sense of being regarded as respectable and reason-able), the lower the value of belonging to it, and this eventually re-sults in widespread defection."[16]

While writing before some of the more important studies on this topic were published, Neuhaus anticipated this line of argu-ment and put a theological spin on it. During the twentieth centu-ry, he claimed, and particularly during the latter half, the mainline churches began to abandon their theological distinctiveness in favor

14. Neuhaus, "The Post-Secular Task of the Churches," 1.

15. Roger Finke and Rodney Stark, *The Churching of America 1776–1990: Winners and Losers in Our Religious Economy* (New Brunswick, N.J.: Rutgers University Press, 1992), 249–55.

16. Ibid., 238.

of political relevance. Rather than leading culture, the Christian churches all too often fell behind and began to allow secular culture to take the lead. It was, argued Neuhaus, a time of the "great accommodation."[17] Central to Neuhaus's critique of mainline Protestantism was that although it was "long an extremely influential force, it has lately been on the decline. Its membership is shrinking, and many of those who remain seem more committed to certain political and social objectives than to traditional gospel values."[18]

The "great accommodation" became an increasingly problematic phenomenon to Neuhaus once the churches abandoned a self-confident Christianity that could function as a check on secular political counterparts. Mainline church leaders were increasingly capitulating to secular political interests and in doing so were allowing the world to set the agenda for the church, thus turning the proper order of things on its head. This tendency weakened the voice of the churches and, contrary to their intentions, limited any real influence they might have in shaping the political and social order.[19]

The marginalization of mainline Protestants did not diminish the importance of the legitimating role these religious groups had played throughout much of American history. Even with their passing the need was still there and the task still had to be done. With mainline Protestantism becoming increasingly irrelevant to this process, if the American experiment were to remain vibrant, this legitimating role had to be assumed by another group. As a way to provide an intellectual framework to make sense of this process, Neuhaus turned to Vilfred Pareto's idea of the "circulation of elites." As Neuhaus explained it, "social functions ... are performed by groups that, after a while, constitute themselves as elites. After a longer while, the elite (whether economic, military, governmental,

17. Neuhaus, *The Naked Public Square*, 213–18.

18. William J. Gould Jr., "John Paul and the Catholic Moment," *Washington Post*, September 6, 1987, B2.

19. Avery Dulles, *The Resilient Church: The Necessity and Limits of Adaptation* (Garden City, N.Y.: Doubleday, 1977), 84–85.

or religious) become flabby or disillusioned and no longer perform the function by which it acquired its privileged social position. When that happens, the function is not simply neglected. Rather, some other group, usually a quite different group, moves in to displace the old elite. And so elite functions circulate from one group to another."[20]

Surveying the religious landscape, Neuhaus tried to determine which religious group was in the best position to take the place of mainline Protestantism and examined three in particular: the fundamentalist Christians, the Lutherans, and the Roman Catholics.[21] He paid most of his attention to the fundamentalist and Catholic options. Neuhaus first focused on the fundamentalist Christian churches that had reappeared in American public life during the previous decade. In an early essay he noted their impressive use of technology and communications, and their effective electoral strategy in gaining political influence, but downplayed their chances of success given their tendencies toward apocalypticism and premillennialism. In important ways these latter characteristics were too far outside the mainstream to ever become a dominant vision guiding most Americans' lives. Even if they happened to win some elections, he thought it unlikely that they would ever win over many converts who did not already subscribe to their worldview.[22]

A few years later, Neuhaus expanded on his critique of fundamentalist Christianity in his book *The Naked Public Square*. Here he became more critical of fundamentalist Christianity's harsh tone and style, the intellectual substance of the Moral Majority, or lack thereof, and related contemporary forms of right-wing Christianity. He further argued that fundamentalism's sectarian language both prohibited the development of a commonly shared public ethic and,

---

20. Neuhaus, *The Naked Public Square*, 261–62.

21. Neuhaus also briefly looked at Protestant Evangelicals as a possible replacement but dismissed that option almost out of hand. We will thus not take the space to address his objections here.

22. Neuhaus, "The Post-Secular Task of the Churches," 15.

in fact, tended to marginalize the value of religious language in the public square for those not already in agreement with a fundamentalist worldview.[23] The biblicism, literalism, and private interpretative framework at work in this worldview, while providing a comprehensive worldview to the individual believer, did not provide a useful vantage from which the believer can engage the non-believer.[24] The narrowly defined rhetoric from which fundamentalists draw undermined any constructive public debate with those who disagree. Neuhaus argued that "by separating public argument from private belief, by building a strict separationism between faith and reason, fundamentalist religion ratifies and reinforces the conclusions of militant secularism."[25] In other words, the fundamentalist approach to the encounter between religion and politics does little more than support the divorce of the one from the other. It unwittingly participated in the establishment of the naked public square.

With fundamentalist Christianity an unlikely successor to mainline Protestantism, Neuhaus turned his attention to Lutheranism. A Lutheran himself before his conversion to Roman Catholicism in 1991, one might be inclined to think that he would hold Lutheranism as the likely heir to mainline Protestantism. This was not the case. A European-style Lutheranism, he argued, with its two-kingdoms theology and tendency toward authoritarianism, does not have much to offer as it lacks a religious rationale that could be useful in defending a democratic style of government. American-style Lutheranism, which had moved beyond the limits of the European tradition, held some promise but had not matured enough to be ready to fulfill the responsibilities that were being slowly abandoned by the mainline churches.[26]

Having discussed possible options in the Protestant community, Neuhaus also looked at the possible role that Roman Catholicism

23. Neuhaus, *The Naked Public Square*, 36–37.
24. Ibid., 16–18.
25. Ibid., 37.
26. Neuhaus, "The Post-Secular Task of the Churches," 16–17.

could play in strengthening the idea of the American experiment. From the mid-seventies to the late eighties, his assessment of the Roman Catholic Church as a viable alternative to mainline Protestantism shifted back and forth from a passing optimism, to a qualified suspicion, to, finally, a strong conviction that only the Catholic church could fill the role of mainline Protestantism. In one of his earliest discussions on this issue he noted, almost in passing, that "the quality of moral discourse in American public life depends, I believe, in large measure upon the nerve with which American Catholics join in the struggle to revitalize and redefine the terms of our common covenant."[27] Whether this would occur depended largely on how American Catholicism adjusted its identity now that it had finally become "American" in the post-World War II era. The Catholic church now had an opportunity, in a way that it did not in earlier years, to engage and shape American culture directly.

In an essay written a few years later Neuhaus took a more skeptical tone regarding the Catholic church's ability to provide a leadership role in the coming decades. He worried that the Catholic church had been welcomed into American society only recently and that anti-Catholicism, still alive and well in society, could alienate American Catholics from taking a leadership role.[28] He expressed concerns over the credibility of current church leadership and worried that the Catholic leadership had grown out of touch with its own tradition. On this point he wrote that "Catholic leadership, so eager to be 'Americanized,' has emulated mainline Protestantism to the extent that it too has struck out, but before it even got a proper turn to bat. A comparison of the public positions on both foreign and domestic issues of the National Conference of Catholic Bishops with the National Council of Churches is not encouraging. And it is best not to even mention the captivity of influential religious orders and other organizations to the 'liberationist' mentality,

27. Neuhaus, *Time Toward Home*, 148.
28. Neuhaus, "The Post-Secular Task of the Churches," 16.

which—whatever its merits—disqualifies them from taking part in the redefining of America."[29] Such a critique presupposed that the Catholic church leadership had abandoned a formative role and, like mainline Protestantism, merely accommodated itself to political positions put forth by the world. Not surprisingly, such a perspective hardly instilled confidence that the Catholic church could step up and play an important role in the defense of the American democratic experiment. At this point, Neuhaus did not seem hopeful that the Catholics, the Lutherans, or the fundamentalists were likely to take the place of mainline Protestantism. The essay ended with a pessimistic observation, lamenting the fact that "in this drama of relating Christian faith and public life, the old actors are exhausted and the new ones are impossible. Post-secular America has a religious role in search of religious leadership that has the nerve for it."[30]

Only a few years later, Neuhaus reversed this position and instead argued that the Catholic church, as the single largest religious group in the United States, remained in a prime position to play an important culture-forming role. He claimed that by the mid-eighties it appeared that the institutional church seems to have "weathered the storm" that arose in the immediate aftermath of Vatican II, although, he quickly added, there was still the threat that Catholics would replicate the behavior of mainline Protestantism. While he did not expand on the role of the Catholic church in the United States at any great length at this point, it is notable that he was already making reference to it being the "Catholic moment."[31]

It was in his book by that name that Neuhaus fully embraced the contributions that the Catholic church could make to American political life. In his earlier works he often voiced concern about the church's capitulation to secular politics, particularly of a leftist variety. While he continued to express some unease in this regard, he began to highlight competing trends that could function as a

---

29. Ibid.   30. Ibid., 18.
31. Neuhaus, *The Naked Public Square.*

counterweight to these tendencies. Perhaps foremost of all stands the figure of Pope John Paul II and, at his right hand, that of Joseph Ratzinger.

Although Neuhaus only briefly mentioned the role that John Paul II might play in the church in his earlier writings (and not a word on Ratzinger), in *The Catholic Moment* he spent an extensive amount of time on both. Most important for our purposes is the way that each tried to redirect the church during the eighties and particularly in the manner that John Paul II engaged controversial theologians and bishops. No longer, according to Neuhaus, could Catholic theologians say what they wanted without consequence. Theology must be done in a context wherein certain ideas are authoritative; there are, in other words, limits to theological speculation that have to be respected. The reining in by John Paul II and Ratzinger of theological speculation run wild, claimed Neuhaus, was an act of *renewal* following a post-Vatican II period that witnessed a collapse of Catholic identity.[32] While focusing on the international Catholic scene, Neuhaus pointed out the important implications that this renewal process has for the American Catholic church. The task that John Paul II had taken up in relation to the universal church coincided with the concerns that Neuhaus had regarding the American one. Neuhaus highlighted John Paul II's call for the American church "to resist the forces of modern accommodationalism. Accommodationalism can take the form of tailoring the truth to serve the civil religion of American democracy, or to gain respectability in the eyes of the secularized academe, or to advance the revolutionary struggle."[33]

"Accommodationalism" is the same term Neuhaus used to describe the collapse of mainline Protestantism. During the twentieth century mainline Protestantism engaged in a "great accommodationalism" that effectively undermined its spiritual authority and

32. Neuhaus, *The Catholic Moment: The Paradox of the Church in the Postmodern World* (New York: Harper and Row, 1987), 97–110.

33. Ibid., 102.

made it little more than a partisan in political affairs. By reiterating this term here, he is linking certain trends in American Catholicism with the failure of mainline Protestantism and warning Catholics that their church could meet a similar fate if they do not follow the lead of the pope. Neuhaus is also calling out segments of the Catholic church who are, as he saw it, engaged in accommodationalist activities. Within the larger context of his thought this accusation of accommodationalism consisted in a veiled criticism of the American bishops who too often engaged in partisan political bickering. In this vein, Neuhaus expressed his concern that "instead of being engaged in a new intensity of reflection ... people on all sides of the political divides come to view the bishops as simply one more set of actors in the familiar play of politics as usual."[34]

While Neuhaus did not oppose in principle the bishops' desire to engage political life, he argued that they often go about it in the wrong way. Their primary responsibility is not to stake out positions on every pressing political issue of the day, but to work at forming culture by imbuing it with a Catholic sensibility. If it were to do this, the Catholic church would have an opportunity to take up the torch that was dropped by mainline Protestant churches in recent decades. It was for Neuhaus the "Catholic moment." At this point his discussion intersected with the thought of George Weigel. Highlighting a then recently published book, Neuhaus claimed that Weigel's *Tranquillitas Ordinis* provided a road map that would help American Catholics recover their tradition in the modern world and lead them to fulfill the role once occupied by mainline Protestantism. Weigel's arguments offered, Neuhaus believed, a framework that could help the church understand what it means to be both Catholic and American.[35]

---

34. Ibid., 275.
35. Ibid., 240.

George Weigel: Up from the Middle Ages

Richard Neuhaus's emphasis on the "Catholic moment" in American life provides a useful segue into the thought of George Weigel. Similar to Neuhaus, Weigel recognized in the Catholic church an institution that has available to it a range of resources that could contribute to the renewal of the American experiment. In this respect the intellectual vision of John Courtney Murray played an indispensable role in the development of Weigel's thinking on the matter. His use of Murray committed him not only to a conceptual scheme that helped make sense of the world, but also to a historical framework that shed a particular light on the American democratic tradition.

Throughout his writings, Murray looked at both the state of Catholicism in mid-twentieth-century America and at the importance of medieval Catholic thought on American political thought. During the nineteenth century one of the key debates that raged in Protestant circles was the compatibility of Roman Catholicism with American republican values. Protestants of this era often "charged that Catholicism was an irrational religion based upon blind submission to an arbitrary teaching authority" and held that "Catholicism and American republicanism were historically, practically and theoretically incompatible."[36] The supposed incompatibility between these two traditions dogged the Catholic community well into the following century. By the post-World War II period, the source of these criticisms began to shift. While plenty of Protestants remained skeptical of the Catholic church, secularist thinkers began to speak out more loudly against the activity of religious communities in the public sphere.[37]

---

36. Patrick W. Carey, "American Catholic Religious Thought: An Historical Overview," *U.S. Catholic Historian* 4, no. 2 (1985): 126.

37. Robert McElroy, *The Search for an American Public Theology: The Contribution of John Courtney Murray* (New York: Paulist Press, 1989), 32–37. The most outspoken secular opponent of the Roman Catholic Church in the late forties was Paul Blanshard. See, for example, Paul Blanshard, *American Freedom and Catholic Power* (Boston: Beacon Press, 1949).

Murray's defense of the Catholic church's involvement in the public sphere can be read as a two-front attack against both Protestant antagonists and their secular counterparts. At the core of this defense is the idea that "all that is best in modern democracy is a reviviscence of ... 'the eternal Middle Ages.'"[38] In other words, he argued that one of the important tap roots for American republicanism rests in the intellectual resources that were nurtured and developed in medieval Catholic political thought.[39] Protestant claims to the contrary, not only is the Catholic church compatible with American democracy, it was an indispensable intellectual source for it. Because medieval Catholic political thought functions as a central support for the American democratic experiment, the secularist critique also becomes more tenuous. Secularists sought to banish religion to the margins of public life and, in doing so, replace any notion of a religiously grounded political tradition with a secular substitute. Doing so would, Murray contended, leave a spiritual vacuum that would open the door for an array of political abuses. Without some form of spiritual substance that would reinforce the value system inherent in American republican thought, the only thing that would remain is the state.[40]

The assertion that the scholastic period functioned as one of the fundamental sources for the American experiment in democracy is not novel to John Courtney Murray. This connection extends at least as far back as the early twentieth century. In his book *The Survival of American Innocence*, William Halsey traced this link to the growing confidence and optimism of the American Catholic church during this period. Halsey highlighted James Walsh's *The Thirteenth: Greatest of the Centuries* as one of the clearest and earli-

38. Cited in McElroy, *Search for an American Public Theology*, 24.

39. According to Murray, the roots of American republican thought actually extend back as early as Pope Gelasius I and his formulation of the "two swords" idea, but they mature during the scholastic period, in what he refers to as the medieval synthesis. For a brief but useful overview, see McElroy, *Search for an American Public Theology*, 20–25.

40. John Courtney Murray, "Contemporary Orientations of Catholic Social Thought on Church and State in the Light of History," *Theological Studies* 10 (June 1949): 187, n. 28.

est examples of this attempt.[41] In this book, Walsh aimed at painting "Catholicism as the inspirational element in the creating of universities, trade schools, libraries, Gothic architecture, literature, art and the early beginnings of democratic liberties."[42] In the decades following its publication, American Catholic intellectuals sought to demonstrate the extent to which their identity as Catholics was linked closely with their identity as Americans. Not only was Catholicism not an alien faith, but it was essential to the emergence of the American political tradition.

This type of argument culminated in the writings of John Courtney Murray. More intellectually refined and less romantic than his precursors, Murray contended that one of the essential sources for the American constitutional system, or the American proposition as he often referred to it, was to be found in medieval Catholic philosophy and theology.[43] Accordingly, "the heart of the Catholic social tradition could best be discerned in the medieval synthesis, and he saw in that synthesis compelling declarations of fundamental theological importance which had been recognized and enshrined in the American polity."[44]

The ideas that became enshrined in the American polity were reflected in what Murray referred to as the "public consensus," which is "an ensemble of substantive truths, a structure of basic knowledge, and an order of elementary affirmations that reflect realities inherent in the order of existence."[45] It was Murray's contention that these elementary affirmations functioned as a commonly held framework through which political conversation in the public

41. James Walsh, *The Thirteenth: Greatest of the Centuries* (New York: Catholic Summer School Press, 1912).

42. William H. Halsey, *The Survival of American Innocence: Catholicism in an Era of Disillusionment, 1920–1940* (Notre Dame, Ind.: University of Notre Dame Press, 1980), 66–67.

43. Ibid., 76–77.

44. Robert W. McElroy, "Catholicism and the American Polity: Murray as Interlocutor," in *John Courtney Murray and the Growth of Tradition,* ed. J. Leon Hooper et al., 6 (Kansas City, Kan.: Sheed and Ward, 1996).

45. Murray, *We Hold These Truths,* 27.

sphere was made possible. What troubled Murray was the growing sense that this consensus was slowly breaking down and what remained was an array of political opinions, the truth of which could not be measured by an appeal to some higher standard. The total breakdown of this consensus would, he worried, undermine the viability of the American experiment in democracy. A transcendent and autonomous standard that can function as a check on political power and decision making was an important anchor for the continued viability of the American system, without which political life would likely devolve into a system of interest-based, power politics.[46]

By the late sixties, the threat to this consensus had become more pronounced, as cultural, political, and religious upheavals fractured political debate and further undermined any common ground that might have existed in earlier decades. Growing skepticism surrounding the consensus influenced Catholic intellectual life, as much as it did some of their secular counterparts. An early biographer of Murray explained that after Murray's death in 1967, the American Catholic church lurched leftward and many therein grew skeptical of the American liberal tradition.[47] As Murray was a staunch defender of the public consensus and of the American political tradition, he began to be taken by some as quaint, irrelevant, and perhaps even dangerous.[48] At one point Garry Wills noted that it was not uncommon for Murray to be considered as being impossibly passé during the height of the sixties.[49] As late as 1978 another author wrote of Murray that "time is moving him deeper into the shadows of memory and interest."[50]

While segments of the Catholic left were rejecting Murray in

46. Neuhaus, for example, expressed concern about the de-transcendentalizing of truth as it relates to culture. Doing away with the transcendent brings with it the illusion of a value-free public sphere when in fact competing values are still pursued, albeit absent an overtly moral language; Neuhaus, *The Naked Public Square,* 125–40.

47. Donald E. Pelotte, *John Courtney Murray: Theologian in Conflict* (New York: Paulist Press, 1975), 189.

48. Ibid.

49. Neuhaus, *The Catholic Moment,* 255.

50. John Deedy, *Seven American Catholics* (Chicago: Thomas More Press, 1978), 152–53.

favor of other political and religiously grounded philosophies, by the mid-seventies other influential Catholic scholars were beginning to recognize again the important contributions that Murray made to American Catholic and political life. The sociologist John Coleman, for example, argued that John Courtney Murray was one of only three deceased American Catholic theologians worth reading at the time, given the insights that he provided on the intersection between Catholic theology and modern political life.[51] Shortly thereafter, David Hollenbach penned an essay expressing general agreement with Coleman and calling for a "critical re-evaluation of the American civil liberties tradition which Murray brought into creative contact with the American Catholic social tradition."[52] Three years later, in 1979, a symposium that focused specifically on the contributions of John Courtney Murray was held at Georgetown University. Participants included many of the thinkers who stood on the cusp of what would be the vanguard of the Murray revival.[53] Other Catholic scholars arose to answer their call to reengage some of the questions advanced by Murray, George Weigel among them.

Weigel expressed general agreement with Murray that the public consensus provided an intellectual framework that made the American experiment in democracy viable. Further, he also agreed that the principles comprising the consensus had their roots in medieval political thought. These principles included the state/society distinction; the notion that America is ultimately a nation under God's judgment; the principle of the people's consent to be governed; the idea that virtue is the basis for freedom; the notion of human rights; and the constitutional character of American political life.[54] Given

51. John Coleman, "Vision and Praxis in American Theology: Orestes Brownson, John A. Ryan, and John Courtney Murray," *Theological Studies* 37, no. 1 (March 1976): 3–40.

52. David Hollenbach, "Public Theology in America: Some Questions for Catholicism after John Courtney Murray," *Theological Studies* 37, no. 2 (June 1976): 291.

53. "Theology and Philosophy in Public: A Symposium on John Courtney Murray's Unfinished Agenda," *Theological Studies* 40, no. 4 (December 1979).

54. George Weigel, *Tranquillitas Ordinis: The Present Failure and Future Promise of American Catholic Thought on War and Peace* (Oxford: Oxford University Press, 1987).

the intellectual sources of the republican tradition, Weigel was also convinced that the Catholic church was an important player in any attempt to reaffirm the values of American political life.

The problem, Weigel argued, was that while the church possessed the resources to defend and revitalize the American experiment in democracy, church leaders had in recent years rejected this tradition. In the preface to his book *Tranquillitas Ordinis,* he expressed his concern that the "Church in the United States has not only failed to develop its heritage of thought over the past generation; the Church's most influential teaching centers have, in the main, largely abandoned that tradition."[55] *Tranquillitas Ordinis,* as is evident from its subtitle, *The Present Failure and Future of American Catholic Thought on War and Peace,* is primarily interested in the Catholic understanding of war and peace. Nevertheless, there is a more fundamental issue at stake here. There has developed within the Catholic tradition, Weigel argued, the notion of *tranquillitas ordinis,* or the tranquility of order, which can be traced back to the thought of Augustine and Aquinas.

Weigel argued that the American experiment in democracy has, in the context of modernity, best embodied the rightly ordered political community that is implied in the idea of the "tranquility of order." Weigel is not arguing that American-style democracy is the only valid expression of this vision, but in a world that has been buffeted by totalitarianisms of every variety, it is a model that the Catholic church should uphold and affirm. Further, it is not only consistent with, but also a legitimate formulation of, the Catholic political tradition that preceded it. His affirmation of republican political thought and its compatibility with Catholic teaching is not without some controversy. As Weigel noted, throughout much of the nineteenth century, and well into the twentieth, there was some resistance to the liberal political tradition. "Even if alone among Western institutions," he wrote, the Catholic church "would not

55. Ibid., ix.

accommodate to the intellectual challenge mounted by modern historical, literary, sociological, psychological, political, and scientific theory."[56]

Throughout this period, the Vatican expressed skepticism regarding liberal political thought and often viewed it as a threat to its own authority. On one level this reaction was understandable, for as liberalism spread across the European continent, anticlerical sentiment found greater influence in many areas of society, and anti-Catholic feeling became pronounced. This motivated church leadership to react harshly to the modern world, and to seek ways of reestablishing the church's authority in European life. One of the goals "of the post-1815 Roman Church was to salvage what rights and independence it could in the face of an expansion of state power and influence."[57]

While caution and even animosity toward liberalism became a common reaction of the church in Europe, the American church maintained a more confident posture with respect to the compatibility of these two traditions. Picking up on this tendency, Weigel alleged that many within its leadership ranks early on developed a positive intuition that "Roman Catholicism's traditionally incarnational ... imagination about human history, and the social ethic derived from it, were not merely congruent with an experiment in democratic pluralism, *but in fact implied in it.*"[58] Consequently, the American bishops recognized that the experiment in democratic pluralism was not a Protestant or Enlightenment invention, however much either of these traditions may have contributed to it, but was an extension and modern expression of an Augustinian/Thomistic tradition of what constituted a rightly ordered political community.[59]

It is in this context that Weigel links Murray's notion of the

56. Ibid., 74–76.

57. Gary Lease, "Vatican Foreign Policy and the Origins of Modernism," in *Catholicism Contending with Modernity,* ed. Darryl Jodock, 36 (Cambridge: Cambridge University Press, 2000).

58. Weigel, *Tranquillitas Ordinis,* 52.

59. Ibid.

American proposition with his notion of the *tranquillitas ordinis.*[60] The promise of this tradition was affirmed by most of the American church up until Vatican II. But for all its promise, in the decade that followed the tradition became increasingly peripheral to Catholic thought and was, for all intents and purposes, abandoned by the American Catholic leadership. Similar to Neuhaus's critique of the leadership in the mainline Protestant churches, Weigel argued that church leadership had become more interested in prophetic politics and political relevance than in affirming and upholding the millennia-old Catholic tradition. He wrote that many of the Catholic intellectual elite "set themselves the task of delegitimating the American proposition—although what many of them understood themselves to be doing was undertaking a 'prophetic' critique of the American system of political economy and of U.S. foreign policy."[61]

Weigel understood it as partly his responsibility to draw attention to this failure and call the church back in the process. This process of recovery required that the church reject the overtly prophetic, left-wing Catholicism that looks at America as worthy of condemnation for its inequities and sins, a tendency that was apparent throughout the writings of publications like *The National Catholic Reporter.*[62] While left-wing Catholicism posed a challenge, it was not the only threat to the intellectual integrity of the American Catholic church; the traditionalist wing that rose up in reaction to Vatican II was also a danger to be avoided. Holding up *The Wanderer* as a preeminent example of this temptation, he held that the traditionalist Catholics look to the post–Vatican II era as a period in which the "heresy" of Americanism and modernism had finally gained the upper hand and modernism infected the church. What

60. George Weigel, "John Courtney Murray and the American Proposition," *Catholicism in Crisis,* November 1985, 8.

61. Ibid., 12.

62. Weigel, *Catholicism and the Renewal of American Democracy* (Mahwah, N.J.: Paulist Press, 1989), 47–69.

was needed was a new era of restoration that would bring Catholicism back to the church of Popes Leo XIII and Pius IX.[63]

The stark divisions that had arisen in the church and the problems associated with them are, for Weigel, not merely of ecclesiological importance because of the direct bearing these divisions could have on American political life. Given his conviction that the church had a useful set of resources that could help strengthen the American democratic experiment, the deep fissures within the church prevented it from taking advantage of these resources in an effective manner. Furthermore, these divisions merely reflected the fractured state of society.

Echoing the thought of Alasdair MacIntyre, whose argument we touched on briefly above, Weigel claimed that modern Western society had effectively devolved into a state of moral chaos. The shift to emotivism as the dominant moral paradigm in which modern society functioned made it extremely difficult to provide objective and reliable foundations for any sort of moral claims related to political life. This is clearly untenable for someone like George Weigel, who argued that the American democratic vision is built on a set of shared moral propositions that takes seriously a set of self-evident truths that are, in turn, affirmed as the basis for the American political system. The philosophical pluralism that underlies the moral relativism that both Weigel and MacIntyre hold is part of the modern condition and cannot account for such self-evident truths.

To counter this, Weigel argued that what the West needs to recover is an appreciation for natural-law thinking, which would provide a religiously neutral moral grammar that people of all faiths could use to analyze pressing moral questions. Drawing on the supposed neutrality of natural law and citing Murray, Weigel argued that at its core are three fundamental presuppositions: "that man is intelligent; that reality is intelligible; and that it [reality] be obeyed in its demands for action or abstention."[64] Furthermore, he argued

63. Ibid., 70–82.
64. Weigel, *Catholicism and the Renewal of American Democracy,* 93.

that almost all men and women of good will could use natural law as a basis for arriving at moral conclusions.[65] He goes so far elsewhere as to claim that it might be possible to argue that natural-law thinking is inherent in the human condition and that, whether we realize it or not, we regularly think in terms of natural-law categories, even if we do not realize that we are doing so.[66]

While appealing to the natural-law tradition as a solution to this chaotic state of affairs, the case that he makes during this period falls short of its intended target. His failure to provide a theoretical defense of natural law, something he readily admitted he was not trying to do, is the very case that he needed to make so as to provide a convincing brief for his argument. Another book written by Alistair MacIntyre, *Whose Justice? Which Rationality?*, demonstrates why this is so. Here MacIntyre argued that the Thomistically grounded moral thought of natural law, on which Weigel depended, is itself a tradition that in a modern context is in competition with competing moral traditions. Part of this competition entails debates over the meaning of such terms of justice, rationality, and, more specifically, practical reason.[67]

Some sense of what we mean by the terms "justice" and "rationality" are constituent to any understanding of the natural law. How someone understands these terms is dependent on the intellectual tradition to which one commits herself. MacIntyre wrote that "Aquinas' account is only fully intelligible, let alone defensible, as it emerges from an extended and complex tradition of argument and conflict" that included Aristotle and Augustine, not to mention the debates that occurred during the thirteenth century and later.[68] Further, Aquinas's appropriation of these terms is at odds with the way in which competing traditions, such as liberalism, use these same terms. Needless to say, MacIntyre's emphasis on the tradition-based

---

65. Ibid.   66. Ibid., 199.

67. Alasdair MacIntyre, *Whose Justice? Which Rationality?* (Notre Dame, Ind.: University of Notre Dame Press, 1988), 2.

68. Ibid., 205.

reality of natural law highlights why Weigel's argument, that "man is intelligent; that reality is intelligible; and that it be obeyed in its demands for action or abstention," is not in itself an adequate defense of the natural law. The terms that are presupposed in this observation have to be fleshed out much more fully if they are to be made convincing to others who have a competing understanding of what these terms mean.[69] To make the case for the adequacy of natural law to address contemporary problems, he would need to develop a more systematic defense of this approach. Failing to do so here reveals, if not a deficiency in his argument, at least an opening where more work would have to be been done in the coming years.

Michael Novak: Catholic Social Teaching and the State

The historical narrative that Novak constructs signifies somewhat of a departure from that of his neoconservative Catholic allies, insofar as he is hesitant to give religion as central a role in his political vision as they do in theirs. Already noted in the previous chapter, and to Neuhaus's dismay, Novak argued that at the heart of American life is an "empty shrine," a claim that sounded too much like the naked public square to Neuhaus. Even though Novak admitted that the Christian tradition helped to shape the political and cultural vision in a Western context, Christianity was not for him, and at least at this time, a necessary presupposition to the democratic capitalist experiment.[70] Deemphasizing the role of religion in this way results in a subtle but marked contrast to Neuhaus and Weigel.

It will help to recall that both Neuhaus and Weigel argued that the American democratic experiment emerged out of the Christian political and social teaching tradition. Weigel held that the seeds of this experiment were planted in the medieval period and par-

---

69. To be fair, he indirectly noted this when recognizing that certain strands of Protestantism take the condition of original sin as having clouded man's rational faculty to such an extent as to make natural-law thinking impossible. In response, he merely states that he thinks they are incorrect; Weigel, *Catholicism and the Renewal*, 201.

70. Novak, *The Spirit of Democratic Capitalism*, 67–68.

ticularly in the thought of Thomas Aquinas. In the centuries following Aquinas, these ideas slowly matured and finally became an important philosophical basis for the American experiment in democracy. While perhaps not as explicit as Weigel, and working out of a more general Christian framework, Neuhaus defended the idea that American political life is largely an expression of a Christian worldview. Political ideas are, in effect, the result of a shared moral and religious framework of a given people. In the case of Western society, Christianity became the primary resource out of which the ideas expressed in the Constitution emerged.

Novak's writings during this period do not share this vision. He does not hold to the proposition that the American political tradition *emerges* out of the Catholic tradition. Instead, he essentially argues that over the course of the twentieth century the American political tradition slowly *converges* with the Catholic social teaching tradition. Although he voiced a different vision, there is in all three an important correspondence: each holds to the idea that Catholic social teaching and the American experiment in democracy are not at odds with one another, but are complementary. The convergence that Novak envisioned signifies a process of reconciliation, primarily due to developments in Catholic social teaching that began in the nineteenth century.

Two elements in this evolution are of particular importance to Novak. First is his contention that human rights have become central to modern Catholic social teaching. Second, poverty in the developing world has become a problem that the church had to confront in a more forceful manner. This latter feature has become increasingly evident due to the growing importance of economic development in post-World War II Catholic thought. In sum, Novak wrote that "more clearly in the 1980s than in the 1890s, Catholic social thought now recognizes two overarching ideals ... these are the ideals of 'development' and 'human rights.'"[71] Not only have

---

71. Novak, *Catholic Social Thought and Liberal Institutions: Freedom with Justice* (New Brunswick, N.J.: Transaction, 1989), 29. By development, Novak is here referring in

these two elements become central to modern Catholic social teaching but, as we will see, he argued that they can best be promoted through institutions that are congruent with democratic capitalism.

Human Rights and Catholic Social Teaching

Novak was not alone among Catholic intellectuals of that period in recognizing that the Catholic church had come to embrace the human-rights tradition. In his book *Claims in Conflict* David Hollenbach examined this development and traced the church's changing take on human rights during the previous century.[72] Its eventual embrace of human rights contrasted with what the church held in an earlier age, when democratic self-governance and free speech were condemned, religious freedom was scoffed at, and other liberties inherent in liberalism were held in low regard. From Pope Leo XIII, who laid the groundwork for the modern appreciation of human rights, through Pope Paul VI, this growing appreciation was rooted in the church's concern for the dignity of the human person.[73]

While not relying on him explicitly, and in places criticizing Hollenbach's analysis, Novak's thought nevertheless reflected the general arc that Hollenbach laid out in his writings on the subject. The church's resistance to the liberalism in a European setting promoted skepticism about the idea of human rights proclaimed by liberals everywhere. By the eve of the Second Vatican Council the church's position on human rights and liberal forms of democracy had been turned on its head. Remarking on John XXIII's encyclical *Pacem in Terris,* Novak proclaimed that the pope had finally solidified the tradition of human rights, "many of them borrowed almost directly from the U.S. Bill of Rights, into the universal patrimony of the church."[74]

---

particular to economic development in political life and the central role that it has come to play in Catholic social teaching.

72. David Hollenbach, *Claims in Conflict: Retrieving and Renewing the Human Rights Tradition* (New York: Paulist Press, 1979), 1.

73. David Hollenbach, "Human Rights in Catholic Thought," *America,* October 31, 2005, 17.

74. Novak, *Catholic Social Thought and Liberal Institutions,* 131.

Beyond a strictly theoretical engagement with the issue, a fundamental emphasis during this period was on the importance of the institutionalization of human rights.[75] Such institutions would include, for Novak, structures that support a representative democracy, a free press, the proliferation of mediating institutions, and a federal government that was kept in check but was by no means impotent. Not only are human rights important for their domestic significance, they also have relevance on the international plane. It was important for the U.S. government to challenge countries like the Soviet Union that do not have in place the infrastructure to support a human-rights ethic. Such governments pose a continual threat to those countries, like the United States, who exalted such a framework.[76] George Weigel echoed this concern, noting that an important objective of the neoconservative Catholics during the eighties consisted in the revitalization of the "American commitment to human rights ... as the indispensable antidote to the poison of Marxism-Leninism."[77]

The Catholic church's slow embrace of human rights during the twentieth century signified to Michael Novak an important advance in her social teaching. It demonstrated not only an advance in the church's understanding of the inherent dignity of the human person, but also laid the groundwork for a deeper appreciation of democratic forms of government. This was particularly important

75. Michael Novak, *Human Rights and the New Realism: Strategic Thinking in a New Age* (New York: The Freedom House, 1986), 7. It is also worth noting here that shortly after Reagan was elected president, Michael Novak was named to the U.S. delegation to the U.N. Human Rights Commission. For a collection of his statements when he was on the commission, see Michael Novak and Richard Schifter, *Rethinking Human Rights: Speeches by the United States Delegation to the 37th Session of the United States Commission on Human Rights* (Washington, D.C.: The Foundation for Democratic Education, 1981). For a discussion of his time on the commission, see Michael Novak and Richard Schifter, *A Conversation with Michael Novak and Richard Schifter: Human Rights and the United Nations* (Washington D.C.: American Enterprise Institute, 1981).

76. Novak, *Human Rights and the New Realism*, 17–24; Weigel, *Tranquillitas Ordinis*, 368–69; Neuhaus, "What We Mean by Human Rights and Why," *Christian Century*, December 6, 1978, 1177–80.

77. Weigel, "The Neoconservative Difference," 139; see also Richard Neuhaus and George Weigel, "Could Glasnost Make a Difference in Human Rights?" *Wall Street Journal*, January 28, 1988, 22.

in an age that had witnessed the rise of totalitarianism as exemplified by the Soviet Union and the Marxist threat.

A theoretical appreciation and even embrace of the human-rights tradition was not adequate, nor was the mere affirmation of institutional structures that would protect and promote human rights. For democratic institutions to remain vital, and perhaps even take root in the first place, and for human rights to be taken seriously, economic development is an important correlative step. The poor must be lifted out of their poverty and provided the opportunities and resources that will allow them to become politically and socially proactive.[78] As the twentieth century progressed the church began to take notice of this need and increasingly emphasized the need for economic development.

Economic Development and Catholic Social Teaching

Following World War II, Catholic social teaching began to take on a focus beyond Western Europe and turned toward the developing world. Partly as a consequence of this wider outlook, there emerged a more fully developed international perspective in her social teaching.[79] While even the earliest social encyclicals affirmed moral principles applicable to international relations, they typically favored topics of Western European interest. In *Rerum Novarum*, for example, Pope Leo XIII paid extended attention to the problem of an exploited working class and the responsibilities of both the working class and management toward one another. This emphasis reflected the heightened importance of labor relations at the end of the nineteenth century and the conflict between proponents of a socialist and free-market economy.

As social, political, and economic conditions changed during the

---

78. Novak, *The Spirit of Democratic Capitalism*, 15.

79. For an extended analysis of the internationalization of the common good in Catholic social teaching, see William A. Barbieri, "Beyond the Nations: The Expansion of the Common Good in Catholic Social Thought," *The Review of Politics* 63, no. 4 (Autumn 2001): 723–54.

twentieth century, Catholic social teaching was regularly applied to newly emergent problems. One problem of particular importance during the post-World War II period was the growing interdependence of the international community. Partially in response to changing political and economic conditions, the Vatican began to address the issue of economic and political development and, along with it, globalization. In the years preceding the formation of the United Nations, Pope Pius XII called for the creation of international, institutional structures that would help to alleviate poverty worldwide.[80] Following Pius XII's lead, John XXIII further developed this focus on the international community and gave extensive attention to the promises and perils accompanying globalization, the growing interdependence of the world community, and underdevelopment.[81] He taught that it is the responsibility of more technologically advanced nations to assist their less developed counterparts in acquiring "the scientific, technical, and professional training they need, and to put at their disposal the necessary capital for speeding up their economic development with the help of modern methods."[82]

Novak argued that while it was during the leadership of John XXIII that the political liberties inherent in the human-rights tradition were emphasized, it was during the rule of Paul VI that economic development became a central theme. He cited in particular the final passage of *Octogesima Adveniens,* which states that "development is the new name for peace," and claimed that this pronouncement falls squarely in line with the worldview of Adam Smith, who asserted that "economic activists in the fields of commerce and industry would bring about the interdependence of the world, development, and peace."[83]

Not only does Novak argue that democratic capitalism is the most effective mechanism to raise the poor out of poverty, he also

---

80. William Au, *The Cross, the Flag, and the Bomb: American Catholics Debate War and Peace, 1960–1983* (Westport, Conn.: Greenwood Press, 1985), 163–66.

81. *Mater et Magistra,* May 15, 1961.

82. Ibid., no. 163.

83. Novak, *Catholic Social Thought and Liberal Institutions,* 137.

asserts that an underlying commitment to democratic capitalism is reflected in recent developments in Catholic social teaching. Because the church has embraced human rights and takes seriously the importance of economic development in the developing world, the church is implicitly committed to the institutional structures that will realize these value commitments. Ideas alone are not enough. In a political context, for ideas to work they must become embedded in and find expression through institutional structures. To make value commitments viable, it is essential to move the discussion from the more abstract character of political theory to the concrete character of political and economic institutions that will help to realize these intellectual commitments.[84] With this in mind Novak argued that, while he may not have realized it at the time, Pope Paul VI's "commitments to human rights and to economic development commit him to liberal institutions."[85]

Novak's affirmation of democratic capitalist institutions and his assertion that the church had, as a consequence, committed herself to these institutional structures—given the value commitments she made during the twentieth century—were not without controversy. There were others in the church who were more skeptical of the capitalist enterprise, and who instead thought it to be the source of many problems in the modern world. While Pope Paul VI's teaching signified an advance in some respects, Novak worried that, when paired with certain interpretations of the Second Vatican Council documents, the same teaching could be used for a more pernicious effect. Paul VI's establishment of the Vatican Justice and Peace Commission in 1967, followed by a series of synods throughout the seventies, and the Latin American conferences at Medellin and elsewhere, both inspired and gave credibility to the rise of liberation movements.[86] Suffice it to say, liberation theologians gener-

---

84. Michael Novak, "Democracy and Development," *Catholicism in Crisis*, September 1983, 41.

85. Novak, *Catholic Social Thought and Liberal Institutions*, 143–44.

86. Ibid., 144–48; Novak, *The Spirit of Democratic Capitalism*, 272–73.

ally held that the international structures that ordered the economy were weighted heavily in favor of the developed world and to the enormous disadvantage of underdeveloped countries. Capitalism is, they argued, an unjust economic system that should be overturned in favor of a system that is more equitable.

Novak argued that many of these movements had perfectionist and romantic tendencies that sought to wipe out sinful structures once and for all. They aimed at eliminating injustice and leveling hierarchies. They also often abandoned traditional Catholic teaching altogether. Worse still, for Novak, these aberrant tendencies were not restricted to a minority of Latin American theologians who were fighting against legitimate injustices, albeit, according to Novak, while proposing the wrong solutions. It was not exclusive to a handful of academics in a few universities. The destructive tendencies at work in the church following the Second Vatican Council had become influential among large segments of the Catholic leadership.[87] The "war to eliminate hunger, discrimination, war, and every human evil, that illusory war waged by our own idealism … the ancient name for such idealism as now suffuses so many of our elites in Western and non-Western societies is gnosticism."[88]

Many of the American bishops and Catholic leaders in general had, according to Novak, lost their way and failed to apply properly Catholic social teaching to the major problem areas of the day. While there were unfortunate trends in this direction, Novak remained confident that the development of Catholic social teaching was, from the perspective of the Vatican, more congruent with his own teaching than it was with these heterodox teachings. By the late eighties he was increasingly confident that John Paul II had taken concrete steps "concerning the importance of liberal democratic institutions to the fulfillment of Catholic moral teaching," and thus once again put church teaching back on firm ground.[89]

---

87. Novak, *Confession of a Catholic*, 46, 183–206.
88. Ibid., 193.
89. Novak, *Catholic Social Thought and Liberal Institutions*, 220.

From the neoconservative Catholics' perspective, it is they who are aligned nicely with papal teaching, in contrast to much of the American Catholic leadership, including more than a few bishops, who stood in opposition to church teaching. It should therefore come as no surprise that each of the neoconservative Catholics turns to John Paul II as a pivotal figure in the life of the church. On one occasion Weigel declared of him that he was "standing firmly across the flood crested river of cultural collaborationism and appeasement and urging, 'Stop.'"[90] The pope was the one who had, from their perspective, validated neoconservative Catholic concerns and given the seal of approval to many of their solutions. In this way neoconservatives engage in a process of triangulation. Criticizing the American bishops for many of their political stands, the neoconservative Catholics proceeded to argue that the Vatican and, more specifically, John Paul II held views that were largely consistent with their own.

The struggle between these competing parties, the neoconservative Catholics on one side and progressive theologians and bishops on the other, took shape at distinct moments throughout the eighties. The most apparent of these moments were in the debates surrounding the bishops' letters on the economy and on war and peace and in discussions related to Latin America and liberation theology. Not only were the neoconservative Catholics fighting to save the church, they were doing so in the context of the Cold War. Before turning our attention to these matters, it is worth highlighting one of the central issues that has divided Americans for the past half century: abortion. This issue highlights some surprising nuances in the neoconservatives' thought and also provides a springboard to better understand political conditions that gave rise to their thinking on the eve of the Reagan presidency.

90. Weigel, *Catholicism and the Renewal of American Democracy*, 41.

3 ❖ FROM ABORTION TO REAGAN

THROUGHOUT THE MIDDLE DECADES of the twentieth century American Catholics had traditionally sided with the Democratic Party in national elections and were reliable constituents in the New Deal coalition built by FDR. But for the first time since the Gallup organization began in 1935, the Democratic Party was unable to maintain its Catholic backing in the presidential election of 1972. Nixon secured 52 percent of the national Catholic vote, which was up from a mere 33 percent just four years earlier.[1] This shift was due "in part because the Democratic Party in the heady years between 1968 and 1972 became associated with a cultural liberalism that some Catholic voters, especially working-class whites, found unsettling.... Humphrey, during the bitter days of the 1972 Democratic primaries, inaccurately but effectively tarred McGovern as favoring 'abortion, acid, and amnesty.'"[2]

One of the pivotal events that contributed to the disruption of the New Deal Democratic coalition during the seventies was the *Roe v. Wade* decision. While the decision did not drive Catholics en masse to the Republican Party, it helped to siphon off conservative,

---

1. William Prendergast, *The Catholic Voter in American Politics: The Passing of the Democratic Monolith* (Washington, D.C.: Georgetown University Press, 2007), 157.
2. John McGreevey, "Catholics, Democrats, and the GOP in Contemporary America," *American Quarterly* 59, no. 3 (2007): 670.

pro-life Catholics during the next decade. Debates as to whether Catholic, pro-choice politicians—a contradiction for many conservative Catholics—ought to be allowed communion and whether the average lay Catholic can in good conscience vote for such a figure and remain in good standing with the church have become commonplace in recent election cycles. While abortion quickly became a defining issue for many conservative Catholics, by the late seventies that broader church had integrated enough into American culture that there was little difference between non-Catholics and their Catholic counterparts on this issue. During this period Catholic voters as a whole "were only modestly less pro-choice than the general population ... and tended not to make abortion a voting issue."[3] The same could not be said for the American Catholic hierarchy, which had been vocally opposed to abortion even before the *Roe* decision.

In his book *Catholic Bishops in American Politics* Timothy Byrnes declared that "the Catholic bishops' most significant political act in the late 1960s and early 1970s was their identification with the movement to ban abortion. With the help of the bishops' attention and resources, abortion became a prominent item on the conservative social agenda, and in time conservatives made abortion the centerpiece of their effort to draw socially conservative Catholics away from the Democratic Party."[4] Throughout the late sixties and into the 1970s the hierarchy issued a number of statements opposing the liberalization of abortion laws, including *Human Life in Our Day,* released in 1968, and subsequent statements issued in 1969, 1970, and 1972. In each of these publications the bishops cited Catholic doctrine and American legal principles as the basis for their opposition.[5] In the first statement, for example, they reasserted the importance of protecting human life from the moment of conception and declared that

3. Ibid., 671.
4. Timothy Byrnes, *Catholic Bishops in American Politics* (Princeton, N.J.: Princeton University Press, 1991), 65.
5. Ibid., 56.

attempts to soften moral or legal prohibitions against abortion are "contrary to Judeo-Christian traditions inspired by love for life, and Anglo-Saxon legal traditions protective of life and the person."[6]

In addition to periodic pastoral and theological statements that sought to clarify and reaffirm the church's position on abortion, the bishops also became politically active in their opposition. In the pre-*Roe* period various bishops made efforts to rally lay Catholics against the liberalization of abortion laws. In the last major statewide referendum before *Roe v. Wade,* the Michigan Catholic Conference helped to rally the Catholic working class against the referendum, an effort that proved decisive in its defeat.[7] A couple of years earlier, in 1967, the New York bishops issued a pastoral letter urging the laity to oppose the Blumenthal bill, which would have permitted abortion when the physical or mental health of the mother was at stake, when the infant would be born with a physical or mental defect, when the pregnancy was a result of incest or rape, or when the mother was unwed and under fifteen years of age.[8] With over six million Catholics in New York State alone, this gave the bishops a good deal of potential clout, even though Catholics were not in ideological lockstep on the issue.[9] The bill went down to defeat that spring.

A *New York Times* article at the time noted that it was the position of most political observers that the Blumenthal bill had little chance of passage, "primarily because of the Catholic opposition."[10] A few months later, Richard Neuhaus attributed the defeat of the bill primarily to the presence of Catholics in that state.[11] Although crediting the bishops for this success he also shared some harsh

6. National Conference of Catholic Bishops, *Human Life in Our Day* (Glen Rock, N.J.: Paulist Press, 1969), no. 84.

7. McGreevey, "Catholics, Democrats, and the GOP," 671.

8. "Abortion Reform," *New York Times,* February 14, 1967, 42.

9. Michael Sean Winters, *Left at the Altar: How the Democrats Lost the Catholics and How the Catholics Can Save the Democrats* (New York: Basic Books, 2008), 117–19.

10. Sydney Shanberg, "State's Eight Catholic Bishops," *New York Times,* February 13, 1967, 1.

11. Richard John Neuhaus, "The Dangerous Assumptions," *Commonweal,* June 30, 1967, 408.

words, claiming that the bishops had a serious credibility problem on the issue of human rights. Recognizing their influence in debates over abortion Neuhaus lamented that "judging from their public statements, the bishops' role of championing the unborn child's right to life is in stark contrast to their sublime indifference to the slaughter of the innocents in Vietnam," and further quoted a friend who said that seeking advice from the bishops on the rights of the disinherited is "somewhat like getting advice about academic freedom from the Inquisition."[12] Three years later he reiterated a similar concern, stating that "the Roman Catholic hierarchy is one of the least credible witnesses to social morality in American life."[13]

The *Roe v. Wade* decision turned the entire debate over abortion on its head. With the decision, the focus shifted away from state-level initiatives to the national level. Responding to the decision the bishops formed the National Committee for a Human Life Amendment and issued the *Pastoral Plan for Pro-Life Activities* (1973), which provided a proactive political strategy that sought to educate the public on issues from a pro-life perspective, called for the provision of pastoral care for those who were facing difficult child-bearing circumstances, and issued a blueprint for public policy efforts on behalf of the pro-life cause. That same year the bishops stated explicitly that passage of a pro-life amendment to the Constitution was a priority of the highest order.[14] Surveying the work of the bishops on the abortion issue at the time of and following the *Roe v. Wade* decision, Michael Cuneo concluded that "it is doubtful that the Catholic leadership of any country in the Western world (with the possible exception of Ireland) has been more outspoken on abortion, or more actively engaged in fighting it, than the American bishops."[15]

12. Ibid., 409.

13. Richard John Neuhaus, "American Ethos and the Revolutionary Option," *Worldview* 13, no. 12 (December 1970): 6.

14. Byrnes, *Catholic Bishops in American Politics,* 56–57.

15. Michael Cuneo, "Life Battles: The Rise of Catholic Militancy within the American Pro-Life Movement," in *Being Right: Conservative Catholics in America,* ed. Mary Jo Weaver and R. Scott Appleby, 278 (Bloomington: Indiana University Press, 1995).

While the bishops were steadfast in their opposition to abortion, going so far as to call for a constitutional amendment to ban the practice, both Michael Novak and Richard Neuhaus were less strident than the bishops regarding how to deal with the problem of abortion. As early as 1967, when the above-mentioned Blumenthal bill was under discussion in New York, both Neuhaus and Novak published articles that focused on the legal and ethical implications of the issue. Both also shared a similar starting point that helped to guide the development of their thought on this matter over a period of at least two decades. That starting point centered on the question of when life begins and at what point the fetus should be considered a person worthy of moral protection.

In an editorial written for the *Christian Century* Novak admitted that he found his "conscience divided" as to whether or not he should support an expansion of abortion in cases in which the mother's physical or mental health was at risk, in instances of rape or incest, or in the likelihood of a deformed baby. On the one hand he took for granted that the right to life is not unconditional; war, the death penalty, and self-defense are notable instances in which another's life is taken without culpability. Nevertheless he admitted the importance of protecting those who are most vulnerable and defenseless. He concluded that the key question with regard to abortion, "although not the only question, is whether the fetus is to be considered a human being and so entitled to human rights," the answer to which he admitted ignorance.[16]

Given his admitted uncertainty about the answer to a question of such gravity, but also preferring to err on the side of caution, Novak expressed a deep discomfort with abortion but entertained the caveat that perhaps "we ... should legalize abortion under certain circumstances."[17] The caveat emerged primarily out of concern for the very poor who often have no option, unlike the wealthy among us, but to seek abortions under "unspeakable" and "hideous" con-

---

16. Michael Novak, "Abortion Is Not Enough," *The Christian Century*, April 5, 1967, 430.
17. Ibid., 431.

ditions. At the time when he wrote these words, abortion was not legally accessible in most cases and where it was provided, the conditions could vary widely. Admitting that under certain narrow circumstances it might be proper to allow legal abortion, Novak believed that the most basic reason for most abortions, and particularly those in underprivileged areas, was socioeconomic. Given the economic underpinnings of most abortions it would perhaps be imprudent to legalize abortion across the board as "it does not seem right to seek a medical solution to a socioeconomic problem." A better option than providing legislative support for abortion would be to provide tax-funded financial assistance and medical support, a greater accessibility to contraception, and more widespread availability of adoptive services for those are most likely to seek an abortion. Where such forms of outreach still failed, Novak begrudgingly admitted that perhaps abortion should be legally accessible.[18]

Over the next decade he wrote a series of articles focusing on abortion that reiterated many of the same themes that emerged in his 1967 essay. In what was perhaps the most forthright statement in any of them, Novak stated bluntly that "I would not like to see abortion forbidden in law, even though I believe it to be forbidden by a genuine humanistic morality. For there is no way ... to eliminate abortion entirely. Better, if it happens, that it happens with good medical care."[19] While abortion might always be with us in some form or other, Novak again reiterated the importance of trying to diminish the number of abortions that occurred. In a second essay he again conceded that abortion should not be outlawed. Here he wrote that "since there is moral disagreement, and since abortion occurs in any and every society, I would rather have the law permit abortion. I would rely upon moral argument to dissuade men and women ... from choosing abortion."[20] It should be through moral

18. Ibid.

19. Michael Novak, "Personal Morality and Abortion," *The News and Courier,* August 10, 1977, 8A.

20. Michael Novak, "The Abortion Controversy," *The News and Courier,* January 10, 1978, 11A.

suasion that people choose against abortion and in favor of other alternatives, such as adoption.

While Novak overtly stated on at least two separate occasions that abortion ought not be forbidden by law, in other places he seemed at least open to limitations on its availability. By early 1978 he was growing convinced that, although there was still disagreement on the issue, a moral consensus against abortion was in fact forming. His evidence for such a claim relied on an article published in the *Population and Development Review* that claimed available polling data demonstrated that support for the pro-choice position never exceeded 50 percent and in some instances was as low as 30 percent. Based on the hypothesis that these polls were accurate and that an increasing proportion of Americans believe that the fetus is a human life that deserves protection, Novak concluded that the "movement to recognize the human and civil rights of the unborn is growing in political power. Only a willful minority can frustrate this moral consensus." It is thus time for the Supreme Court to revisit the issue and, at the very least, "reduce the number of months within which abortion is legal."[21] While outright prohibition might not be the proper course, it was legitimate to consider placing limitations on its availability.

During the late sixties and early seventies, Michael Novak's position on abortion shifted slightly. In his earliest commentary on the matter he admitted that the permissibility of abortion hinged on whether or not the fetus is worthy of being considered a person whose rights ought to be respected and protected. In 1967 he was undecided on the issue but, because of this uncertainty, felt more comfortable erring on the side of caution and assumed that it was. Nevertheless, because there was little consensus on the matter he argued that abortion should not be made illegal. His stated moral opposition to the practice, paired with his acknowledgment that

21. See Michael Novak, "The Rights of the Unborn," *The News and Courier,* February 28, 1978, 11A, and "Referendums on Abortion Would Be Interesting," *The News and Courier,* November 24, 1978, 9A.

abortion ought at least for the time being remain legal, seems identical to the "personally opposed ... but" position that caused more than one Catholic politician a good deal of strife in later years. His situation is more complex than that.

In 1984, Novak explicitly took on this rationale held by some Catholic politicians and argued that such an approach is illegitimate. Responding to the presidential bid of Mario Cuomo and his "personally opposed, but I must uphold the law permitting abortions" logic, Novak argued that Cuomo missed a fundamental step in the analysis. That step consists in "argument, public advocacy, persuasion, the slow creation of a new majority. This is politically difficult for those Catholics in public office who represent substantial numbers of citizens in favor of abortion. But it is morally helpful."[22] Presumably such an argument would be in pursuit of a goal. One could imagine that such a goal would be for politicians to use their public presence to try and convince people of the immorality of abortion. More likely it would seem to include using the power of the position to prohibit or at least limit abortion legally. In Novak's case he seems to want a little bit of both.

During the seventies he objected to the prohibition of abortion and supported using moral argument to convince others not to have abortions. Such an approach seemed to reject legislation as a proper mechanism for addressing the issue. In other instances he seemed in favor of using the democratic process as a mechanism to restrict abortion. If, through a national referendum or some similar mechanism, it could be demonstrated that a broad moral consensus against abortion existed within the American electorate, a basis could thereby be established for setting legal limits on the practice. It would seem that his general approach during this period under study provides support for putting limitations on abortion through the legislative process, but not prohibiting it. What is left unclear is where such limitations should begin and where they should end.

22. Michael Novak, "Archbishop, Governor, and VEEP," *National Review,* September 21, 1984, 45.

In 1989 Novak concluded that modern science has demonstrated that the fetus has "an autonomous genetic code of its own; it is an unmatchable individual; and it is human both in form and in its natural ... development."[23] This represents a significant shift in his thinking compared to the position staked out in the essay he wrote some twenty years earlier. In the earlier piece he expressed some uncertainty on this very point. Even though he had become more confident in the fact that the fetus is a person deserving of legal rights, he was not committed to an outright ban on abortion. He seems to believe that the decision to allow abortion or impose restrictions on it should be something that is decided by the American electorate. Because of the fundamental nature of this debate it is essential that the American people decide, through the legislative process, what limits will be implemented on this issue. Taking a more federalist tack, he admitted that when all is said and done a variety of "local" solutions might prove the best way forward. This will certainly not provide a perfect solution, but one that amounts to a tolerable peace.[24] What is perhaps most interesting is the fact that what appears to be his morally grounded opposition does not translate into an immediate call to arms for the legal prohibition of abortion, but rather the conviction that the American people ought to make a decision as to how to address the legal and moral questions surrounding the issue.

Just as Novak had ventured to write an article in 1967 that analyzed some of the ethical and legal implications related to the attempt to liberalize abortion laws, Neuhaus also commented on these efforts. Recognizing that there may be instances where abortion is permissible, such examples lay on the outskirts of human experience and not at its center.[25] Regardless of the myriad arguments that people make in support of liberalization, when all is said and

---

23. Michael Novak, "The Abortion Fight: It's Not Just a Matter of Religion," *Washington Post,* November 20, 1989, A15.

24. Ibid.

25. Neuhaus, "The Dangerous Assumptions," 413.

done, "the argument would seem to turn on whether or not the fetus is to be considered a human being."[26] Given the apparent continuum in which life develops, it is difficult to draw any clear lines at which point one can positively determine when the fetus is not a person deserving of human rights and when it is. For this reason, those who support liberalizing abortion laws have a difficult case to make determining when this dividing line actually exists.

Given his reservations as to the moral legitimacy of abortion, the complete legalization of the process was not a viable course of action for Neuhaus. Reflecting on Neuhaus's life, the Catholic legal scholar Robert George argued in a 2009 article that the abortion issue was one of the primary factors that alienated Neuhaus from political liberalism. He supported civil rights and opposed the Vietnam War for the same reason that he opposed abortion, because of "the conviction that human beings, as creatures fashioned in the image and likeness of God, possess a profound, inherent, and equal dignity. This dignity must be respected by all and protected by law ... he believed in 1984 what he believed in 1974 and 1964."[27] The embrace of the abortion issue by political liberals as a central issue of their political platform was a factor that motivated Neuhaus to align himself with conservative circles, which supported the legal abolition of abortion. Nevertheless, George's analysis oversimplifies the case somewhat and overlooks the more nuanced positioning of Neuhaus.

In his earliest writing on the subject, Neuhaus recognized that there might be instances in which abortion is a regrettable option, although even here he was uncomfortable with the procedure and opposed widespread legalization. Instead he argued that the United States ought to address the issue through effective family planning and wider use of contraception, and simultaneously tackle the socioeconomic problems that often underlie a woman's decision to

26. Ibid., 412.
27. Robert George, "He Threw It All Away," *First Things,* March 20, 2009, available at http://www.firstthings.com/onthesquare/2009/03/he-threw-it-all-away (accessed April 10, 2013).

have an abortion in the first place. This is a similar tack to that of Novak. In both cases, reducing the prevalence of underlying causes like poverty and other forms of social insecurity would be an important step in reducing the appeal of abortion.[28] At one point Neuhaus contended that our apparent move to a system of universal healthcare is a most encouraging phenomenon. Such a system could help to minimize the incidence of abortion insofar as the accessibility of medical services would be one less thing that women would have to worry about when experiencing an unwanted pregnancy.[29]

During the mid-seventies Neuhaus focused more extensively on the relationship between Christian faith and its implications for public policy. One area of interest consisted in the role that the state should play in the regulation of private decision making and human relationships. Although the issues that he focused on extended well beyond abortion, the rationale that he used was pertinent to his position on abortion. With respect to his specific areas of interest, Neuhaus asserted that contraception should be available to both adults and minors. Laws which try to regulate sexual activity between consenting adults should be eliminated. This includes all laws relating to homosexuality, sodomy, and other private sexual behavior. Discrimination in hiring procedures that is based on "sexual orientation should be legally proscribed," including cases related to the military, school teachers, and public positions such as fire fighters and police. Prostitution should not be a crime, pornography should be regulated but not tightly restricted, and we as a society ought to seriously reconsider the usefulness of the legal prohibition of many drugs currently proscribed by law.[30]

The rationale underlying these judgments consisted in his contention that they are "victimless crimes" and, as such, the state should generally avoid legislating against such activities. He recog-

28. Neuhaus, "The Dangerous Assumptions," 412.

29. Richard John Neuhaus, *Christian Faith and Public Policy* (Minneapolis: Augsburg Publishing House, 1977), 117.

30. Ibid., 141.

nized that the notion of "victimless crime" is more complex than is generally understood; the line between public and private morality and the consequences of each are much more ambiguous than this term suggests. Nevertheless, he was clear in his conviction that the sorts of behaviors discussed above, and particularly those that were currently criminal, may be sinful but "it is not the state's business to monitor and repress sin as such.... What the law may call a crime is not necessarily a sin.... Neither is all sin a crime."[31] Crimes that are "victimless," even if objectively sinful, should not necessarily be prohibited by law. In contrast to these kinds of behaviors, abortion is not such a crime; in pregnancy another life has to be taken into consideration.[32]

Even admitting to the fact that abortion affects not only the mother but the fetus, Neuhaus did not at this point advocate for an outright prohibition on the practice. Instead, he admitted that while "in the statistically slight instances of rape or serious deformity of the unborn child, perhaps the choice of abortion should be legally available," unregulated access to it should not be made available.[33] He worried about the possibility that if that were to occur society could be slowly overcome by an "abortion mentality" that would begin to look at human life through a utilitarian lens and, in doing so, perceive the destitute, the sick, and the lame as expendable.

Focusing on the unregulated nature of the availability of abortion in the United States following the *Roe* decision, Neuhaus promoted the possibility of a human life amendment. *Roe* was "regressive and reactionary, a great leap backward in humanity's moral and political struggle. It excludes rather than includes. It panders to the convenience of the strong and neglects the defense of the weak. It must be reversed."[34] The purpose of the life amendment would be to restrict in law the availability of abortion and simultaneously reaffirm the inherent value of life. While he admitted that it would be

---

31. Ibid., 111. 32. Ibid., 116.

33. Ibid., 114–17.

34. Neuhaus, "Two Views on the Human Life Amendment," *U.S. Catholic,* April 1977, 28.

impossible to "eliminate all abortions, whether legal or illegal ... we can reestablish in law and in its moral commitment an ever expanding definition of life that is to be protected and cherished."[35]

Traditionally social progress in Western society has been marked by an expansion of liberty and the inclusion of those who had been cast to the outskirts of society. Progress of this sort was admittedly uneven. The *Dred Scott* case of 1857, which excluded African Americans from many legal protections, wrongly empowered the state to arbitrarily define who constitutes a person worthy of respect and who does not. Such was also the case in the *Roe v. Wade* ruling. Both decisions had the practical effect of empowering the strong at the expense of the weak.[36] At its best, liberalism as a political vision had been on the forefront of expanding the definition of what it meant to belong to the human community, most recently during the civil rights debate and in its support for black empowerment. In recent years, unfortunately, liberalism had morphed from a philosophy that seeks to expand legal protections to those who live on the outskirts of society to a philosophy that embraces an atomizing individualism obsessed with individual rights disconnected from communal obligations.[37]

Neuhaus argued that it was due time for liberalism to return to its roots and again reaffirm the expansion of freedom and inclusivity that functioned as one of the pillars of liberal thought. To do so, he proposed three objectives that the pro-life movement ought to pursue. First, it is important to reaffirm in law and in culture an expanding definition of life that ought to be protected, one that is "compassionately caring rather than coldly utilitarian, morally attuned to the vulnerable than the rights of the strong." It is important, second, to pursue a course that seeks to dramatically reduce the number of abortions and, third, to create voluntary and public pro-

35. Ibid., 29.
36. Ibid., 28.
37. Richard John Neuhaus, "Hyde and Hysteria," *The Christian Century*, September 10–17, 1980, 849.

grams that support the birth of children into the world.[38] As part of the effort to reduce abortion, it is crucial for the community at large to create systems of support for mothers who are pregnant and help provide the resources necessary to support them in this process.

Neuhaus's hope that the liberal political heritage, most likely through the Democratic Party, would embrace such a vision was not fulfilled. While it was unclear how the abortion issue would play out in party politics in the early seventies, within a decade the pro-choice position had become mostly established within the ranks of the Democratic Party and the pro-life one within the Republican. Such an alignment had begun to take shape during the 1976 election between Jimmy Carter and Gerald Ford. Throughout much of the general election Carter effectively finessed the topic, as he sought to appeal to both socially liberal and conservative constituencies. By the summer and into the early fall, however, he took steps that clarified the general parameters within which he would address abortion as president. In an interview with the National Catholic News Service in June 1976 he declared his personal opposition to abortion but noted that he would not support a constitutional amendment that would ban all abortions.[39] In response to the interview, Archbishop Joseph Bernardin said that "despite his personal opposition to abortion, we regret that he continues to be unsupportive of a constitutional amendment to protect the life of the unborn. His reiteration of this stance reveals an inconsistency that is deeply disturbing to those who hold the right to life to be sacred and inalienable."[40] Carter reiterated his stance against a constitutional amendment on the eve of the election, in the October 22 debate with Gerald Ford.

In the course of the debate the candidates were asked for their

38. Neuhaus, "Two Views on the Human Life Amendment," 29.

39. "Jimmy Carter's Views on Abortion, Excerpt from NC News Service Interview," reprinted in *Origins* 6, no. 11 (September 2, 1976).

40. "Comments of Archbishop Joseph Bernardin Regarding Jimmy Carter's Views on Abortion," reprinted in *Origins* 6, no. 11 (September 2, 1976).

position on a constitutional amendment that would overturn *Roe v. Wade.* Both took positions consistent with their respective party platforms. President Ford voiced support for such an amendment, while Carter did not. The latter said in response, "I am strongly against abortion. I think abortion is wrong. I don't think the government ought to do anything to encourage abortion, but I don't favor a constitutional amendment on the subject. But short of a constitutional amendment, and within the confines of a Supreme Court ruling, I will do everything I can to minimize the need for abortions with better sex education, family planning, with better adoptive procedures. I personally don't believe that the Federal Government ought to finance abortions, but I draw the line and don't support a constitutional amendment."[41]

The importance of Carter's position on the abortion issue for our purposes has less to do with party politics or even the institutional church's reaction and more to do with the position that Novak and Neuhaus took in respect to his bid for president. Neuhaus endorsed him. Novak, while not following Neuhaus's lead, expressed some positive words for Carter in the lead-up to the election and quickly warmed to the possibilities of a Carter presidency soon after his victory. In addition to their sympathetic demeanor toward a Carter presidency was the fact that his "personally opposed, but" approach to abortion did not seem to deter Neuhaus from an endorsement or undermine Novak's growing support for him.

In April 1976 Novak wrote an essay that focused on Jimmy Carter's bid for the presidency, the religious identity he brought with him to the public stage, and both the obstacles and advantages that this identity would bring with it during the election. Numbering thirty-one million to as many as forty million believers, and representing two-thirds of all white Protestants, evangelicals represented a significant religious power base in American politics. This group

---

41. "Presidential Campaign Debate between Gerald R. Ford and Jimmy Carter," October 22, 1976, transcript from the University of Texas, http://www.ford.utexas.edu/library/speeches/760947.htm (accessed July 27, 2012).

thus represented to Jimmy Carter, an evangelical himself, a natural constituency that he could draw on for votes. His "role for evangelical Christians may be rather like John F. Kennedy's for Catholics," wrote Novak, and as such could help to consolidate this base in his favor.[42] On the downside, Carter's religious identity could prove off-putting to northern Catholics who had traditionally formed an important part of the Democratic base. The question which Carter had to answer was whether or not he could respond to the needs of constituencies outside of the evangelical world and get from them enough support to win the nomination and, eventually, the presidency.[43]

Following the election and Carter's victory, Novak admitted in an editorial that he had not wanted Carter to win and, in a later article, stated that he had privately supported Gerald Ford during the general election.[44] In the primaries he had in fact campaigned on behalf of Senator Henry "Scoop" Jackson, one of the figureheads in the emergence of political neoconservatism.[45] His reservations about Carter hinged on the conviction that "he didn't have a plan, a direction, for the future," and because a Democratic presidential win under the likes of Carter would make it difficult to reestablish the party on a "new intellectual and political base."[46] Furthermore, the base to which Carter appealed would not be a lasting source of strength for the party. On the one hand, his strongest base was in the South, which was a generally conservative constituency. Tellingly, this demographic had in recent years voted increasingly more Republican and thus was becoming a less reliable part of the electorate for Democrats running for national office. On the other hand, Carter consistently made concessions to the left wing of the Dem-

42. Michael Novak, "The Hidden Religious Majority," *Washington Post,* April 4, 1976, 29.
43. Ibid.
44. Michael Novak, "'Family Democrats' Elected Carter," *The News and Courier,* November 11, 1976, 10A; on his support for Ford, see Michael Novak, "A Switch to Reagan for a Strong America," *Commonweal,* October, 24, 1980, 24.
45. J. David Hoeveler, *Watch on the Right: Conservative Intellectuals in the Reagan Era* (Madison: University of Wisconsin Press, 1991), 247.
46. Novak, "'Family Democrats' Elected Carter," 10A.

ocratic Party that, on its own, was not representative of the American electorate and thus could not function as a base for a party that hoped to win elections. Appealing to a sector of the country that was becoming more Republican every election cycle or to a vocal but unrepresentative segment of the electorate was not a recipe for long-term success.[47]

Concerned about Carter's electoral strategy, Novak remained positive about the prospects for long-term Democratic success and held to the conviction that Carter was "in a position to construct a new ideological base, a new political philosophy, and a new practical politics for the Democratic Party." To be successful in later elections would require Carter and his party refocus their attention on the part of the electorate that had given Carter his greatest support, "union workers, lower income voters, the less highly educated—ordinary folks." Such an electorate would be family-centered, oriented toward a more ethnic and Catholic base, and could "liberate American politics from the sterile liberal-conservative arguments of the last two decades, and put the Democratic Party on a fresh, creative, and truly popular basis, as strong as Roosevelt's in 1933."[48]

In the run-up to the 1976 election Richard John Neuhaus endorsed Jimmy Carter for president, claiming "that a Carter presidency would benefit race relations, help the poor, overcome a sterile and secular Enlightenment liberalism, and provide a new beginning for the democratic experiment."[49] He expressed disappointment regarding Carter's opposition to a constitutional amendment on the abortion issue, but was simultaneously unimpressed with what he referred to as Ford's "reluctant endorsement" of returning the abortion issue to the states. On this issue, at least, both had failed to think through abortion and the fundamental responsibility of the state to protect the most vulnerable members of society, including the unborn.[50] In

47. Ibid.
48. Ibid.
49. Richard John Neuhaus, "Why I Am for Carter," *Commonweal*, October 22, 1976, 683.
50. Ibid.

fact, Richard Neuhaus not only supported Carter in 1976, but agreed to organize on his behalf, explaining that "Carter is an embarrassment to the press because he prays for his campaign in public.... I'm supporting him because it is important to our national health that we rediscover American character and we're not going to rediscover it if it continues to be defined by a small elite contemptuous of the majority."[51]

Neuhaus supported Carter in part with the sense that a Carter presidency would help to provide the "cultural and political climate that will bring moral discourse and public policy into a closer and more candid alliance. The abortion debate ... will undoubtedly benefit from that alliance."[52] Neuhaus is not entirely clear how this benefit would accrue from the rest of his argument. Presumably Carter's courageous approach to race-related issues and his concern for the poor and the related desire to institute policies that will lift people out of poverty would dispose his administration to a concern for all those who are vulnerable, including the unborn. In a related way, Neuhaus was confident that Carter's religious sensibility, paired with his political acumen, could "signal the end of the public hegemony of the secular Enlightenment in the Western world."[53] Carter's religious convictions, Neuhaus seemed to assume, could open up perspectives on the unborn that are not fully appreciated in the midst of a secular culture inspired by the Enlightenment.[54]

While Neuhaus held out hope for the Carter presidency going into 1977, by the end of his first term Neuhaus had developed serious reservations regarding Carter's leadership and the direction he was taking the country. Nevertheless, even as late as 1979 Neuhaus accepted an appointment by Carter to participate in the White House Conference on the American Family. This conference had

51. Richard Neuhaus quoted in J. Brooks Flippen, *Jimmy Carter, the Politics of Family, and the Rise of the Religious Right* (Athens: University of Georgia Press, 2011), 80.

52. Neuhaus, "Why I Am for Carter," 684.

53. Richard John Neuhaus, "A Carter Presidency and the Real Watershed," *Worldview* 19 (September 1976): 29.

54. Ibid., 685.

initially been proposed by Carter during his presidential campaign three years earlier. Addressing the annual convention of Catholic Charities, he promised to convene such a conference to highlight the importance of the American family and reinforce its relevance to policy making. As Carter made clear in his opening address to the conference a few years later, its purpose was "to examine the strengths of American families, the difficulties they face, and the ways in which family life is affected by public policies."[55]

While there is no reason to doubt his sincerity on this subject, Carter was likely trying to curry Catholic support for the upcoming election, something that he had lost just four years earlier.[56] There was some concern among Carter's advisors that the Democratic Party had developed a "Catholic problem." Regardless of his intentions, the Conference on the American Family that he had promised to convene did not occur until a full three years after his promise was initially made. There was difficulty agreeing on an agenda, a failure to appoint an advisory staff that could push things ahead, and an apparent inability to even set a date for the event. Even the name of the conference was eventually changed to the White House Conference on Families, "in order to highlight a 'neutral model' of the family."[57]

In his book on the neoconservative Catholics, Damon Linker argued that Neuhaus immediately resigned from his position on the conference's advisory committee when the Carter administration moved "to pluralize the title of the conference (from 'Family' to 'Families')."[58] The evidence does not support such a claim. As late as May 15, 1980, not even one month before the first of three confer-

55. Jimmy Carter, "White House Conference on Families Statement Announcing the Conference," January 30, 1978. Online at Gerhard Peters and John T. Woolley's website, *The American Presidency Project*, http://www.presidency.ucsb.edu/ws/?pid=29884 (accessed July 23, 2012).

56. Leo Ribuffo, "Family Policy Past as Prologue: Jimmy Carter, the White House Conference on Families, and the Mobilization of the New Christian Right," *Review of Policy Research* 23, no. 2 (2006): 320–21.

57. Ibid., 321.

58. Linker, *The Theocons*, 44.

ences convened, Neuhaus was still listed as a member of the national advisory committee.[59] He continued to be listed as a member on the summary report to the president on the findings and conclusions of the conference, which was dated November 1980.[60] In both cases, the letterhead clearly lists the name of the conference in the plural, as the "White House Conference on Families," a change that had occurred much earlier in the organizational process.[61] The political historian Leo Ribuffo reported that the change from the singular to the plural was suggested as early as the period preceding Carter's inauguration in 1977.[62]

It does not appear that Neuhaus ever officially disassociated himself from the conference. Regardless of his official connection, in later years he did express some exasperation at the change in the name insofar as it occurred in response to pressures imposed on the White House by groups of homosexual activists and feminists. What was particularly problematic for Neuhaus was that they were trying to broaden the definition of the family to include "alternative lifestyles," which included expansion of the notion of marriage to include homosexual unions. It was a move that Neuhaus opposed. While some were calling for the admission of homosexual unions into the definition of marriage, he thought it "absurd" to change the Western understanding of marriage and family law in response to the outcry of a tiny minority. Even if such a change were ever to take place, it was not the role of a national conference that costs millions of dollars to do so. Traditional values were alive and well in America and ought not be overturned or ignored by partisan delegates assigned to a White House conference.[63]

59. White House Conference on Families, *National Organizations Issues Resource Book* (Washington, D.C.: Department of Health, Education, and Welfare, 1980), http://www.eric.ed.gov/PDFS/ED198925.pdf (accessed July 25, 2012); the White House actually convened three conferences around the country that constituted the overarching conference.

60. White House Conference on Families, *Listening to America's Families: Actions for the 80's* (Washington, D.C.: U.S. Government Printing Office, 1980).

61. White House Conference on Families, *National Organizations Issues Resource Book.*

62. Ribuffo, "Family Policy Past as Prologue," 321.

63. Neuhaus, *The Naked Public Square,* 96–97.

Michael Novak, who referred to the White House Conference on Families as a "monster," expressed similar concerns. He claimed that the organizers of the event handpicked appointees whose politics were conducive to a more open-ended definition that rejected the "nostalgic family" and instead hoped to include "homosexual liaisons, childless and unmarried couples living together, communes, and similar affinity groups" as part of the definition. His point was not to argue that childless couples, for example, were not a "family" as such, but that the "nostalgic family" referred to by White House planning staff—husbands and wives with children and even single parents—comprised the overwhelming majority of family units in the United States. Furthermore, although there are some exceptions, an even greater majority of the population was presumed not to regard the traditional family with such contempt.[64]

The importance of the traditional family, Novak argued, beyond the fact that it accounts for the overwhelming type of family structures in American life, is due to the role that it plays in education and value formation. In short, the bourgeois family that is predominant in American life nurtures the values that make possible the political economy of the modern West. The communal nature of the family offsets the exaggerated emphasis on the individual that is ever the temptation of capitalist economists, but by virtue of its being an independent and self-supporting entity it functions as a buffer against the temptations of statists.[65]

By the time the White House Conference on Families ended, both Neuhaus and Novak had grown disillusioned with Carter and had begun the search to find an alternative. For Neuhaus, the 1980 election was a time of transition. Having lost his faith in Carter and being unwilling to support him for a second term, he was "still unprepared to publicly embrace the Republicans, despite having quietly supported Reagan during the 1980 campaign."[66] During the 1980

---

64. Michael Novak, "In Praise of Bourgeois Values," *Society* 18, no. 2 (January/February 1981): 60.

65. Ibid., 61.   66. Linker, *The Theocons*, 45.

primary season Michael Novak initially floated the idea of Daniel Patrick Moynihan taking a run at Jimmy Carter for the Democratic nomination in 1980. Bill Buckley accused him of clinging to nostalgia for the Democratic Party and wanting to continue to vote for it but having problems doing so. While Novak initially expressed discomfort with the idea of voting for Reagan, Buckley reassured him that they would soon find each other "mutually endearing."[67] By this time Novak had clearly begun to shift his allegiances, if not in fact then in principle, from the Democratic to the Republican Party.

While still clinging to the possibility of finding a Democrat for whom he could vote in good conscience, Buckley's reassurance soon proved prescient as Novak began to express some interest in a potential Reagan bid for the presidency. On the eve of the election Novak endorsed Reagan's bid for the White House. One characteristic that attracted Novak to this possibility was that Reagan had clearly been teaching himself "about the language of working people, particularly—but not only—that of ethnic workers in the large industrial states. He talks constantly about the basic moral realities of their life: family, work, neighborhood."[68] This talk of neighborhood and family reflected the mediating institutional framework that was central to neoconservative Catholic thought.

Another area that swayed Novak toward Reagan was foreign policy. Novak contended that Carter had no vision and that he promoted a foreign policy that weakened America and threatened its security in the face of the Soviet Union. Under Carter the United States had lost its military effectiveness in the Middle East, witnessed the collapse of the shah of Iran, sat idly by during the invasion of Afghanistan, and failed to respond to Soviet-supported Marxist inroads all across Latin America. Novak contended that

67. William F. Buckley, "Why Not Moynihan in 1980?" *The News and Courier,* June 1, 1979, 4A.

68. Michael Novak, "Choosing Our King," *The News and Courier,* March 19, 1979, 12A.

given the stakes of this confrontation, how one understands the Soviet empire was the *primary* political issue of the day. Based on his policy decisions, Carter had shown that he did not understand the Soviet Union well at all and thus put America in a much more vulnerable situation as a result. In contrast, Novak contended that Reagan's foreign policy, while more confrontational than that of Carter, enhanced the prospect of peace: "The only way to prevent war is to be willing to resist Soviet probes. Reagan's policies show higher probabilities of peace than Carter's do. The American left, egging on the worst in Carter, is leading the country into war with silly protestations of peace."[69]

69. Novak, "A Switch to Reagan for a Strong America," *Commonweal*, October, 24, 1980, 590.

4 ❖ A WORLD SPLIT APART?

ON MAY 22, 1977, President Jimmy Carter gave the 132nd commencement address at the University of Notre Dame. The most memorable and often-cited phrase came after he praised the values of democracy and declared that "being confident of our own future, we are now free of that inordinate fear of communism." Such fears had, according to Carter, been costly. They had led the United States to cooperate with any dictator or authoritarian ruler who was an ally against the Soviet Union, contributed to the abandonment of American values and the adoption of the "flawed and erroneous principles and tactics of our adversaries," and cost American lives through the involvement of the United States in foreign wars, most notably Vietnam.[1] Instead of continuing along this course he promoted a set of different priorities that he promised would guide his administration over the course of his presidency, first among them being "America's commitment to human rights as a fundamental tenet of our foreign policy."[2]

The emphasis on human rights in the Notre Dame speech built on a similar commitment made during his inaugural address, where he stated that our "commitment to human rights must be absolute.... Our moral sense dictates a clear-cut preference for those so-

---

1. Jimmy Carter, commencement address at the University of Notre Dame, May 22, 1977, http://www.presidency.ucsb.edu/ws/index.php?pid=7552 (accessed May 20, 2012).
2. Ibid.

cieties which share with us an abiding respect for human rights."[3] He followed this with the promise to actively oppose human rights abuses everywhere, regardless of whether they were committed by America's allies or adversaries and followed on this commitment by restricting foreign and economic aid to countries like Nicaragua and Iran, which had traditionally been allied with the United States during the Cold War.[4]

Carter's foreign policy was met with hostility by his conservative critics, who accused him of projecting weakness internationally and embracing a "naïve concern for human rights (that) had undermined vital interests."[5] The fall of the shah of Iran and the collapse of the Somoza regime in Nicaragua were used as evidence to support these accusations. Michael Novak voiced a related criticism, arguing that Carter "attempted to be 'evenhanded' and to balance every accusation against an opponent of the United States with an accusation against a friend ... and pretended that all nations erred against human rights more or less equally. No distinction was made between totalitarian nations and authoritarian nations."[6]

Jeane Kirkpatrick had originally developed this critique three years earlier in her influential essay "Dictatorships and Double Standards." Here she argued that while seeking to eliminate human rights abuses perpetrated by allied governments, the Carter administration implemented punitive measures that weakened America's Cold War allies. This undermined U.S. interests overseas insofar as it contributed to the ouster of "moderate autocrats friendly to American interests with less friendly autocrats of a more extremist persuasion."[7] While noting Carter's rhetorical support for human

3. Hauke Hartmann, "US Human Rights and Policy under Carter and Reagan, 1977–1981," *Human Rights Quarterly* 23 (2001): 405.

4. Ibid.

5. Leo Ribuffo, "Jimmy Carter: Beyond the Current Myths," *Magazine of History,* Summer/Fall 1988, 22.

6. Michael Novak, "Human Rights and White Sepulchers," in *Human Rights and U.S. Human Rights Policy: Theoretical Approaches and Some Perspectives on Latin America,* ed. Howard Wiarda, 82 (Washington, D.C.: American Enterprise Institute, 1982).

7. Jeane Kirkpatrick, "Dictatorships and Double Standards," *Commentary,* November

rights, Kirkpatrick asserted that his actual policies hindered the realization of human rights as they contributed to the destabilization of allied governments. This had the unintended effect of strengthening the Soviet Union's position in international affairs.[8]

Although criticizing his specific foreign policy strategy, Kirkpatrick emphasized that the central problem was not Carter's emphasis on human rights per se but his naïve application of a human rights paradigm to foreign policy. In the foreword to Joshua Muravchik's book *The Uncertain Crusade,* Jeane Kirkpatrick admitted as much when she wrote that "the notion that policy should not reflect concern with human rights is as far-fetched as the notion that foreign policy should not express the nation. In the American view, human rights are universal and the very purpose of government is their protection."[9] Human rights should be taken seriously as part of the political framework that informs the development of American foreign policy. This was only the first step. Human rights had to be effectively implemented through the construction of viable political institutions if they were going to be effective as a political instrument. Picking up on this point, George Weigel argued that the Carter administration fell short because it "failed to make the essential linkage between 'human rights' and political systems. That human rights were protected by the growth of democracy in the world was not an idea that gripped the imaginations of the Carter administration's human rights officials."[10] Similarly, Novak argued that "the protection of human rights depends upon the erection of institutions that embody a certain vision of human dignity. More than that, such protection depends upon the convictions, habits and active associations of citizens who hold such institutions to their pur-

---

1979, http://www.commentarymagazine.com/article/dictatorships-double-standards/ (accessed March 26, 2012).

8. Hartmann, "US Human Rights and Policy," 419.

9. Joshua Muravchik, *The Uncertain Crusade: Jimmy Carter and the Dilemmas of Human Rights Policy* (New York: Hamilton Press, 1986), ix.

10. George Weigel, "Book Review: *The Uncertain Crusade: Jimmy Carter and the Dilemmas of Human Rights Policy,*" *World Affairs* 148, no. 2 (Fall 1985): 133.

poses."[11] From the perspective of practical politics ideas are not very useful if one does not take seriously the means of their institutionalization. This is a recurring theme in the thought of the neoconservative Catholics: ideas have to be institutionalized if they are going to have any long-term political relevance and the institutions most effective at protecting and promoting human rights are those found in liberal democracies.

Carter's critics contended that his foreign policy failed in part because it expected that allied governments would embrace a human-rights-based political framework without recognizing the importance of developing institutions that would protect such a framework in practice. Because many Middle Eastern and Central American countries did not have in place the institutional structures that were conducive to an American-style human rights regime, it was highly improbable that such a framework would succeed. Instead of undermining American allies in this way it would be more effective to work with them to build up institutions that would be capable of providing human rights protections. This would not be easy, since it is impossible to "democratize governments anytime, anywhere, under any circumstances"; it can take decades and a little good fortune for an autocratic government to evolve into a democratic one.[12] Nevertheless, making the effort to institutionalize political and social structures that would respect human rights was crucial to an effective foreign policy. Fine-sounding rhetoric about the importance of human rights was no replacement for the hard work that it would take to establish institutions that would be capable of nurturing a culture that respects human rights.

These themes were reiterated in a more formal setting during a presidential debate between Jimmy Carter and Ronald Reagan. Asked if, while president, he would back oppressive regimes that were friendly to the United States' foreign policy goals but weak on

11. Michael Novak, *Human Rights and the New Realism: Strategic Thinking in a New Age* (New York: Freedom House, 1986), 11.

12. Kirkpatrick, "Dictatorships and Double Standards."

human rights, Reagan accused Carter of advocating policies toward friendly governments that contributed to the emergence of an even worse situation. Too often, Reagan argued, because a given country's leadership "didn't meet exactly our standards of human rights, even though they were an ally of ours, instead of trying patiently to persuade them to change their ways, we have, in a number of instances, aided a revolutionary overthrow which results in complete totalitarianism.... This is a kind of a hypocritical policy when, at the same time, we're maintaining a detente with the one nation in the world where there are no human rights at all—the Soviet Union."[13] In contrast, he promised to pursue a more aggressive foreign policy that did not downplay the abuses of the Soviet regime. His approach marked a resurgence of an aggressive anticommunism that was more consistent with policies promoted in the period between World War II and Vietnam and that sought to contain "the expansion of Soviet power and influence, adopting a 'hands off' attitude toward the domestic policies of pro-Western governments and resisting radical movements in the third world."[14]

The divisions between the two parties on foreign policy are in large part a product of the political fallout from the Vietnam experience. It was during this period that many on the left began to reexamine America's role in the world and became more sympathetic to the drawing down of American power from overseas. Those on the right, by way of contrast, often doubled down on American power and argued that even if Vietnam was a poorly chosen war it signified a discrete failure in the application of American values and not an inherent corruption of the American system. Consequently, the debate over Vietnam challenged American leadership to reconsider the proper role of American power in the world. To what extent did American military intervention function as a positive or negative

13. 1980 Ronald Reagan/Jimmy Carter Presidential Debate, October 28, 1980, http://www.reagan.utexas.edu/archives/reference/10.28.80debate.html (accessed May 22, 2012).

14. Richard Burt, "Presidential Candidates Stake Out Divergent Ground on Foreign Policy," *New York Times,* October 19, 1980, 1.

force on the international scene? What is the priority of values that America should project in its foreign policy and what kind of social, economic, and political strategies should be put into place based on a consideration of these values? Given the context of the Cold War, the debate often hinged on perceptions related to the Soviet threat and the dangers that communism posed to American security.

In the immediate aftermath of World War II, most liberal intellectuals shared a general consensus regarding the important achievements of the American past and a strong support for international anticommunism. Although they often differed on the question of means, these differences were typically understood in the context of shared ends, which included an aversion to communism and a belief in America's positive influence in the world.[15] What is often referred to as the "liberal consensus" reaffirmed "the capacity of American capitalism, assisted by a moderate degree of economic management by the government, to create economic prosperity; the desirability of preserving and modestly extending the New Deal legacy; and the necessity of combating the threat of world communism."[16]

While a potent force in the immediate aftermath of the war, by the late sixties this consensus had fractured and was replaced by a diversity of perspectives regarding the value of the American experiment and the role of America in the world. As a central actor in the breakdown of this consensus, "the Vietnam War became the gateway from the optimism of the 1960s to the pessimism of the 1990s, and the specific catalyst that fragmented the postwar liberal consensus."[17] Robert Tomes neatly summarizes the geography of American intellectual life and the differences that emerged when he writes that "the war transformed the consensus into an array of distinct intellec-

---

15. Robert Tomes, *Apocalypse Then: American Intellectuals and the Vietnam War, 1954–1975* (New York: New York University Press, 1998), 9–15.

16. Ewan Morgan, *Beyond the Liberal Consensus: A Political History of the United States since 1965* (New York: St. Martin's Press, 1994), 2. For one of the seminal works on the idea of the liberal consensus see Louis Hartz, *The Liberal Tradition in America* (New York: Harcourt, Brace and World, 1955).

17. Tomes, *Apocalypse Then*, 8.

tual groups—neoconservatives, democratic socialists, New Leftists, disillusioned liberals, and conservatives, each of which approached the new postwar America with a fresh and unique outlook heavily influenced by their wartime experiences.... Generally contentious toward each other, the new groups shared few of the old assumptions which had bolstered the consensus. These assumptions, like America's international responsibilities, faith in democratic institutions and a belief in capitalism as the inviolable economic system, became a springboard of disagreement."[18]

The failed presidential bid of Senator George McGovern in 1972 illustrates some of the tensions at play between competing factions in American political life. Throughout the campaign, McGovern promoted a more cooperative and less confrontational approach to the Soviet Union. His campaign slogan, "Come Home, America," while targeted at the United States' involvement in Vietnam, was taken by some to be a call for a renewed form of American isolationism.[19] One group that was particularly vocal in the face of McGovern's call were the political neoconservatives, who interpreted it "as a call to leave not simply Vietnam but much of the world as well.... The McGovern vision seemed to suggest that America's active involvement in the world ... was immoral, imperialistic, and corrupting."[20] Richard Neuhaus, having not yet allied himself with the conservative- and neoconservative-leaning intellectual classes, provided a different take on McGovern's plea. McGovern's call was not an appeal to isolationism but a call to resume the pilgrimage toward the fulfillment of America's destiny as a "good and decent land. The return he [McGovern] advocates is always to 'the task,' 'the challenge,' 'the dream' of America's potential, never to a past point of achievement."[21] In

18. Ibid., 234–35.

19. John Ehrman, *The Rise of Neoconservatism: Intellectuals and Foreign Affairs 1945–1994* (New Haven, Conn.: Yale University Press, 1994), 60.

20. Jay Winik, "The Neoconservative Reconstruction," *Foreign Policy* 73 (Winter 1988–1989): 138.

21. Richard John Neuhaus, "Going Home Again: America after Vietnam," *Worldview* 15, no. 10 (October 1972): 35–36.

short, Neuhaus took McGovern's call more figuratively, as a plea to return to American roots, while political neoconservatives took it as a call to American isolation.

While at the time not sharing the political outlook of the neoconservatives, Richard Neuhaus, and Michael Novak for that matter, drifted in that direction during the seventies and by the early eighties shared many of the convictions that the political neoconservatives embraced. Peter Steinfels was one of the earliest thinkers to provide a comprehensive analysis of neoconservatism, publishing a critical study of its adherents' thought in 1979. Since the publication of his book, a standard narrative of the emergence of political neoconservatism has become widely accepted.[22] Typically the narrative begins with a group of New York intellectuals in the 1940s, some of whom, including Sydney Hook and Irving Kristol, flirted at one time or another with Marxist thought.[23] For the most part that was a passing phase, however, and this group of intellectuals soon positioned themselves as stalwart, liberal anticommunists who embraced a New Deal Democratic worldview that became dominant in the post–World War II years.

In response to the political and cultural upheavals of the 1960s, the neoconservatives became disenchanted with the thinking of many on the left whom they worried had radicalized and, in doing so, gone soft on communism and embraced a neo-isolationist foreign policy. On the domestic front, neoconservatives developed misgivings regarding Lyndon Johnson's Great Society and the wider governmental "war on poverty."[24] By the late sixties the political

22. Peter Steinfels, *Neoconservatives: The Men Who Are Changing American Politics* (New York: Simon and Schuster, 1979). Since Steinfels's book, other commentaries on neoconservatism include, in addition to Ehrman's *The Rise of Neoconservatism,* Gary Dorrien, *The Neoconservative Mind: Politics, Culture and the War of Ideology* (Philadelphia: Temple University Press, 1993); Gary Dorrien, *Imperial Designs: Neoconservatism and the Pax Americana* (New York: Routledge, 2004); and Murray Friedman, *The Neoconservative Revolution: Jewish Intellectuals and the Shaping of Public Policy* (New York: New York University Press, 2005).

23. Max Boot, "Myths about Neoconservatism," in *The Neocon Reader,* ed. Irwin Stelzer, 45 (New York: Grove Press, 2003).

24. Joshua Muravchik, "The Neoconservative Cabal," in *The Neocon Reader,* ed. Irwin Stelzer, 244.

neoconservatives had, perhaps most notably through their flagship journal *Commentary,* begun to denounce the growing radicalism of the left. The "New Left," whom Norman Podhoretz once accused of embracing an indiscriminate anti-Americanism, often functioned as a standard bearer of this radicalization.[25]

Neoconservatives' growing aversion to the liberal politics espoused by Democratic Party leadership was accompanied by a rightward shift. In the fall 1973 issue of *Dissent* magazine, Michael Harrington published an article in which he criticized the political neoconservatives for misreading, if not distorting, the social and political context of the sixties. In particular, he argued that they greatly exaggerated the degree to which the federal government had intervened in social, economic, and political life during the sixties, and overestimated the extent to which unintended consequences, generally negative, were a product of this intervention.[26]

Focusing on social policy in the early 1970s, Nathan Glazer criticized what he understood to be a widely held worldview among the liberal elite of his day. Such a view maintained that modern industrial society had brought with it a system of entrenched power and wealth that only reinforced and exacerbated widespread economic and political disparities that were already present in a preindustrial context. Under such circumstances, "most men lived in squalor while a few, profiting from the labor of the many, lived in great luxury."[27] The stark disparity between rich and poor required the implementation of systemic reforms to alleviate these inequalities.

Given that private charity proved to be incapable of achieving this objective, government was called on to step in, provide solutions, and, in doing so, establish some degree of equity and security to the marginalized members of society. By the early seventies Glazer had grown increasingly skeptical of the effectiveness of this

25. Thomas Grubisich, "Norman Podhoretz: New Left's Enemy from Within," *Washington Post,* April 11, 1971, G1.

26. Michael Harrington, "The Welfare State and Its Neoconservative Critics," *Dissent,* Fall 1973, 435–54.

27. Nathan Glazer, "The Limits of Social Policy," *Commentary,* September 1971, 51.

type of government intervention and held that while social policy initiatives on the federal level may have ameliorated some problems, they almost inevitably gave rise to equally grave ones. Appeals to the government for solutions to social problems create a dependence on government that simultaneously undermines traditional sources of security like the family, neighborhood, and voluntary associations.[28]

Just a month before Glazer's article, Irving Kristol expressed a similar set of concerns and further questioned whether further government intervention in the economy would provide workable solutions to the problems of domestic inequality and strife, or merely make things worse. Specifically, Kristol questioned why there had been significant growth in the welfare population during a time in which America was experiencing unprecedentedly low levels of unemployment. One would have assumed that during a period of prosperity there would be a notable drop in the welfare rolls because employment opportunities were generally plentiful. He concluded that "this 'explosion' was created—in part intentionally, in larger part unwittingly—by public officials and public employees who were executing public policies as part of a 'War on Poverty.'"[29]

During the "war" on poverty, he continued, a number of factors contributed to the growth in the welfare population. First, the official definitions of "poverty" and "need" were changed during this period, thus making more people eligible to participate in various welfare programs. Second, as welfare benefits were increased more people began to apply for welfare when eligible because of the larger benefits accrued. When such benefits begin to compete with low wages, the rational choice would be for welfare benefits, which could be collected without having to work. Finally, Kristol pointed to various campaigns that were launched during the early and mid-sixties which aimed at diminishing the stigma of welfare and signing more people up. While striving to provide economic securi-

28. Ibid., 53–54.

29. Irving Kristol, "Welfare: The Best of Intentions, The Worst of Results," *Atlantic Monthly*, August 1971, 47.

ty, he concluded, these programs resulted in a range of unintended and perverse consequences.[30]

One of the gravest unintended consequences was the effect of welfare on the family, particularly in black and lower-income communities. For Irving Kristol and other political neoconservatives the welfare system was one of the major contributors to this breakdown. Kristol noted that "the family is, in our society, a vital economic institution. Welfare robs it of its economic function. Above all, welfare robs the head of the household of *his* economic function, and tends to make of him a superfluous man."[31] It should come as little surprise, Kristol concluded, that, demoralized and irrelevant, many men in low-income neighborhoods choose to remove themselves from families that are no longer reliant on them.

Given the newly emergent conservative identity of the political neoconservatives, it is useful to differentiate them from the broader conservative movement that had become an established force by the late seventies. The former were measured critics of the welfare state, not unapologetic adversaries, and were sympathetic to the many of the Depression-era policies of the 1930s. On the domestic front it is reasonable to refer to them as New Deal Democrats. What drove a wedge between the political neoconservatives and the Democratic leadership of the sixties was the further expansion of government programs into diverse areas of American life. Reflecting back on this period, Irving Kristol remarked that "it was when the Great Society programs were launched that we began to distance ourselves, slowly and reluctantly, from the newest versions of official liberalism."[32] Further differentiating the political neoconservatives from their conservative contemporaries was Kristol's claim that the twentieth-century heroes of the political neoconservatives were Franklin Roosevelt and Ronald Reagan.[33] It was an odd pairing

---

30. Ibid.   31. Ibid.

32. Irving Kristol, "American Conservatism: 1945–1995," *The Public Interest*, Fall 1995, 85.

33. Irving Kristol, "The Neoconservative Persuasion," *The Weekly Standard*, August 25, 2003.

from the perspective of popular conservatism, but one that pointed to the role that the neoconservatives believed government could
play in American political and economic life.

In contrast, establishment conservatives often argued that there
was continuity on the left, from the "Old Left" to the "New Left."
In his important book on American conservatism, George Nash
noted that for many conservatives, "radicalism was the 'logical conclusion' of the inherent egalitarianism and relativism of the liberals.
What was the hippie counterculture, with its call to 'do your own
thing,' but 'an extreme extension' of liberalism's relativist assault
on the verities of the West?"[34] Such a perspective would obviously
create a division between conservatives of old and the neoconservatives. While perhaps sharing a general disdain for Johnson's "war on
poverty," the latter would not be inclined to support a conservatism
that viewed the New Deal as antithetical to American ideals, not
to mention any sort of libertarian strain of thought that was active
within some conservative circles.

Economic policy and the effectiveness of government intervention was only one area of interest to the political neoconservatives;
foreign policy and America's proper role in world affairs was also a
focal point in their thought. On the foreign policy front there was
much more continuity with an old-line conservatism that provided
room for agreement. During the Reagan era this was one area in
which the agreement between these two political groups was emphasized. Throughout the seventies the neoconservatives remained
staunchly anticommunist and called for a reassertion of American
power in the world and the rejuvenation of American confidence at
home. This concern became more acute as they became convinced
the Democratic Party had abandoned their traditional anticommunist leanings and had grown soft on the Soviet threat.

Writing a rather somber assessment of the state of American life
at the beginning of the 1980s, Norman Podhoretz exemplified this

34. George Nash, *The Conservative Intellectual Movement in America, Since 1945* (Wilm-
ington, Del.: Intercollegiate Studies Institute, 1998), 285.

perspective when he stated that while he and his cohorts were often labeled "neoconservatives," it might be more accurate to describe them as "neonationalists." Such a designation would highlight their positive view of the values embedded in the constitutional and institutional structure of American civilization and reaffirm their conviction that the survival of liberal democracy required a forceful American presence in the world.[35] As Peter Steinfels noted, the neoconservative Catholics were worried that "a crisis of authority has overtaken America and the West generally. Governing institutions have lost their legitimacy; the confidence of leading elites has been sapped. Social stability and the legacy of liberal civilization are threatened."[36]

For many conservatives, Ronald Reagan promised to be a stabilizing force in this period of economic and political turmoil. If Jimmy Carter had sought to promote human rights as the guiding principle in his foreign policy, even if, as his critiques maintained, it was to the detriment of American security, Ronald Reagan's anticommunist rhetoric represented a reassertion of American power and a commitment to stand firm against the Soviet Union. This was a welcome shift to many of his supporters who were concerned that the West had grown frail and unwilling to confront the threat that the Soviet Union posed. In June 1978 Aleksandr Solzhenitsyn initiated a public debate over this unease in a commencement address that he gave at Harvard.

A Nobel Prize for Literature recipient, Solzhenitsyn had lived in the United States since his exile from Russia three years earlier, and when invited to give the Harvard commencement address gave a speech titled "A World Split Apart." In it he leveled a series of forceful criticisms against the West and its failure to respond effectively to the threat posed by Soviet Union.[37] He argued that the

35. Norman Podhoretz, *The Present Danger* (New York: Simon and Schuster, 1980).

36. Steinfels, *Neoconservatives*, 53.

37. Aleksandr Solzhenitsyn, "A World Split Apart," in *Solzhenitsyn at Harvard,* ed. Robert Berman, 3–22 (Washington, D.C.: Ethics and Public Policy Center, 1980).

world was split between communist and non-communist spheres and that the United States and Western Europe had an obligation to respond forcefully to the aggression of the Soviet Union. Sadly, he complained, both the United States and its allies had in recent years begun to reveal weaknesses that hindered its ability to respond effectively. Solzhenitsyn warned that the Western world was slowly turning into a moral wasteland, with pornography rampant, a press that was willing to distort facts if it was to its own benefit, and a people that had become soft, selfish, and unwilling to make any personal sacrifice for the benefit of the greater good.[38] The underlying reason for this decline was the West's exaltation of the individual and belief in the "autonomy of man from any higher force above him. It could also be called anthropocentricity, with man seen at the center of it all."[39] Echoing that theme during his acceptance speech for the Templeton Prize five years later, Solzhenitsyn proclaimed that "men have forgotten God; that is why all this has happened."[40]

The thesis promoted by Solzhenitsyn in his Harvard address struck a nerve among many of the American intellectual elite. Both the *New York Times* and the *Washington Post* published editorials critical of his address. The former argued that Solzhenitsyn was a religious enthusiast who "believes himself to be in possession of The Truth and so sees error wherever he looks," and who is promoting a holy war that "bespeaks an obsession that we are happy to forgo in this nation's leaders."[41] The *Washington Post,* in its own editorial, declared that the speech was based on a "gross misunderstanding of Western society," and did not appreciate the importance of diversity and pluralism as a source of strength in Western culture. Furthermore, the *Post* accused Solzhenitsyn of engaging in a single-minded campaign against communism and the Soviet Union that would re-

---

38. Ibid., 7–15.

39. Ibid., 16.

40. Aleksandr Solzhenitsyn, "Men Have Forgotten God," address given on the occasion of his acceptance of the Templeton Prize, London, England, May 10, 1983; reprinted in the *National Review,* July 22, 1983, 873–74.

41. "The Obsession of Solzhenitsyn," *New York Times,* June 13, 1978, A18.

sult in an endless Cold War.[42] Still other critics followed suit, finding fault with his understanding of liberal democracy and failing to come to terms with the indispensable role that the idea of tolerance played in a Western context.[43]

While he had his detractors, Solzhenitsyn tapped into important strains of twentieth-century conservative thought. The political historian George Nash highlighted this when he wrote that Solzhenitsyn, in his "searing indictment of atheistic humanism, and in his call for fundamental spiritual renewal transcending the 'ossified formulas of the Enlightenment,' expressed with remarkable force themes espoused by American conservatives from Whittaker Chambers to the Religious Right of today."[44] The political commentator George Will further reinforced this connection when he claimed that "compared to the long and broad intellectual tradition in which Solzhenitsyn's views are rooted, the tradition of liberalism, or modernity, are [sic] short and thin."[45] Solzhenitsyn, Will concluded, drew on a much richer intellectual tradition than those thinkers enmeshed in contemporary liberalism. Solzhenitsyn depended on thinkers as diverse as Cicero, Augustine, Aquinas, and Pascal in the formation of his worldview; it was similar to the tradition that the West had depended on for its own intellectual development.[46] In short, "Solzhenitsyn's critique of the West was to a large extent an internal critique of a society that had increasingly attenuated ties with the best part of its moral and political heritage."[47]

As was true of the conservative pundits, the significance of Solzhenitsyn's thought was not lost on the neoconservative Catholics.

42. "Mr. Solzhenitsyn as Witness," *Washington Post,* June 11, 1978, C6.

43. See, for example, the critiques put forth by Arthur Schlesinger, "The Solzhenitsyn We Refuse to See," and Mary McGrory, "Solzhenitsyn Doesn't Love Us," in *Solzhenitsyn at Harvard,* ed. Berman, 63–74 and 60–62, respectively.

44. George Nash, "On Twenty Years of Great Conservative Thought," *Policy Review* 84 (July/August 1987): 1.

45. George Will, "Solzhenitsyn's Critics," *Washington Post,* June 18, 1978, B7.

46. Ibid.

47. Daniel Mahoney, *Aleksandr Solzhenitsyn: The Ascent from Ideology* (Lanham, Md.: Rowman and Littlefield, 2001), 20.

On September 16, 1980, Michael Novak spoke at a dinner in Washington that was sponsored by the Ethics and Public Policy Center (EPPC). Its official purpose was to launch a new book that analyzed Solzhenitsyn's commencement address at Harvard. The book, appropriately titled *Solzhenitsyn at Harvard,* provided a reprint of Solzhenitsyn's address, a series of previously published articles that were written in its immediate aftermath, and a collection of new essays that were written by specialists on important themes that emerged throughout the address. In his contribution to the book, Michael Novak focused on the theological and religious importance of the speech. Compared with his dinner address, the views presented in his essay provided a different account of Solzhenitsyn's political thought.

While praising Solzhenitsyn as a man and honoring the personal example that he provided to the rest of the world, Novak's speech at the EPPC dinner took a more critical tone regarding Solzhenitsyn's Harvard address than the views reflected in his contribution to the book. The speech, titled "Democracy Takes Sin Seriously," tried to soften Solzhenitsyn's pessimism over the vitality of Western society. Contrary to Solzhenitsyn, Novak contended that the American political tradition in particular had the intellectual resources at hand to counter the communist threat and channel human behavior in such a way that it could lead to human flourishing. A notable failing of Solzhenitsyn focused extensively on ideas and ultimate values and too little on the concrete realities and institutions that are essential for the realization of the ideas to which he was committed. Ideas, values, and moral principles are embodied in social, political, and economic systems and thus the framework for these systems has to be accounted for and taken seriously in any political philosophy.[48]

Novak argued that Solzhenitsyn's apparent lack of interest in practical institutions and his tendency toward political idealism

---

48. Michael Novak, "Democracy Takes Sin Seriously," in *Solzhenitsyn and American Democracy* (Washington, D.C.: Ethics and Public Policy Center, 1981), 11.

reflected the worldview of Karl Marx more than he might have intended, and "turned communism inside out as a vision of effortless Christian civilization, populated not by sinners but the virtuous, organized ... by simple righteousness."[49] Embracing an idealized conception of the "City of God" as a kind of perfect model for social life, Solzhenitsyn then used it as a standard to judge Western society. Such an approach inevitably led to the conclusion that the flesh-and-blood institutions of the "City of Man" are wholly inadequate. Solzhenitsyn failed to recognize the ways in which such institutions could provide a useful check on evil and man's vicious inclinations. According to Novak, liberal democracy "accepts the Jewish and Christian vision of human fallibility, bestiality, will-to-power, world, flesh and devil," and recognizes the importance of providing a check on human sinfulness by decentralizing power and limiting the influence of any single political, economic, or social institution.[50] Failing to appreciate this, Novak worried, Solzhenitsyn came very close to embracing a traditionalist view of the social order that was explicitly religious and potentially theocratic in practice.[51]

In contrast to this critical account, Novak provided a much more positive appraisal of Solzhenitsyn in his contribution to the book *Solzhenitsyn at Harvard.* In a somewhat jarring opening sentence, particularly when compared to the criticisms expressed in his speech, Novak declared that Solzhenitsyn's Harvard address was "the most important religious document of our time, more shattering than *Pacem in Terris,* more sharply analytical of the human condition in our century than any word from the World Council of Churches.... Solzhenitsyn's claim seems classically Catholic."[52] Such high praise contrasts sharply with his criticisms at the EPPC dinner; it is difficult to mesh his assertion that Solzhenitsyn's words are reminiscent of Marx and yet, simultaneously, classically Catholic.

49. Ibid., 12.
50. Ibid., 14.
51. Novak, *The Spirit of Democratic Capitalism,* 51.
52. Michael Novak, "On God and Man," in *Solzhenitsyn at Harvard,* ed. Berman, 131–2.

One explanation for this is that his essay and his speech focused on two different characteristics of Solzhenitsyn's address. In both his written essay and his speech Novak took for granted that modernity was witness to a time of crisis, primarily insofar as the Soviet Union was a threat to international peace and prosperity. In his speech, however, Novak focused on what he understood to be Solzhenitsyn's failure to provide workable solutions to the crisis at hand, whereas in his essay he focused on what Solzhenitsyn understood were the underlying causes of the crisis—humanity's turning their back on God and their embrace of thoroughgoing anthropocentrism. While Novak readily admitted that exceptional men, both atheistic and agnostic, had lived during the twentieth century, exemplified the virtuous life, and expressed courage in the face of great evil, he worried how a society would cope when unbelief became the reigning standard. There have been secular saints, and although "brave and strong individuals continue to adhere to honesty, courage, liberty and compassion, and even to give their lives for values they make central to their being, a *society* based systematically upon the non-existence of God and upon man as the sole measure must, of human necessity, slide further and further into defenselessness and loss of will."[53] Absent a reliable and objective basis that extended beyond personal preference, it was unlikely that such a society could avoid slipping into relativism. In the context of the Cold War this could prove particularly problematic; how would Western society find the will to offer a strong defense against such a great evil as the Soviet Union?[54] The lack of moral will to confront the Soviet Union and to take the steps necessary to prevail over this threat had as much to do with the failure of the Christian churches to take the lead in this effort as it did with any weaknesses present in the political classes.

At their finest, the churches have the moral credibility, the institutional capacity, and the intellectual resources to respond effective-

53. Ibid., 135.
54. Ibid., 139.

ly to the Marxist challenge. Unfortunately, rather than functioning as a bulwark against communism, many of the mainline churches in particular had begun to embrace a vulgar Marxism and, in doing so, failed to appreciate this threat. Novak lamented at one point that in the face of communism "it is the churches that preach disarmament, urge tolerance for the Gulag Archipelago (not directly, of course, but in effect), support the forces of organized authoritarianism if only they will call themselves 'liberation forces,' and spread the doctrine of appeasement under the cloak of Christian charity."[55]

Although he primarily focused on the mainline churches and their supposed embrace of a vulgar Marxism in his essay on Solzhenitsyn, elsewhere he expressed concern about the influence of Marxism in the Catholic church. In an editorial written for the *National Review* in 1985, he claimed that Marxism was no longer only an external threat to the church but was "one of the largest and most rapidly gaining heresies in Church history."[56] His expectation and hope was that John Paul II would cleanse the church of this threat through the selection of cardinals who would provide a hard line against this danger. In retrospect, the magnitude of this threat was clearly exaggerated, but this sentiment exemplified the danger that Novak thought communism posed to the Catholic and other Christian churches.

Given the importance of a religiously grounded resistance to Marxism, it was particularly troubling that, from the neoconservative Catholic perspective, large swaths of the Christian churches supported policies that could be read as sympathetic to a Marxist worldview. Such commitments were typically occasioned in support of social justice, and not as an appeal to explicitly Marxist rhetoric. Nevertheless, in practice these commitments often resulted in a posture that was antagonistic to American foreign policy and at odds with the Christian political tradition.[57]

55. Ibid., 140.
56. Michael Novak, "Red Hats and Hinges," *National Review*, May 31, 1985, 37.
57. Novak, "Errand into the Wilderness," 205.

One of the key developments in this tradition, at least as understood by the neoconservative Catholics, was the important role that it was called on to play in the defense of democracy. Neuhaus's defense of liberal democracy and his desire to support the virtues of the American experiment was evident in his early writings. The failure to defend the American experiment runs the risk of betraying the very tradition that Christians are called on to defend. In an essay titled "Christianity against the Democratic Experiment," he made this point succinctly when he wrote that the American creed "reflects, albeit partially, a universal longing and [is] informed by those insights which we believe are revealed by God. Although in a severely provisional way, the American dream partakes of that absolute future promised by God. If this is true, and to the extent that it is true, betrayal of the American creed is linked to betrayal of the coming Kingdom of God."[58] Given this framework, if the Christian churches were to turn their back on the Democratic experiment, it would be equivalent to rejecting one of their fundamental public purposes: to assist in the fulfillment of humanity's destiny.[59]

Efforts to defend the American political tradition by way of an appeal to Christian thought was not relegated to publications in peer-reviewed journals and popular magazines; the neoconservative Catholics also made efforts to institutionalize their ideas. One such institution was the Institute for Religion and Democracy (IRD), which was initially established as a counterweight to mainline Christian churches that funded overseas organizations and undermined American political institutions. The importance of defending democracy in the face of the Soviet threat was one of the key themes of the IRD's founding document, titled *Christianity and Democracy*, which was penned by Richard Neuhaus in late 1981. In the charter Neuhaus reiterated his conviction that the Christian churches were obligated to provide a strong defense of the American

58. Richard John Neuhaus, "Christianity against the Democratic Experiment," *Cross Currents* (Spring 1969): 133–48.
59. Ibid., 138.

democratic system of government and emphasized that "it is both politically and theologically imperative to assert that Marxism-Leninism promulgates a doctrine that is incompatible with a Christian understanding of humanity and historical destiny. Thus Christians must be unapologetically anticommunist." He proceeded to argue that the best alternative to communism was democracy.[60]

For Neuhaus, the rejection of communism was at its core a rejection of political monism; the Soviet Union merely exemplified this tendency but hardly exhausted it. While the main focus of this document understandably centered on the threat of Marxism-Leninism, given its role in world affairs at the time, his interests extended beyond this specific threat to the broader totalitarian temptation. In contrast to such a temptation, liberal democracy upholds political pluralism, asserts the autonomy of the religious, political, cultural, and economic spheres of life, and affirms a notion of human rights that is not dependent on the state for their legitimacy. Quite the contrary, "the state is bound to acknowledge and respect those rights which have their source in the transcendent dignity of the human person created by God," and which are lived out in the context of society.[61]

The centralization of power that occurred in totalitarian states led to the breakdown of the mediating institutions that provided a check on government power. While economic, social, and other cultural organizations play an important role in offsetting the power of the state, religious institutions are, for Neuhaus, the primary mechanism through which the state could be kept in check. It is thus obligatory for those in the churches to function as witnesses on behalf of democracy, to defend the moral principles that make democracy possible, and to "illuminate the relationship between Christian faith and democratic governance."[62] Religious institutions have the capacity to function as a constant reminder to the state that it is

---

60. Richard John Neuhaus, "Christianity and Democracy," *First Things*, October 1996, 36.
61. Ibid. 62. Ibid., 35.

under transcendent judgment and that it is not an end in itself but rather an institution that is called to be in service to its people.[63]

In a symposium sponsored by the *Center Journal* in the summer of 1982, George Weigel commented approvingly on Neuhaus's *Christianity and Democracy*.[64] He wrote that the IRD charter provided a fresh perspective on how the church could address the communist threat, influence foreign policy, and shed light on the "current situation of the churches' address to questions of America's national security."[65] Soon after the institute's founding, a pair of Washington-based researchers published a report that questioned the motivations and intentions of the IRD's leadership. Erich Hochstein and Ronald O'Rourke, the authors of the publication, focused on the links between IRD and other conservative political organizations and concluded that "the IRD is virtually a religious arm of the neoconservative political segment of the Democratic Party."[66] In particular, they emphasized its close relationship with the Coalition for a Democratic Majority, an organization that was founded nearly a decade earlier by "Scoop" Jackson and other "neoconservative" Democrats who broke ranks partially in response to the nomination of George McGovern. When asked about this connection George Weigel declared that the institute was not an organization of the "New Right," that it was trying to reach out across the spectrum of church life, and that its emphasis on human rights was a priority that could not be pigeonholed into a partisan political perspective.[67]

In an editorial for the *National Review* Michael Novak took issue with the study by Hochstein and O'Rourke and dismissed their claim that the institute shared some membership with the Coalition for a Democratic Majority, calling the similar membership an

63. Ibid., 32.

64. George Weigel, untitled essay, *Center Journal* 1, no. 3 (Summer 1982): 73–74.

65. Ibid., 74.

66. James Mann, "Neoconservatives Aim at Liberals," *The Christian Century*, November 4, 1981, 1115–17.

67. Ibid., 1116–17.

innocuous overlap. This overlap, he claimed, was irrelevant given that the institute's mission was not politically partisan.[68] The IRD was primarily a "religious organization of Christian clergy and laity concerned about the extension of democracy everywhere in the world—and about efforts by some church bureaucracies to funnel church funds and ideological support to non-democratic movements."[69] On a more nuts-and-bolts level the institute was established as a way to provide financial transparency to church groups, so that people would know where their money was going and for what purposes. Far from controversial, all religious organizations, he claimed, ought to be "fair, impartial, pluralistic, open and representative to a reasonable degree" precisely because such organizations represent a wide range of people with varied perspectives.[70]

Responding to Novak's editorial, James Wall, who was then the editor of *The Christian Century,* argued that while Novak called on the National Council of Churches (NCC) and other mainline organizations to be representative of their constituency, and generally impartial in their political activities, many of Novak's conservative allies could be accused of a similar failure. While Wall admitted that the religious left had at times idealized certain political agendas, the religious right had in effect committed the same sin, having "in varying degrees embraced the pursuit of 'democratic values' with such zeal that they show signs of mistakenly identifying the Christian faith with a political ideology.... The religious left has made this mistake in idealizing leftist governments. This does not, however, excuse the right for making the same mistake."[71]

Coming to Novak's support, Richard Neuhaus contended that the IRD was established as a non-partisan organization that would not break down along liberal and conservative lines, but in favor of

68. Michael Novak, "The Snoop Report," *National Review,* December 11, 1981, 1488.
69. Ibid.
70. Ibid.
71. James Wall, "Reds: A Timely Film on Political Religion," *The Christian Century,* December 23, 1981, 1331–32.

those who affirmed a fundamental connection between Christian faith and human freedom and those who did not.[72] Nearly a quarter of a century after its founding Neuhaus reaffirmed this vision for the institute and argued that its existence had demonstrated a "Christian effort in the latter part of the twentieth century to retell the American story relative to God's providential purpose and most specifically to God's creation of human beings wired for freedom."[73] Notwithstanding Neuhaus's contention that IRD was nonpartisan, its critics contended something very different. One article written for the *Christian Century* argued that the institute was a thoroughly political institution that exploited religious language and institutions to push a worldly agenda.[74] Another essay claimed that the IRD was "the official seminary of the Reagan administration" and was taken seriously by the media as a credible outlet because both Neuhaus and Novak sat on its board, thus giving it immediate credibility.[75]

The sharp political debates of the early eighties between representatives of the mainline Protestant churches and the leadership of the IRD was exacerbated when the latter's accusations received extensive coverage in both a lengthy article published in *Reader's Digest* and a segment on *60 Minutes* in January 1983.[76] The *60 Minutes* segment, titled "The Gospel According to Whom?" examined the ways in which the NCC distributed funds collected during

72. Richard John Neuhaus, "Christianity and Democracy," 36.

73. Richard Neuhaus, *Reflections on IRD*, October 2005, http://www.theird.org/Page.aspx?pid=1128 (accessed November 8, 2010).

74. Wall, "Neoconservatives Aim at Liberals," 1115–17.

75. James Wall, "Anticommunism Binds IRD to White House," *Christian Century*, November 28, 1984, 1115. See also James Wall, "They Come to Listen in Cherry Blossom Time," *The Christian Century*, May 1, 1985, 44. Other essays critical of IRD in *The Christian Century* include James Wall, "Playing for Peace on the World Stage," December 4, 1985, 1107–8; James Wall, "Reds: A Timely Film on Political Religion," December 23, 1981, 1131–32; "IRD Denies Charge," January 22, 1986, 64; Robert McAfee Brown, "One Sided Terms for Dialogue," May 25, 1983, 530–31; James Wall, "The True Shame of IRD as Informant," February 16–23, 1983, 139–40.

76. James Mann, "More Red Controversy for Church Council," *U.S. News and World Report*, February 13, 1983, 36.

Sunday services at churches across the country. The accusation that Morley Safer suggested throughout the segment was that "officials of the NCC may be using Sunday offerings to promote Marxist revolutions."[77] The *Reader's Digest* article, which was titled "Do You Know Where Your Church Offerings Go?" levied a similar set of criticisms. Funds were being misused by the NCC leadership to support political causes that, if made public, would alienate many of the parishioners who were contributing these funds in the first place—or so implied both outlets in their coverage of IRD.[78]

The executive director of the National Council of Churches, Reverend Paul McCleary, responded to the IRD's accusations, declaring that "our interest is in helping those who are in need and in furthering justice.... We do not fund or support communism. In countries with communist governments, like Vietnam or Cambodia, we determine how we can help people who are suffering only by providing specific material for specific purposes."[79] Defenders of the NCC argued that their critics were so obsessed with the threat of Soviet totalitarianism that they ignored the many institutions and organizations that the NCC funded that were in no way political, and claimed that the IRD was little more than a small band of conservatives who were distorting a religious message for overtly political ends.[80] Furthermore, according to a representative of the council at that time, less than one-tenth of one percent collected during Sunday services each week was actually destined for NCC coffers.[81]

Following the *60 Minutes* episode, James Wall accused the pro-

77. Kenneth Woodward and David Gates, "Ideology under the Alms," *Newsweek,* February 7, 1983, 61.

78. Colman McCarthy, "The Council of Churches and an Attack from the Right," *Washington Post,* February 27, 1983, H5.

79. Paul Taylor, "National Council of Churches under Sharpest Attack Ever," *Washington Post,* January 26, 1983, A25.

80. Paul Herbutt, "Church Council Policies 'Leftist,' Institute Charges in New Booklet," *Washington Post,* March 19, 1983, B6; Charles Austin, "Protestant Leaders Debate the Role of Religion in Public Affairs," *New York Times,* March 25, 1982, A16.

81. Taylor, "National Council of Churches"; see also Woodward and Gates, "Ideology under the Alms."

duction of containing an array of "distortions, innuendos and half-truths," and blamed the IRD as the primary source of information for these errors. Reporting on a discussion with a then-unnamed representative from the IRD, Wall wrote that his correspondent claimed that the point of the *60 Minutes* segment and *Reader's Digest* article was to help spur a "creative dialogue."[82] Wall scoffed at the notion and concluded that the real intention of the IRD leadership was to damage the credibility of and undermine the unity of the mainline churches. What the IRD was trying to achieve was "a church stance that parallels U.S. foreign policy. The IRD strategy, both in its own publications and in its 'leaks' to both the *Digest* and CBS-TV, is to support a Reagan foreign policy. Church groups have sought to build bridges to such communist nations as the People's Republic of China, the Soviet Union and Poland, but IRD almost completely ignores these involvements. Instead it concentrates on precisely those smaller countries which the Reagan administration has chosen as its battlefields against communism.... It is quite clearly pushing a political foreign policy congenial to the Reagan White House."[83]

Jim Wall's unnamed correspondent was Richard Neuhaus. Responding to these accusations Neuhaus reiterated his desire for a dialogue regarding the church's role in foreign affairs. He admitted that the *60 Minutes* episode provided a highly editorialized account of the issue, but that there were no glaring errors of fact. Standing by his participation in its production, Neuhaus reiterated his concern that there were operative assumptions against liberal democracy and toward totalitarianism at work in the NCC.[84] It is this question, he claimed—namely, to what extent the churches ought to defend and support democratic values—that should form one of the bases for a creative dialogue. Needless to say, Neuhaus was of

82. Wall, "The True Shame of IRD as Informant," 139.
83. Ibid., 140.
84. Richard John Neuhaus, "The IRD and Church Dialogue," *The Christian Century*, April 6, 1983, 317–19.

the conviction that such a defense of democratic values should be made forcefully and without apology. He concluded his letter by claiming that the strident criticism aimed at the IRD by their critics undermined any hope that the church might provide a collective social witness in defense of democratic values and in opposition to the totalitarian tendencies of Soviet Marxism.[85]

Politically, such a rigorous defense of democracy brought with it the risk of confrontation with the Soviet Union. While direct conflict had so far been avoided, a perceived slight or mistaken strategic calculation by one side or the other could conceivably give rise to tensions that would not easily be diffused. With the ever-present possibility of total war and with the invention of weaponry that could devastate entire populations in an instant, such miscalculations would have proved dire. It was on this problem—the problem of war—that George Weigel spent his energy in the late seventies and mid-eighties. One of the core problems confronting statesmen in their standoff against the Soviet Union, he contended, was that we lived with the constant threat of total war and in an age in which the threat of tyranny constantly pushed us to the brink.

What became particularly problematic for the makers of foreign policy, he contended, was that attempts to counteract one threat—total war—risked providing an opening for the other: totalitarianism. On the one hand, discounting the usefulness of war as a foreign policy tool to keep one's enemies at bay risked betraying weakness, which was a particularly dangerous disposition in the face of an enemy that would not shy away from using force of arms to further its own ends. On the other hand, the invention of nuclear weapons and modern warfare could threaten disaster for any country that used military means to fight off foreign powers who were trying to expand their international influence. Would it be possible to avoid sliding into a state of total war if the West engaged in direct military confrontation with the Soviet-dominated Eastern bloc?[86]

85. Ibid., 320.
86. Weigel, *Tranquillitas Ordinis*, 1–20.

The only apparent choice for Western society was a rather precarious either/or. The United States could resist totalitarian expansion at all costs, thus risking the possibility of total war and along with it destruction on an unprecedented scale. The other option was to downplay resistance to totalitarian aggression and reduce the risk of total war, but increase the likelihood of totalitarian expansion. From this vantage point, "between the fire of war and the pit of totalitarianism, moral imagination in the modern world is in schism. Our choices seem reduced to either/or propositions: either resist total aggression, even by war, or run the risk of a world in Gulag; either end the threat of war, even by appeasing totalitarians, or run the risk of global holocaust."[87] In popular parlance the United States seemed to be left with the uncomfortable choice between an international ethic of "better dead than red" and one of "better red than dead." With such a decision at hand debates over our future foreign policy were at an impasse, but fortunately it was a false choice. Weigel argued that an appeal to the Catholic tradition on war and peace provided a possible solution to this problem and would allow us to avoid being committed to totalitarian subjugation or a condition of total war.

The Catholic just war tradition aims, somewhat ironically, at peace, since it seeks the "reestablishment of a bond of community that will allow both attacker and attacked to resume their responsibilities for the common good of their peoples.... Just war is ordered to the common good, both of one's own community and of the enemy."[88] War and politics thus form an intimate relationship. To address the moral problem of war, political leaders must work to realize a "dynamic, rightly ordered political community" that relies on practical wisdom rooted in a perspective of moderate realism.[89] To understand what exactly Weigel meant by this, it is crucial to examine some of the influences that helped shape his thought during that period.

87. Ibid., 17.   88. Ibid., 37.
89. Ibid, 394–95.

Although a self-professed defender of the Catholic just war tradition, Weigel was deeply influenced by other strains of thought including, perhaps surprisingly, the pacifist one. One of the more profound influences on his thinking occurred during the time that he spent as a fellow during the late seventies at the World Without War Council (WWWC), a think tank established by the pacifist Robert Pickus a decade earlier. In 2003, a quarter-century after they first met, Weigel referred to his initial encounter with Pickus as one of the most important meetings of his life.[90] While never fully embracing the pacifism of Pickus, Weigel integrated much of Pickus's philosophical framework into his writing on just war during the Reagan years.

Throughout the Cold War Pickus remained a staunch critic of what he viewed as a faulty paradigm of American foreign policy—the reliance on military buildup and the consequent militarization of American foreign policy as an effective means of maintaining peace. In one interview he referred to the theory of deterrence as an "insane framework" since it centered the pursuit of peace on the threat of military destruction, rather than exploring new economic and political frameworks that could temper the appeal to mass warfare as a way to settle disputes.[91] While critical of American foreign policy, Pickus remained staunchly anticommunist throughout his life and refused to engage in an anti-American rhetoric that he believed permeated large segments of the peace movement.

His involvement in peace organizations in the decades following World War II was constantly in flux as discrete organizations consolidated, fractured, and sometimes disappeared altogether. Following a brief stint with the American Friends Service Committee, a Quaker peace group, during the late fifties, Pickus became involved with an "organization called 'Acts for Peace'. . . which became 'Turn

---

90. George Weigel, "Robert Pickus—A Life Lived Vocationally," *The Catholic Difference,* November 5, 2003, www.eppc.org/publications/pubID.1926/pub_detail.asp (accessed September 1, 2007).

91. Robert Pickus, "Full Turn Toward Peace," *MANAS* 15, no. 6 (February 7, 1962): 3.

toward Peace' and then 'Negotiation Now,' that finally became known as the 'World Without War Council.'"[92] It was through his involvement with the WWWC and, in large part, through the influence of Pickus that Weigel was able to secure a fellowship at the Woodrow Wilson International Center for Scholars in Washington and write one of his major works during this period, *Tranquillitas Ordinis*.

Tranquillitas Ordinis is the culmination of a decade's worth of research and writing on the question of war and peace. Tracing the development of his thought from his earlier work, and particularly during his time at the WWWC, will shed light on the ways in which both the secular pacifist and Catholic just war traditions influenced his thought. In one of his earliest essays on the problems confronting America in the foreign policy realm, Weigel projected an idealistic and far-reaching vision. He wrote that "the goal of American policy must be general, universal, complete and inspected disarmament in the context of a world order in which war is no longer an acceptable means of conflict resolution, because other alternatives are available."[93] While he recognized that in the earthly city conflict will never disappear in human relations, he remained confident that for at least the next decade political structures and strategies could be put into place that make unnecessary an appeal to mass, organized violence—war—as a viable strategy to resolve conflict. In other words, war is only one of multiple mechanisms that can be used to provide a resolution to human conflict; it is not a necessary one and could, in theory, be largely eliminated. To do so it would be important to initiate something like a "peace-initiatives strategy" that could provide alternative mechanisms for dealing with international crises.

Such a strategy would avoid abrupt solutions like American uni-

92. Norman Podhoretz, *Breaking Ranks: A Political Memoir* (New York: Harper and Row, 1979), 191.

93. George Weigel, "Hard-Nosed Idealism: A Model for Disarmament," *America,* October 1, 1977, 186.

lateral disarmament, which would serve only to open America up to attack without putting into place institutional structures that would prevent such a response. At the other extreme, Weigel was also skeptical of a strategy that relied on mutually assured destruction, which would likely escalate the arms race and in doing so jeopardize any possibility for a long-lasting and reliable peace.[94] In a later essay Weigel recognized that for some four decades a deterrence strategy based on mutually assured destruction had worked, but "working" does not necessarily make something morally legitimate. It might be the most useful strategy for the moment, but in the long run there must be put into place a strategy that directly addresses the arms race and emphasizes the importance of arms reduction. This "peace initiatives strategy" was influenced by the thought of Robert Pickus, who defined it as a policy that "recognizes that any final settlement must be based on common consent, but asserts that there are situations in which only independent action taken without prior agreement can create a situation in which agreement becomes possible."[95]

Arms reduction was one of the primary objectives as it would commit the United States to implement initiatives that would build momentum toward peace. Such initiatives would consist in a series of carefully determined steps that anticipated reciprocation by its enemies and thus provide an opportunity for additional steps that could further the process of disarmament. For example, Weigel suggested that the United States unilaterally halt underground nuclear testing and call on the Soviet Union and other nuclear powers to do the same. If reciprocation ensued then the United States could take further measures, such as halting the test firing of ICBMs and calling for further reciprocation. Such an approach would take small steps that would result in significant changes to geopolitical rela-

94. Ibid., 187–88.

95. *Peace and Freedom: Christian Faith, Democracy and the Problem of War* (New York: Institute on Religion and Democracy, 1983), 20–30. Robert Pickus and Robert Woito, *To End War* (Berkeley, Calif.: World Without War Council, 1974), 188.

tions between the United States and the Soviet Union and would lead to the establishment of new safeguards against armed conflict. He pointed to successes in the past where this approach had born fruit, such as with the partial test ban treaty, a success that gave him reason to believe that such a strategy could work again in the future.[96]

The obvious drawback to this approach is that absent reciprocation, the strategy dies a quick and early death. Given that there was no overarching political structure that could help manage political relations on the international plane, individual nations functioned within what was a de facto state of anarchy in relation to each other. In an essay published in 1979, Weigel highlighted this problem when he wrote that "the fundamental reason why nations rely on military means of security is that there is, at present, no viable, credible alternative means of nonviolent international conflict resolution.... Work for disarmament must simultaneously be work for alternative means by which the inevitable conflicts among sovereign states are processed, adjudicated, and resolved without resort to the mechanism of mass, organized violence—war."[97]

In another context he reiterated a similar sentiment, writing that "the root cause of the problem of war today lies in a system of independent nation states, each claiming absolute sovereignty over its own affairs, and none accountable to a transnational political authority."[98] A strategy that depended on mutual cooperation alone would probably not provide an adequate, long-term framework to secure peace. At any time one or more of the nations involved could refuse to reciprocate, thus effectively ending any practical advances that had been achieved. A dependence on mutual reciprocation could thus function only as an intermediate stage until more fundamental changes could be made to the international system. Weigel

96. Ibid., 188.
97. George Weigel, "The Catholics and the Arms Race: A Primer for the Perplexed," *Chicago Studies* (Summer 1979): 176.
98. Weigel, *Peace and Freedom,* 61.

contended that structural changes needed to be introduced into the international framework that would constrict and channel decision making on a national level. In the following years he began to flesh out these structural issues and, in doing so, began in earnest to draw on the thinking of both Robert Pickus and twentieth-century Catholic thought.

In a small booklet that was published by the Institute on Religion and Democracy, George Weigel noted that to achieve a lasting peace it was important to understand what was meant by the term *peace*. When speaking of peace in a public context, he emphasized that he was not talking about an inner peace that is brought about through a right relationship with God, nor was he speaking of a peace conditioned by a complete absence of conflict. Such a peace is utopian and presupposed that humans could bring the Kingdom of God to earth. The peace of which Weigel spoke was constituted by a public order secured through a common authority in which social and political structures are put into place that provide rational, non-violent ways of dealing with conflict on the international level.[99] Political structures would have to be implemented on an international scale that would assist in this process. Weigel insisted that these newly devised international structures would not replace the current system of nation states but instead complement it. It was a framework that had a four-part structure.[100] In short, a world without war "would be a disarmed world, under law, where there was a sufficient minimum of political community to sustain that law, and in which the political and economic development problems of the Third World were being solved."[101]

It is here that the strong influence of the peace activist Robert Pickus on George Weigel is evident. The framework discussed above is in many respects reminiscent of Pickus's approach to war and

99. Ibid., 46.

100. Weigel, *Tranquillitas Ordinis*, 197.

101. George Weigel, *The Peace Bishops and the Arms Race: Can Religious Leadership Help in Preventing War?* (Chicago: World Without War Council, 1982), 24.

peace. In an interview given in 1962, Pickus stressed the importance of eliminating war as a viable alternative to solving conflict between nation states. The goal of his efforts was "total and general disarmament" that would be achieved through a "growth toward world law," and a "sense of community adequate to sustain world law." This would be further matched by American support for "economic and political policies that challenge colonialism and feudalism."[102] Just a few years following this interview, Pickus summarized these interconnected themes in a book he co-wrote, titled *To End War*. Here he wrote that "a world without war is a world in which agreement on universal, complete and enforceable disarmament has been achieved and put into effect. But disarmament is not a sufficient objective, for it cannot be maintained without alternate procedures for resolving conflict and establishing justice in world affairs. It cannot be maintained without law. But there can be no law without the sense of a world community."[103] Furthermore, as those in third-world countries will likely be little concerned about laws governing international affairs so long as their condition remains poor, it is essential to create effective mechanisms for economic development.[104]

In addition to the four themes listed above, Weigel also emphasized the importance of democracy as a principle that ought to guide affairs both nationally and internationally, because "the advance of democracy is the advance of peace."[105] The American experience of democratic institutions had proven, with the significant exception of the Civil War, to be an effective mechanism that had been used to support non-violent conflict resolution and could function as a model for international institutions. The problem of war was at its core a political problem; the establishment of political institutions that have been shown to have a track record for avoiding violence as

102. Pickus, "Full Turn Toward Peace."
103. Pickus, *To End War*, 181.
104. Ibid.
105. Weigel, "Christian Century Foundation Colloquium," *Catholicism in Crisis*, May 1983, 25.

a solution to conflict on a national level could provide a model that could be used to avoid war on the international plane.[106] Further still, in the context of the Cold War, the rhetoric promoted by and the example of democratic societies could provide a strong moral voice against the Soviet Union's political rhetoric.[107]

While clearly influenced by the thought of Robert Pickus, Weigel's worldview also overlapped with that of the political neoconservatives, particularly in his emphasis on the usefulness of democratic institutions in an international context. The political neoconservative Joshua Muravchik provided a clear defense of this principle in his book *Exporting Democracy*. In a post-communist world, he argued, the spread of democracy would make war a less likely phenomenon as democracies tend not to go to war with one another. Further, given both the interests of the United States and its political value system, the spread of democracy ought to be one of the basic principles upon which American foreign policy is based.[108]

Writing about neoconservative political philosophy, the military historian Max Boot emphasized that the neoconservative take on democracy paralleled that of Woodrow Wilson. The appeal of Wilson had less to do with the usefulness of multilateral institutions like the United Nations, but in the neoconservative appreciation for the usefulness of American power to spread American ideals. The spread of American democracy is a particularly important objective, "not only out of sheer humanitarianism but because the spread of liberal democracy improves American security."[109]

The vision proposed by Muravchik and Boot signified both a similarity and a disjunction between Weigel and the political neoconservatives. Both valued democracy and believed that as a politi-

---

106. Weigel, *Tranquillitas Ordinis*, 144–46.

107. George Weigel, "Exorcising Wilson's Ghost: Morality and Foreign Policy in America's Third Century," *Washington Quarterly* (Autumn 1987): 38.

108. Joshua Muravchik, *Exporting Democracy* (Washington, D.C.: American Enterprise Institute, 1992), 7–12.

109. Boot, "Myths about Neoconservatism," 49.

cal philosophy it was generally superior to the existing alternatives. George Weigel and the political neoconservatives further stressed the benefit that it would bring to American security in particular and international relations more generally if it were to be embraced by nations that were not currently democratic. Nevertheless, unlike his political counterparts, Weigel strongly and repeatedly reaffirmed the value of international institutions and law if such institutions were constructed properly. His entire thesis regarding the possibility of creating a "world without war" depended on the creation of such institutions.

Weigel held international systems in such high regard because of the influence of Robert Pickus on his thought, but he was not the only influence. The Catholic political tradition, particularly as expressed in modern papal teaching, is also an important source for his positive appraisal of international institutions. While Weigel was critical of Pope John XXIII on some accounts, including a failure to properly spell out human rights and develop an adequate understanding of the relationship between peace and justice, he provided a largely favorable account of many of the themes that emerged in the pope's encyclical *Pacem in Terris*. For example, Weigel lauded Pope John XIII for linking "the goals of disarmament, international organization and law, human rights, democracy and economic and social development. This was an important advance over previous church teaching on peace as dynamic political community."[110]

It is important to emphasize that for Weigel the emphasis by John XIII constituted an advance in Catholic thought and not something new. One of the central premises of Weigel's book *Tranquillitas Ordinis* is that the notion of rightly ordered political community extended as far back as Saint Augustine, was developed in the thought of Saint Thomas Aquinas, and further advanced with the founding of the United States. The role of international insti-

110. Weigel, *Tranquillitas Ordinis*, 91.

tutions was simply the next step in the evolution of this concept. Weigel's call for the establishment of democratic institutions internationally was not, at least in theory, based on the sheer projection of American power and American interest, but rather signified a further unfolding of the Catholic political heritage. He claimed that in a modern context this heritage "proposed an approach to the problem of international political community that allowed international institutions to control the bellicosity of nation-states without requiring their abandonment or abolition.... It persistently argued that the peace of political community was a necessity on the international level, and thus had to be created."[111]

Unfortunately Weigel lamented that, just as Catholic leaders were beginning to recognize the importance of advancing the church's teaching on war and peace into the international sphere, these same leaders effectively abandoned the tradition. While the bishops continued to embrace an international perspective, Weigel argued that it became unmoored from the broader social ethic that the church had nurtured and helped develop over the course of centuries and which, in the modern period, found its most complete expression in the American system of government. This abandonment was in large part due to the way in which the Vietnam War played out and the way leadership in the American Catholic church responded to the war. In the words of Weigel, Vietnam signified a definitive turning point in which "the central components of a distinctively Catholic context for thinking about the moral problem of war and peace ... were twisted and bent in such a way that the net effect was a virtual abandonment of the heritage as a horizon for moral analysis."[112]

For Weigel, the institutional Catholic church's response to Vietnam was largely a failure that brought with it ominous consequences. These failures were both analytic and theological in nature.[113]

---

111. Ibid., 142. 112. Ibid., 235–36.
113. Ibid., 216.

On the first point he claimed that many within the American Catholic leadership, which included lay and religious alike, consistently made empirically flawed judgments. This included the strong Catholic support for the corrupt Diem regime and the failure to push for economic and political reform in the region. It included a mistaken analysis concerning the relationship between the North Vietnamese and the Chinese, Russians, and Vietcong. Finally, the analytical errors included a selective condemnation of American atrocities, during the massacre at My Lai, on the one hand, and the relative silence regarding the massacres committed by the Vietcong during, for example, the massive civilian executions in the city of Hue during the Tet offensive.[114] The failure to properly analyze the situation on the ground, while not an exclusively Catholic problem, severely retarded the ability of Catholics to implement an alternative strategy rooted in the Catholic tradition of war and peace.

Weigel attempted to illustrate this error through an analysis of a series of statements released by the bishops from 1966 to 1971 related to Vietnam. The statements grew progressively more critical of U.S. involvement. The first, issued in November 1966, aimed at applying the teachings of Vatican II on war and peace to the Vietnam War and asserted a relative degree of confidence in the decision-making process of the government on this issue. Over the next few years the bishops continued to support the war effort, although cracks began to develop in their support for this cause. From a position of strong affirmation in 1966, the bishop's position included a growing sense of doubt regarding the war's legitimacy.[115]

By 1971 their position on U.S. involvement in Vietnam had notably shifted from the position held just five years earlier. As William Au notes, the experience of Vietnam "helped to move them in the direction of a greater willingness to address negative judgments against major government policies."[116] In contrast to their vote of

114. Ibid., 230–32.
115. William Au, *The Cross, the Flag, and the Bomb: American Catholics Debate War and Peace 1960–1983* (New York: Praeger, 1987), 178–79.
116. Ibid., 180.

support for U.S. government policy then, the bishops now called for an immediate end to the war, although they did not come out in support of immediate withdrawal. This adversarial position was not exclusive to Vietnam, but became more common over the following years, particularly in the critical tone they took in their pastoral letters on war and peace and on the economy.

While it was intellectually justifiable to question the ethical legitimacy of America's involvement in Vietnam, George Weigel criticized the position taken by the bishops in their 1971 document *Resolution on Southeast Asia,* because it "failed to discuss how America might disengage wisely, or what the relevant moral standards to guide such a policy might be."[117] He claimed that the bishops' failure to provide a comprehensive framework for American withdrawal dramatically oversimplified the problems confronting any attempt to end the war. There was thus a failure by the bishops to take advantage of the Catholic tradition on war and peace and apply that tradition to important questions of foreign policy, in this case Vietnam. Rather than trying to come to terms with questions related to when the use of force and intervention overseas was a legitimate response, Weigel contended that large segments within the American Catholic leadership instead embraced a neo-isolationist approach to foreign policy, an all too common anti-anticommunist outlook, and an outright refusal to use military force to defend human rights.[118]

The failure of the bishops to correctly understand and apply the church's traditional teaching on war and peace had important consequences over the next decade, according to Weigel. First, it placed the American Catholic church in a politically vulnerable position; it became increasingly difficult for the church to provide an alternative to secular, or at least non-Catholic, political perspectives. Second, it became increasingly difficult for the leadership of the church to promote authentic teaching as it related to the church's tradition

117. Weigel, *Tranquillitas Ordinis,* 233.
118. Ibid., 233–34.

on war and peace, particularly as it pertained to the Soviet threat to the Western way of life. The way in which Catholic leaders understood this threat highlighted an intellectual division between them and the neoconservative Catholics. The next two chapters will pick up on some of these divisions by examining the way in which Catholic anticommunism played out in the church during the seventies and eighties both in a global context and in a Latin American one. During the eighties, the disruptions in Central America signified one such place; particularly in conservative circles, concerns over Soviet influence in the region took on a greater urgency. For the neoconservative Catholics, these concerns applied not only to secular politics but to distortions that were playing out in certain sectors of Catholic life.

5 ❖ U.S. CATHOLICS AND THE ANTICOMMUNIST CRUSADE

FROM THE MID-NINETEENTH CENTURY onward, anticommunist sentiment was a staple of Catholic political thought. In his encyclical "On Faith and Religion," Pope Pius IX decried the pernicious effect of the communist worldview, declaring that if such a philosophy were embraced "the complete destruction of everyone's laws, government, property, and even of human society itself would follow."[1] Similar sentiments were reiterated in the writings and public pronouncements of the popes that followed. Pope Leo XIII declared that communism, alongside socialism and nihilism, signified a "hideous deformity of civil society," and Pope Pius XI asserted in his encyclical on atheistic communism that such a worldview was "full of errors and sophisms" and was contrary to divine revelation.[2] Pope John Paul II is often noted for his opposition to communism

---

1. Pope Pius IX, *Qui Pluribus (On Faith and Religion)*, November 9, 1846, no. 16, translation available at http://www.ewtn.com/library/encyc/p9quiplu.htm (accessed April 2, 2013).

2. Pope Leo XIII, *Diuturnum (On the Origin of Civil Power)*, June 29, 1881, no. 23, http://www.vatican.va/holy_father/leo_xiii/encyclicals/documents/hf_l-xiii_enc_29061881_diuturnum_en.html (accessed April 2, 2013); Pope Pius XI, *Divini Redemptoris (On Atheistic Communism)*, March 19, 1937, no. 14, http://www.vatican.va/holy_father/pius_xi/encyclicals/documents/hf_p-xi_enc_19031937_divini-redemptoris_en.html (accessed April 2, 2013).

and credited as one of the leading figures who helped to bring down the Soviet Union, through both his moral voice and his political engagement in Eastern Europe.

The anticommunist sentiments expressed by Rome were reflected in American Catholicism, which functioned as one of the leading voices in the American anticommunist crusade. In addition to some of the more infamous figures like Joseph McCarthy, the church produced prominent spokesmen in the likes of Msgr. Edmund Walsh, who in the words of his biographer became "the leading advocate of the national security state, a highly respected interpreter of Soviet political objectives for the Truman administration, and the leading Catholic participant in the idealist-realist debate surrounding American foreign policy."[3] His emergence as a Cold War warrior was nurtured by a church leadership that had traditionally maintained an adversarial stance toward Marxism and, upon its creation, the Soviet Union.

Opposition to communism was also evident in the activities of millions of lay Catholics during the middle decades of the twentieth century, many of whom participated in a range of lay organizations, including the Catholic War Veterans, the Cardinal Mindszenty Foundation, and the Blue Army of Our Lady of Fatima, the last of which was dedicated to propagating the anticommunist message purported to have been revealed during the Marian revelation at Fatima.[4] The Fatima revelation highlighted the important intersection that existed between devotionalism and Catholic anticommunism during the Cold War; opposition to communism was not merely an intellectual or philosophical endeavor, but was embedded in the religious lives of countless American Catholics. Following the popularization of the prophecies on the American home front

3. Patrick McNamara, "'The Argument of Strength Justly and Righteously Employed': Edmund A. Walsh, Catholic Anticommunism, and American Foreign Policy, 1945–1952," *U.S. Catholic Historian* 22, no. 4 (Fall 2004): 57–58.

4. David Laurence O'Connor, "Defenders of the Faith: American Catholic Lay Organizations and Anticommunism, 1917–1975" (Ph.D. diss., State University of New York at Stony Brook, 2000).

after 1942, Catholics turned to the rosary as a weapon that allowed them to participate in the spiritual war against the evil that Soviet communism brought with it. In her study on the political significance of these revelations, one commentator noted that the Fatima prophecies "were heralded as Mary's having seen and attempted to communicate to humanity at the dawn of the Bolshevik Revolution the full magnitude of the danger facing the world."[5]

While a potent force for a time, American Catholic anticommunism, according to the historian Richard Gid Powers, had begun to diminish in its influence by the mid-sixties. The American Catholic church's opposition to communism was at least partly rooted in sociological conditions that defined Catholic identity up through the mid-twentieth century, and particularly due to the impression that it was under siege by the non-Catholic majority. On this point, Powers claimed that "at a time when American Catholics felt themselves at war with much of America, their anticommunism was an expression of their defiant separation from the American mainstream."[6] Catholic support for Franco in Spain, for example, placed them on what they understood to be the side of the Catholic church and against the communist-controlled government. Many non-Catholic Americans, on the other hand, viewed Franco's uprising as an attack on democracy, thus further alienating them from his Catholic supporters. During World War II, Catholic criticism of Stalin was seen as weakening the alliance between the United States and the Soviet Union against Hitler and thus a threat to national security. For their opposition, liberal organs such as *The Nation* and *The New Republic* accused the Catholic press of being pro-fascist.[7]

As American Catholics began to enter into the mainstream in

5. Una Cadegan, "The Queen of Peace in the Shadow of War: Fatima and U.S. Catholic Anticommunism," *U.S. Catholic Historian* 22, no. 4 (Fall 2004): 7; Thomas A. Kselman and Steven Avella, "Marian Piety and the Cold War in the United States," *The Catholic Historical Review* 72, no. 3 (July 1986), 403–24.

6. Richard Gid Powers, "American Catholics and Catholic Americans: The Rise and Fall of Catholic Anticommunism," *U.S. Catholic Historian* 22, no. 4 (Fall 2004): 34.

7. Ibid., 21–24.

the decade following the end of World War II, and with anticommunism becoming more prevalent among non-Catholic Americans, the anticommunism of the Catholic church had a different function than it had years earlier: it provided American Catholics with the opportunity to prove their patriotism. The Soviet Union was the enemy of the state and American Catholicism's opposition to it and its guiding philosophy demonstrated the church's loyalty to America. Nevertheless, the anticommunist extremism expressed by the likes of Joseph McCarthy and others eventually brought this crusade into some disrepute. Given their newfound respectability in American society it was in the interests of Catholics to downplay those attributes that might undermine their rising credibility. As Powers put it, with the end of their isolation in American society, "Catholics began to cast off the attributes of their ghetto mentality, and it turned out that their anticommunism was one of the ghetto rags they gladly shed."[8]

Although cultural politics in the United States played an important role in the downplaying of America Catholic anticommunism, of at least equal importance were developments occurring in Rome. While never abandoning its opposition to communism, the way in which the Vatican engaged the Soviet Union shifted in the period between the papacies of Pius XII and John Paul II. Throughout the reign of Pope Pius XII, the church maintained an adversarial stance toward the Soviet Union, during which time he vocally opposed the repression of the church in the Soviet Union and its satellite states and promoted a moral message that emphasized the transcendent dignity of the human person, highlighted the limited authority of the state, and denounced Marxism and its materialist philosophy.[9]

Pope John XXIII and Pope Paul VI initiated a shift in strategy. Whereas Pius XII's approach hinged on refraining from any sort of contact with Soviet leadership, John XXIII initiated a thaw in relations between the Vatican and Moscow. Through limited engage-

8. Ibid., 29.
9. J. Bryan Hehir, "Papal Foreign Policy," *Foreign Affairs* 78 (Spring 1990): 28–29.

ment with Soviet authorities, the pope promoted a strategy referred to as "Vatican *Ostpolitik,*" which sought to provide some "breathing room" for the Catholic church in Eastern Europe. Through his writings, and in particular *Pacem in Terris,* he laid the groundwork for a dialogue that could occur between the church and communists, recognizing that even movements that were based on false ideas could "contain elements that were positive of approval."[10]

In addition to pursuing a warming of relations between the church and the communist party, John XXIII also expanded on the focus of the church's mission. *Mater et Magistra, Pacem in Terris,* and the Second Vatican Council's *Gaudium et Spes* emphasized the protection of human rights, the alleviation of global poverty, and the importance of the global South, with a less pronounced emphasis on the communist threat. This created more space for the pursuit and realization of the social mission of the church in the world. Pope Paul VI expanded on John XXIII's *Ostpolitik* diplomacy and, in his encyclical *Populorum Progressio,* further highlighted the importance of focusing on the developing world and responding to the unjust international structures that currently defined international relations.[11] This represented a shift away from the focus on the East/ West divide that had preoccupied Pope Pius XII.

While Pope John Paul II is properly credited with reaffirming the church's opposition to communism and in helping to bring down the Soviet Union, he also furthered the themes that had preoccupied both Pope John XXIII and Pope Paul VI. As with his predecessors, he focused on a much broader set of issues, including the role of nuclear weapons in international politics, global poverty and its connection to the developed and developing worlds, and the role of institutional structures in geopolitical relationships.[12] The shift away from Pope Pius XII's single-minded focus on the communist threat in world affairs to the more comprehensive perspective of

10. Ibid., 29–31.   11. Ibid., 32–33.
12. Ibid., 39.

later popes was reflected in the teachings of the American bishops. By the mid-seventies they rejected nuclear deterrence, which had functioned as the cornerstone for America's containment policy, and by the mid-eighties had begun to reevaluate the global political situation as it related to Soviet/U.S. relations and the international economic system.

Richard Gid Powers argued that the shift away from a strident anticommunism by broad swaths of American Catholics, including many bishops, left Catholic anticommunists a "fringe group within the Catholic community led by a few (though prominent) Tories like Buckley."[13] Such a perspective also included the neoconservative Catholics whose anticommunism remained steady, if not more pronounced, during the seventies and eighties. George Weigel also maintained a strong anticommunist streak, urging church leadership to resist the temptation to downplay the Soviet threat and properly assess the conflict between the United States and the Soviet Union. Of particular concern to him was the tendency of many bishops to engage in political judgments that maintained a generalized denunciation of American society and a mistaken understanding of its role in a world fraught with an array of geopolitical challenges.[14] As we will see below, this critique became most pronounced in the debates that occurred over the bishops' pastoral letter *The Challenge of Peace*.

Richard Neuhaus recognized that communism as embodied by the Soviet Union provided the preeminent example of contemporary statism, in which the state bureaucracy aimed at swallowing up any competing voices in the public square. Attempts in modern American life to eliminate, in particular, religion from public debate was disconcerting because, if successful, it would help to lay the groundwork for domestic forms of totalitarianism. On this point Neuhaus asserted that because the "naked square cannot remain naked (from

13. Powers, "American Catholics and Catholic Americans," 30.

14. George Weigel, "Beyond the Challenge of Peace: *Quaestiones Disputatae*," *Center Journal* (Winter 1983): 108–10.

the religious voice), the direction is toward the state-as-church, toward totalitarianism.... The available form of totalitarianism—an aggressively available form, so to speak—is Marxist-Leninism."[15]

Of the three, Michael Novak provides perhaps the most interesting case in this matter, primarily because his views on the communist threat changed over an approximately twenty-year period. The most commonly noted transition in both the secondary literature and in his personal reflections is his break from socialism and eventual embrace of democratic capitalism. Overlooked in this same literature is a shift in his understanding of the relationship between communism and the Western political tradition. The hard-line approach that he took against communism by the mid-eighties was of recent vintage. During the sixties and into the seventies he embraced a much less militant and occasionally even conciliatory disposition toward Marxism. In the following two decades his attitude toward communism shifted from a position of cautious accommodation to one of uncompromising opposition.

One of the earliest accounts of Novak's approach to communism surfaced in an essay pertaining to America's involvement in Vietnam. Here he provided a critical account of the way in which popular American political culture evaluated Marxism. It was not unusual for popular political commentary of that period to assess the communist threat as a clearly defined war of good versus evil, an apocalyptic struggle between a religiously grounded Western worldview and an anti-Western, atheistic, international conspiracy. He criticized as "simple" political perspectives that viewed the Cold War as a "battle for civilization" in which struggle "the forces of light against the forces of darkness." Unfortunately, he continued, there are "those on both sides of the Cold War who delight in the apocalyptic style and who thrive on the division of all human beings into two rival camps."[16]

---

15. Neuhaus, *The Naked Public Square*, 89.
16. Novak, "Stumbling Into War and Stumbling Out," 14–16.

Such a dichotomization of geopolitical relations is deeply flawed, he argued, because communism is not a monolithic force; no single organ directs its activities globally.[17] Further still, while philosophically problematic, communism is not the primary danger to the United States that many make it out to be. Not communism but "hunger, poverty, ignorance and disease" are the primary threats to world peace; "communism and modified capitalism are two rival strategies for coping with these necessary and inevitable revolutions of our age. But neither communism nor modified capitalism are monoliths; both are capable of indefinite evolution and development, according to the individual genius of each nation. The more diversity and open development our government can promote by its flexible conduct in world affairs, the more it will assist in the evolution of communism in a direction more compatible with the interests and safety of our own people and all others."[18]

Such a view understands communism and American capitalism as competing "strategies" for dealing with more fundamental problems confronting humanity. A pair of essays written by Novak around the same time buttressed this point. The first, which appears to be a revised and expanded version of the article quoted above, reiterated his conviction that the primary threat to world peace was economic underdevelopment. Novak then situated the struggle against poverty in the context of the Cold War and added that "to some Americans, the following statement is obvious: 'We are engaged in a struggle to the death with communism, and the sooner we recognize that the better.' To others, among whom I count myself, the main struggle of our generation is against poverty, disease, and political, social, and economic underdevelopment. From this perspective, communism represents one family of responses by which heretofore underdeveloped nations can solve their grievous problems of reorganization."[19]

Consistent with the earlier version of this essay, Novak held that

---

17. Ibid., 13–16.   18. Ibid., 17.

19. Michael Novak, "Our Terrorism, Our Brutality," in *A Time to Build* (New York: Macmillan, 1967), 407–28.

communism constituted an alternative approach to underdevelopment and poverty and not necessarily a metaphysical threat to the Western political tradition. In contrast to the ideological anticommunism that often consumed American political life during the Cold War and that pitted the Soviet Union against the West, Novak took for granted that "there must be, one day, an alliance between cultures describing themselves as 'capitalist' and as 'communist,' for there is increasingly one world and there must one day be one culture. Such a culture must be rich in diversity, not homogenous. It must be open to alternatives and possibilities, not closed. It must be a culture of many philosophies, many theologies, many varieties of economic and political theory and practice. There is no need for all humans to be the same."[20] Here he held out the hope that at some point in the future these competing political cultures would have to work together if the problems confronting the international community were to be effectively addressed. The flip side to his conciliatory tone toward the communist bloc were his criticisms aimed at influential segments of the Catholic community who engaged in "grievous sins of rabid anti-communism" that have only contributed to unhealthy distortions in American political debate.[21]

In the early seventies Novak continued to air his grievances against the strident anticommunist wing in American politics, but this time from a slightly different angle. At one point he argued that America had failed to address the needs of the lower middle class and those beneath them since the Second World War. He said that the primary reason for this neglect was the "influence of the anti-Communist military and intelligence establishment upon the priorities of scientific and technological progress," and further argued that to correct this undue influence "the military budget could, and must be, cut at least in half."[22] The money saved could

20. Michael Novak, "Introduction," in *A Time to Build*.
21. Michael Novak, "The Emergence of Hope," in *A Time to Build*, 294.
22. Michael Novak, "The Politics of the Seventies," in *Politics: Realism and Imagination* (New York: Herder and Herder, 1971), 64.

be used for scholarships, tax rebates, subsidies, and other forms of aid to low-income individuals and families. Novak's willingness to blame the anticommunist establishment's influence for the government's failure to respond to the needs of the poor and his willingness to slash the military point to his continued standing on the "dovish" pole of American foreign policy.

Within a few years this "soft" approach to the communist threat receded and was replaced by a more adversarial one. By 1980, for example, Novak wrote an essay in which he declared that, given the military superiority of the Soviet Union, those who call for less expenditure on military power or who do not fear the decline of U.S. power in the world are setting the conditions for war rather than preventing it: "Peace and justice depend on military readiness."[23] This is quite a shift from less than a decade earlier when he was calling for the military budget to be cut at least in half. The shift to this more hard-line opposition to communism both paralleled and connected to his growing opposition to socialism in favor of democratic capitalism. His conversion to capitalism was informed by pragmatic considerations and his growing conviction that it was the surest mechanism for both domestic and international development.[24] This pragmatic approach conflicted with his earlier theoretical opposition to capitalism, which he later concluded was "bookish" and "abstract" and failed to take into account the practical consequences of the capitalist and socialist economic systems.[25]

In the introduction to his book *The Spirit of Democratic Capitalism*, Novak lauded the practical successes that had followed the introduction of capitalism in the West. An almost total lack of potable water, a dearth of medical knowledge, exorbitantly high food prices, an average life span that did not exceed even thirty years,

23. Michael Novak, "Reflections on the Draft," *National Review*, July 11, 1980, 847.
24. Michael Novak, "The Closet Socialists," *Christian Century*, February 23, 1977, 171–74; "An Underpraised and Undervalued System," *Worldview* (July/August 1977): 9–12.
25. Michael Novak, *Unmeltable Ethnics: Politics and Culture in American Life*, 2nd ed. (New Brunswick, N.J.: Transaction, 1992), xxviii.

and near universal illiteracy—this was the generally expected state of existence for the overwhelming number of human beings in the decades preceding the introduction of capitalism in the in late eighteenth century. From about 1800 onward, he stated confidently, "the invention of the market economy in Great Britain and the United States more profoundly revolutionized the world … than any single force."[26] Real wages increased substantially, medical advances proliferated, life expectancy soared, and the price of bread, which according to Novak cost four-fifths of the average French families' income in the 1780s, became both widely available and cheap. These advances were a direct result of the introduction of capitalist enterprise and, with it, new methods that could be applied to a process of systematic development.[27]

Socialism, in contrast, failed to bring about the promises that it made as an economic system. It promised a better life for all, but brought with it only mediocrity. It guaranteed more widespread and available wealth that could be taken advantage of by more people, but consistently failed to deliver. Capitalism, not socialism, was the mother of invention. Writing some years later on the inadequacies of the latter, Novak wrote that "as I surveyed the economic record of the socialist nations of Eastern Europe, Asia, Africa, and Cuba, I could find none that I admired or would choose for a model of the world. The socialist economic ideal did not work in practice, not anywhere."[28]

Concluding that socialism was an empirically failed experiment, Novak was troubled by its continued popularity, particularly within educated intellectual circles. He concluded that for most advocates of socialism, its practical usefulness was not the most important consideration. Socialism had taken on a veneer of religion that people adhered to through a kind of secular faith. The fact that social-

---

26. Novak, *The Spirit of Democratic Capitalism*, 17.

27. Ibid., 16.

28. Michael Novak, "Errand into the Wilderness," in *On Cultivating Liberty: Reflections on Moral Ecology* (Lanham, Md.: Rowman and Littlefield, 1999), 276.

ism produced few practically beneficial results was largely irrelevant since "certain sorts of piety are immune to empirical tests. American socialists prefer piety to empiricism."[29]

His growing opposition to communism paralleled his opposition to socialism. Like socialism, Marxism projected a religious quality that promised a "great transformation from the present corrupt order into a brotherly, just, and peaceful society."[30] Unfortunately, Novak lamented, having been in practice since 1917, it had proven to be a failure. In some of his writings, he blurs the line between Marxism and socialism and simultaneously points to their failings as though they are one and the same thing. In one essay, for example, he complained that "unable to be empirical or pragmatic, the Marxified mind has no other choice but verbal excess. In practice, the socialist dream is empty; in the caverns of its emptiness many shout the louder." All they have left are a baseless belief in their myths.[31]

By the early eighties Novak had further developed the claim that the intellectual assent to Marxism marked a piety rooted in ideology that remained ungrounded in any pragmatic considerations. In his book *Confession of a Catholic* he argued that it was the most organized form of political idealism in the modern world that sought a total transformation of social and political life.[32] Unfortunately the utopian vision that it promoted functioned in practice as little more than a "gigantic organizing force of tyrannical power" that "preaches class struggle, violence, and hatred."[33] The aggressive and often violent approach to social revolution that it espouses and its utopian, pseudo-religious style can neither be ignored nor overlooked by members of the political, religious, and intellectual classes of the West. As late as 1988, Novak decried intellectuals who denied "the reality of Soviet power, the scope of Soviet ambition, and the

---

29. Michael Novak, "Pious Socialists," *National Review,* February 22, 1980, 227.
30. Novak, *Confession of a Catholic,* 186.
31. Michael Novak, "Extremism as a Virtue," *National Review,* November 9, 1979, 1427.
32. Novak, *Confession of a Catholic,* 192–93.
33. Ibid., 187.

record of Soviet deception" and instead upheld communism as one of the marvel of history. In response, Novak declared that "resistance to communism, principled and militarily effective, is morally obligatory."[34]

One of the central concerns of the neoconservative Catholics pertaining to this threat and to the "morally obligatory" responsibility of the West to confront it was with the American bishops' failure to lead in this respect. The debate that centered on the bishops' pastoral letter *The Challenge of Peace* brought into relief the very different framework that guided the bishops' understanding of the Soviet Union as opposed to that of the neoconservative Catholics. From the neoconservatives' perspective, the bishops had failed to properly conceptualize the Soviet threat and, in doing so, promoted policies that were at odds with the continued military and political security of the Western world. Likewise, the bishops' pastoral letter *Economic Justice for All* provides a second example of the way in which the bishops' engagement with political life shifted as their overt anticommunism diminished. In this letter as well they showed a willingness to be critical of American economic policy and of the national culture. In both cases, the neoconservative Catholics contended that the bishops had become too engaged in the policy-making process. The primary responsibility of the bishops "is to articulate the normative moral framework out of which competent laymen ... with the required technical expertise ... can make morally informed policy judgments."[35] Considering each of the bishops' letters in turn and setting them in the context of the neoconservative Catholic critique will further clarify some of the contours of American Catholic life in the years leading up to the end of the Cold War.

---

34. Novak, "Errand into the Wilderness," 298–99.

35. George Weigel, "Open Letter to Archbishop Bernardin," *Catholicism in Crisis* (January 1983): 15.

The Challenge of Peace

The decision to write a pastoral letter on war and peace was initiated in 1980 at the U.S. bishops' annual November meeting, via a request that Auxiliary Bishop P. Francis Murray made to the National Conference of Catholic Bishops' leadership the previous summer. In the following years the bishops released a series of drafts, one during the summer of 1982 and a second that following November. A final draft was completed and voted on in May 1983, passing with 233 votes in favor and only 9 against.[36]

In the midst of its development, politically conservative-leaning Catholic critics of the pastoral formed an organization called the American Catholic Committee. The committee sought to provide a forum that could effectively counter the bishops' pastoral on war and peace. One proposal included the suggestion to write a "counter-pastoral," a letter written by lay Catholics that would critique the bishops' own. None ever materialized out of this group. However, following the publication of the bishops' first draft, Michael Novak picked up on this idea and, with help from his contacts in the American Catholic community, engaged in a parallel set of deliberations that resulted in the production of his own "counter-pastoral."[37]

The final publication, titled "Moral Clarity in the Nuclear Age," was written by Novak and co-signed by more than one hundred prominent American Catholics. It was widely circulated, initially published in Michael Novak's magazine, *Catholicism in Crisis,* republished in the *National Review,* and eventually admitted into the *Congressional Record* in both the House and the Senate by Rep. Vin

36. Kenneth Briggs, "Bishops, Gratified, Prepare to Teach Letter on Peace," *New York Times,* May 5, 1983, http://www.nytimes.com/1983/05/05/us/bishops-gratified-prepare-to-teach-letter-on-peace.html.

37. Michael Novak, "Reflections on War and Peace," *U.S. Catholic Historian* 4, no. 1 (1984): 94. Michael Novak was a member of the American Catholic Committee, although he was not connected to the subcommittee that was initially given the responsibility to write a lay letter.

Weber (R-Minn.) and Sen. Robert Kasten (R-Wis.).[38] Shortly after the final draft of *The Challenge of Peace* was issued, Novak's statement was published in book form with a series of other essays written by him on related topics.[39] In the introduction William F. Buckley gushed over the statement's importance and declared that, with respect to the bishops, "what will prove historically most important about their own pastoral letter is that it engendered Michael Novak's *Moral Clarity in the Nuclear Age.*"[40]

Novak's "counter-pastoral" was critical of the bishops' approach to questions of war and peace, on the grounds of both tone and substance, and anticipated some of the prominent themes in the thought of the neoconservative Catholics. He criticized many of the bishops for their prophetic tone and for engaging in what he referred to as a kind of religious "enthusiasm" that relied more on emotional excitement than on reason. Novak was particularly critical of religious leaders like Bishops Raymond Hunthausen and Thomas Gumbleton, whose calls for "unilateral disarmament" presupposed a worldview that Novak complained was out of touch with reality. Their pacifist tendencies and prophetic style in the face of the Soviet threat, argued Novak, revealed a naïveté that had led the post-Vatican II generation of American bishops to be "breathtakingly cavalier about the small fragile band of democracies left in the world, about the fate of its flock, about oppression."[41]

Weigel signed on to this critique and argued that the primary motivation behind *The Challenge of Peace* was a sense of fear that embraced a "survivalist ethic." The bishops' approach reflected a popular sensibility that had infected the American churches during the seventies and which embraced a New Testament-style

---

38. Michael Novak, "Moral Clarity in the Nuclear Age," *Catholicism in Crisis* 1, no. 4 (March 1983); reprinted in *National Review*, April 1, 1983.

39. Michael Novak, *Moral Clarity in the Nuclear Age* (Nashville, Tenn.: Thomas Nelson, 1983), 16–17. Henceforth, all references to this publication will refer to this citation.

40. William Buckley, Introduction, *Moral Clarity in the Nuclear Age*, 15.

41. Michael Novak, "Born Again Bishops," *National Review*, August 6, 1982, 960.

apocalypticism.[42] In embracing such a perspective the bishops had engaged in a flight of "reason into panic" that Michael Novak warned against in his "counter-pastoral." It was important, Novak argued, to refrain from a visceral reaction to the nuclear threat. Throughout the biblical tradition God had threatened to destroy the world by fire, plague, and pestilence, and the prophecies contained in the Book of Revelation exceeded the horrors visited on man throughout the twentieth century. We should not, in other words, consider our generation as somehow unique.[43]

Rather than reacting from fear, the neoconservative Catholics argued, it would be more productive if the bishops provided a level-headed analysis of the nuclear threat from within the specific historical context that framed the U.S./Soviet relationship. They criticized the bishops' pastoral for not doing this and for instead focusing too extensively on the nature of nuclear weapons.[44] Weigel noted that using the weapons themselves as the starting point of the discussion, as the bishops' pastoral did, "distorted their entire analysis.... The prism of a nuclear weapons entry point for moral discourse resulted in the bishops' painting a flawed portrait of contemporary reality."[45] The bishops were, according to this view, obsessed with nuclear weapons and failed to take into account the context within which nuclear weapons functioned. To frame the issue somewhat differently, if the United States and Great Britain were the only countries to possess nuclear weapons there would be no reason to write a pastoral letter of this sort. The bishops' focus on nuclear weapons only served to overshadow any proposed solutions that could deal with the bigger problem: Soviet totalitarianism.

The bishops' failure to provide the proper context in which to analyze the nuclear threat skewed their analysis on a number of oth-

---

42. Weigel, *Tranquillitas Ordinis*, 281–82.

43. Novak, *Moral Clarity in the Nuclear Age*, 25–26.

44. Michael Novak, "The Fourteen Families," *National Review*, October 1, 1982, 1222; "Reconciliation and the Russians," *National Review*, July 27, 1984, 37.

45. Weigel, *Tranquillitas Ordinis*, 281–82.

er issues pertinent to the discussion, including the legitimacy of no "first use" of nuclear weapons, the relationship between the just war tradition and pacifism, and a proper understanding of the notion of "peace" and its application to political affairs.[46] Of particular note was the debate that emerged over the legitimacy of deterrence as a foreign policy strategy. The core of the concern on deterrence centered on considerations related to the long-standing tradition of just war theory. One of the central tenets of the theory was the notion that it is illegitimate to target and kill innocent civilians. Given the difficulty of using nuclear weapons in a limited fashion or in a way that isolated military targets and avoided predictable civilian casualties, it would be difficult to justify their use in almost any conceivable scenario. If this were the case could it be moral to possess nuclear weapons as a deterrent force and intend to use them given the moral prohibition in just war theory against the taking of innocent human life?

The American bishops struggled for some time to find a satisfactory answer to this dilemma and fluctuated back and forth during the seventies. Their thinking on this matter was influenced by the teachings of Vatican II, internal debates that occurred during the development of the pastoral letter, and pressures from the Vatican. The council document *Gaudium et Spes* warned that, while the arms race was a "treacherous trap for humanity" that likely only served to aggravate the causes of war, the deterrent function of nuclear weapons might produce a "peace of a sort."[47] The council thus acknowledged that such a strategy could be used as a temporary measure until disarmament could begin in earnest. This grudging acceptance by the council fathers was eventually reflected in the bishops' final draft of the pastoral letter. It marked a departure from the bishops' predisposition against deterrence as expressed in statements during the previous decade.

Ten years after the close of Vatican II the American bishops re-

46. Michael Novak, "Mahonyism," *National Review*, July 9, 1982, 838.

47. *Gaudium et Spes,* December 7, 1965, http://www.vatican.va/archive/hist_councils/ii_vatican_council/documents/vat-ii_cons_19651207_gaudium-et-spes_en.html.

jected deterrence in their pastoral letter *To Live in Christ Jesus,* stating that "as possessors of a vast nuclear arsenal, we must be aware that not only is it wrong to attack civilian populations but it is also wrong to threaten to attack them as part of a strategy of deterrence."[48] The first draft of the bishops' pastoral letter on war and peace reiterated the bishop's 1976 declaration that it was wrong to threaten the use of nuclear weapons and maintained a skeptical tone related to the legitimacy of deterrence. While not unequivocally condemning deterrence in the second draft, the bishops reiterated the claim made in the earlier pastoral letter.[49] From the second to the third drafts the bishops expressed a subtle shift in their thinking. They continued to hold that "mutual deterrence is seen as a dangerous state of affairs, to be escaped whenever possible, but it has lost some of its moral repugnance, which to some extent depended on claims about the wrongness of threatening or intending to do what it is wrong to do."[50] While tentatively accepting deterrence as a viable interim strategy, limitations remained. In particular, they held that "it is not morally acceptable to intend to kill the innocent as part of a strategy of deterring nuclear war."[51]

In contrast to the bishops, the neoconservative Catholics were convinced of the moral legitimacy of deterrence, particularly given the international nature of the Cold War. Michael Novak admitted that deterrence presents a moral problem in light of the just war principles of discrimination and proportionality. But to abandon it in American foreign policy would constitute an abandonment of the duty to defend innocent life, preserve the Constitution, and keep safe the idea of political liberty. The decision concerning the legitimacy of deterrence did not center on whether or not deter-

---

48. National Conference of Catholic Bishops, *To Live in Christ Jesus* (Washington, D.C.: United States Catholic Conference, 1976), no. 79.

49. Robert McKim, "An Examination of a Moral Argument against Deterrence," *Journal of Religious Ethics* 13, no. 2 (Fall 1985): 284.

50. Ibid., 285.

51. National Conference of Catholic Bishops, *The Challenge of Peace: God's Promise and Our Response* (Washington, D.C.: United States Catholic Conference, 1983), no. 178.

rence constituted the use of an evil means (intentionally and directly threatening civilian life through mass destruction) to achieve a good end (preventing nuclear war), but a moral choice that will prevent a greater evil.[52] The central problem was not the destructive threat of nuclear weapons as such but who had possession of these weapons. The Soviet Union posed an existential threat to the United States and for this reason it was crucial to determine the most effective strategy to ensure that the former did not make good on that threat. Deterrence was a useful tactic to achieve this objective.

Novak was concerned that opponents of deterrence underestimated the evil intentions and nature of the Soviet Union. A foreign policy that rejected deterrence could very easily increase the likelihood of war and the loss of human life that would ensue. Lacking the threat of retaliation, and keeping in mind Novak's concern over the Soviet Union's evil intentions, the absence of a strong nuclear deterrent might provide the impetus for Soviet aggression. If a strategy of nuclear deterrence decreased the likelihood of either a conventional or a nuclear war between the United States and the Soviet Union, Novak argued, a deterrence strategy should at least be tolerated for the time being.[53]

In contrast, Weigel expressed more unease with such a strategy, noting that while it had worked for four decades it was based on the notion of mutually assured destruction, which was itself morally questionable. Nevertheless, it was unclear to Weigel what would constitute an alternative and given that there was no apparent better option, a strategy of deterrence remained the best tactic for the time being.[54] Such an approach could provide time for negotiations that could result in future arms reduction and even widespread disarmament.[55]

52. Novak, *Moral Clarity in the Nuclear Age*, 58–62.

53. Michael Novak, "Making Deterrence Work," *Catholicism in Crisis* (November 1982): 4–5.

54. George Weigel, *Peace and Freedom: Christian Faith, Democracy, and the Problem of War* (New York: Institute on Religion and Democracy, 1983), 20–30.

55. Weigel, "Open Letter to Archbishop Bernardin," 17.

While Novak took some credit for changes in the pastoral statement, the more significant source of change, he admitted, was an informal Vatican meeting on January 18–19, 1983, that was held in coordination with the European and American bishops. The Vatican called the meeting to discuss the proposed American bishops' pastoral letter on war and peace that was, at the time, still in its second draft. Although the meeting was closed to the public, a communiqué released by the Vatican reaffirmed the moral authority and responsibility of the church to comment on issues related to war and peace, deterrence, and nuclear weapons, but noted that the gathering was a way to ensure that such teachings were in continuity with church tradition.[56]

The closed-door meeting contributed to a change in tone of the American bishops related to some of the positions laid out in the draft statement. This process benefited the neoconservative Catholics as it played into a strategy of triangulation they used during the eighties. Through this strategy the neoconservative Catholics would publicly stake out a position on a given issue, proceed to argue that their position was more consistent with papal teaching, and then pit the latter teaching against that of the bishops. Not surprisingly, such an approach at times led them to conclude that the American bishops had deviated from church teaching and in doing so supported positions that were not consistent with that teaching, while the neoconservative Catholics allegedly supported a more authentic vision that ought to be supported.

In light of this unspoken strategy, it is not surprising Novak would claim in hindsight that, "with the help of the laity and the Vatican, the U.S. bishops have produced a valiant text."[57] In a follow-up article on the pastoral letter, he noted that quite a few changes were made to the statement during the drafting process, many of which were to his liking. These changes included a more

56. "Vatican Communique on the Informal Consultation on the War and Peace Pastoral," *Origins* (February 3, 1983).

57. Novak, "The Bishops Have Spoken," *National Review,* June 10, 1983, 681.

forthright opposition to Soviet intentions, a conditional acceptance of the deterrence strategy, a clearly defined distinction between the bishops' authority on matters of universal moral principles on the one hand and a more tenuous level of authority on issues of prudential judgment, and a downgrading of the documents' utopian tendencies.[58] Less directly, Weigel echoed this view when he referred to the Vatican consultation as a "moderating influence," and noted that it was a "crucial part of the overall deliberative process."[59]

Economic Justice for All

The neoconservatives' triangulation strategy was not unique to the peace pastoral. It was also at work in their critique of the bishops' pastoral on the economy released three years later. During the 1980 annual gathering of the bishops, Bishop Peter Rosazza of Hartford, Connecticut, proposed that the bishops produce a statement on capitalism. The production of such a statement was particularly important, he thought, given that a pastoral letter on Marxism was released during the same meeting and it would be fruitful to comment on the primary alternative to a Marxist worldview.[60] A decision to move forward on an economic pastoral was agreed to during the same meeting that the bishops initiated the development of a pastoral letter on war and peace

The bishops' pastoral on the economy, like their earlier peace pastoral, went through a series of revisions in coordination with a widespread consultation that included experts from across the country. The bishops issued their final statement in June 1985, which was accepted by a vote of 225 to 9 during the annual gathering in November 1986.[61] As happened with the peace pastoral, the decision

58. Michael Novak, "Rescued from Disaster: The Bishops Speak Out," *Moral Clarity in the Nuclear Age* (Nashville, Tenn.: Thomas Nelson, 1983), 116–17.

59. Weigel, *Tranquillitas Ordinis,* 280.

60. Bishop Ricardo Ramirez, "The U.S. Bishops' Pastoral Letter 'Economic Justice for All' Twenty Years After," Third Annual University of St. Thomas Summer Institute (June 6, 2006), 1, http://www.dioceseoflascruces.org/assets/bp_sp_16.pdf.

61. Ibid., 9.

to use a very public process in developing the pastoral letter opened the door for criticism. One of the most overt critics of the bishops during this period was a group that designated itself the Lay Commission on Catholic Social Teaching and the Economy.

The commission was formed in March 1984 by the American Catholic Committee, the same organization of conservative-leaning Catholics that had been critical of the bishops' pastoral on war and peace.[62] It was headed by William Simon, a former treasury secretary under Nixon, who was active in conservative circles in the late seventies, and Michael Novak, who co-chaired the committee. Included among its other members were prominent Catholics such as Alexander Haig, Clare Booth Luce, and James Q. Wilson. The commission published two major documents during this period. The first, titled *Toward the Future,* was issued just days before the first draft of the bishops' pastoral was released.[63] *Liberty and Justice for All,* the second statement, was released following the final vote on the document *Economic Justice for All.*[64] These statements generally affirmed free-market solutions to economic problems, although they did recognize a limited role for government in economic affairs and thus eschewed a purely laissez-faire approach. The commission objected to the more state-centered approach to the economy that they argued the bishops promoted. One area of particular concern for the commission was the bishops understanding and application of the notion of "rights."

From the first draft onward, the bishops made an appeal to economic rights and emphasized their central place in a just society. Along with civil and political rights, economic rights were important

62. George Cornell, "Catholic Group Praises U.S. Economy Prior To Bishops' Critique," Associated Press, November 7, 1984.

63. Lay Commission on Catholic Social Teaching and the U.S. Economy, *Toward the Future: Catholic Social Thought and the U.S. Economy* (New York: American Catholic Committee, 1984).

64. Lay Commission on Catholic Social Teaching and the U.S. Economy, *Liberty and Justice for All,* reprinted in *Private Virtue and Public Policy* (New Brunswick, N.J.: Transaction, 1990). National Conference of Catholic Bishops, *Economic Justice for All* (Washington, D.C.: United States Catholic Conference, 1986).

in providing for the minimal conditions needed for life in community. In sections 80–84 of the pastoral, the bishops appealed to the importance of economic rights that included a person's basic right to food, clothing, shelter, and medical care. They concluded that access to these elements was "essential to human dignity and to the integral development of both individuals and society and are thus moral issues. Any denial of these rights harms persons and wounds the human community." They further stressed that new economic arrangements would be necessary to ensure access to these fundamental rights. All levels of society, including the private sector and government, would have a role in this process.[65]

The commission's first publication, *Toward the Future,* did not explicitly tackle the question of economic rights, primarily because the document was issued just prior to that of the bishops. While not addressing the issue directly, they did criticize any economic vision that would significantly expand the reach of the state, even if that meant limiting its ability to provide expansive welfare services to those in need. One of the fundamental questions that the commission wanted to raise early on, even if not specifically on the topic of economic rights, was "how to help the poor and the needy without generating an incapacitating dependency" on the state.[66] This question would turn into one of the central criticisms of the bishops' support for economic rights, given the commission's view that the promotion of such rights would in all likelihood require a significant expansion in government services.

The commission's second publication, *Liberty and Justice for All,* expanded on the theme of the pastoral's apparent statist tendencies and on the bishops' appeal to economic rights. While noting that the pastoral was not a socialist document, they claimed it did have statist tendencies. In contrast to what they understood to be the bishops' economic vision, which included a sympathetic view of a

65. *Economic Justice for All,* nos. 80–84.
66. *Toward the Future,* 58–60.

top-down approach to economic activism through political intervention, the commission argued that "economic development begins from the bottom up, through empowering the poor, not from the top down through extending political privileges."[67]

During a speech in which he commended the Lay Catholic Commission's publication *Liberty and Justice for All*, Richard Neuhaus echoed its concerns, claiming that sectors of Catholic leadership had unfortunately followed the path of mainline Protestantism and begun to embrace socialist-leaning economic policies.[68] Both Neuhaus's and the commission's criticisms of the bishops were characterized by a political vision that presupposed the importance of a limited state and that maintained a clear distinction between the responsibilities of government in economic affairs and those of privately run social and economic institutions.

In addition to the specifically political arguments made by Novak and the commission against the idea of economic rights, they also took aim at the bishops and their pastoral letter with regard to a larger, overarching strategy. As with *The Challenge of Peace*, the neoconservative Catholics initiated a triangulation strategy in which they played off comments of the Vatican and recent popes against those of the bishops. The commission argued that the American bishops misappropriated the teaching of Pope John XXIII when they made use of his idea of economic rights as expressed in *Pacem in Terris*, and did so by confusing an important distinction between the notion of "economic rights" and what the commission referred to as "welfare rights."

According to Novak and the commission, "economic rights" included the rights to private property, to safe working conditions, to the opportunity to enjoy work comparable to one's talents that would provide a decent standard of living. These rights point to the development of institutional structures that will protect individuals

---

67. *Liberty and Justice for All*, 9.

68. Richard Neuhaus, "Economic Justice Requires More than Economic Justice," *Journal of Ecumenical Studies* 24, no. 3 (Summer 1987): 379.

from a dependency on the state and also on oppressive economic institutions that might do the individual harm. "Welfare rights," on the other hand, refer to those basic needs of life that are essential to its proper development.[69] Pointing to *Pacem in Terris,* the commission noted that in the section pertaining to welfare rights, John XXIII claimed that a person had the right to food, clothing, medical care, and the like, and thus had "the right to be looked after in the event of ill health; disability stemming from their work; widowhood; old age; enforced unemployment; or whenever through no fault of his own he is deprived of the means of livelihood."[70] The commission stressed the final phrase in this quote, that a person has the right to be looked after *"whenever through no fault of his own he is deprived of the means of livelihood."*[71]

The commission argued that the bishops err in their tendency to collapse what they refer to as "welfare rights" into the same category as "economic rights." The welfare rights to which John XXIII pointed were restricted to a subset of the entire population, those people who *through no fault of their own are deprived of the means of livelihood,* whereas in the bishops' pastoral the failure to distinguish between these two categories of "rights" confused things completely. While the commission was not opposed to government involvement in the economy when it applied to this subset of the population, failing to make this distinction brings with it the risk of introducing a soft tyranny upon society or, as Novak put it, "the state obliged to provide for the daily welfare of all its citizens gains over them exquisite control."[72]

In short, in both the commission's publications and in complementary articles written by Novak, the commission held the position that in the final draft of the pastoral the bishops misappropri-

69. *Liberty and Justice for All,* 11.
70. *Pacem in Terris* (April 11, 1963), no. 11, http://www.vatican.va/holy_father/john_xxiii/encyclicals/documents/hf_j-xxiii_enc_11041963_pacem_en.html.
71. *Liberty and Justice for All,* 11–13.
72. Ibid., 13.

ated the teaching of John XXIII and, in doing so, misunderstood the proper application of Catholic social teaching to the economy. This argument asserted that the bishops had veered away from papal teaching properly understood and that the commission, in calling the bishops to account, was proposing an economic vision in line with the social teaching tradition. In a later essay Novak is somewhat more sympathetic to the bishops but still holds the general position laid out in the commission report. Here he argued that the bishops continue to confuse welfare rights and economic rights in their initial examination of the topic, namely in sections 80–84, but in later sections do demonstrate a more proper understanding of these terms. Regardless, their failure to tease out this distinction in the initial formulation promoted misunderstanding, confusion, and misinterpretation of church teaching.[73]

Michael Novak developed this criticism by appealing to what he referred to as Pope John Paul II's creation theology. He applied this critique initially to a liberationist approach to theology that was popular in the early eighties, and eventually to the broader economic worldview of the bishops. Commenting on Pope John Paul II's encyclical *Laborem Exercens,* Novak contended that the pope "shifts the point of view of Catholic social thought away from 'liberation' and toward 'creation.'"[74] The pope's emphasis on "work" and the importance of work for individual identity and the formation of community is important for Novak because, he argues, it stresses the creative dynamic that is at the core of economic life. Economically and politically, innovation and invention in the modern Western world had propelled society forward; it is what has led to the great technological advances over the past two centuries. Theologically, the notion that creation functions at the center of economic life reflects the principle of the *imago dei:* man is created in the image of God and, being created in that image, becomes a co-creator

73. Novak, "The Future of 'Economic Rights,'" in *Private Virtue and Public Virtue,* ed. James Finn, 70 (New Brunswick, N.J.: Transaction, 1990).

74. Novak, *Catholic Social Thought and Liberal Institutions,* 150.

of the world.[75] This embrace of creativity as the driving force behind all aspects of life came to function as an overarching critique of socialism, liberation theology, Marxism, and other worldviews that downplayed the efficacy of democratic capitalism. So, for example, creation theology "overcomes a nagging difficulty in liberation theology, which rhetorically announces an 'option for the poor' without in any way conceiving of an economic system creative enough actually to raise up the economic standing of the poor."[76]

Novak extended this argument in a section that was included in the commission's publication *Toward the Future*.[77] As was the case with Novak's other publications, this document emphasized the importance of creative initiative on the level of the individual person in community and rejected an overbearing, over-regulating, distributive-oriented government that would only kill creativity. While paying lip service to the notion that the bishops had, by their final draft, begun to affirm the role of creativity in economic life, the commission's publications mention this shift only in passing.[78] Instead, they proceeded to criticize the bishops for embracing the overbearing style of government that would tend to undermine the creative impulse in the first place and argued that the bishops promoted a "preferential option for the state." The drafters of the commission's response did not believe that the bishops' were committed to the creative dynamic in economic life and were more interested in the effectiveness of state intervention to solve the ills of society.[79] Just a few pages later the commission expressed disappointment that the final draft failed to recognize the Madisonian idea that "a regime of personally directed liberty, attracted by incentives, would be more beneficial to unleashing a tide of invention and discovery."[80] Invention, discovery, liberty, and creativity: these are the very

75. Ibid., 161.
76. Ibid., 163. See also Michael Novak, "With Rousseau in Latin America," *National Review*, August 23, 1985, 23, for a similar take on the problems of liberation theology in light of the creation theology that Novak espouses.
77. See in particular 25–52.   78. *Liberty and Justice for All*, 5.
79. Ibid., 8–10.   80. Ibid., 18.

terms that Michael Novak used to develop his notion of creation theology in some of his earlier writings. These are the same terms that the commission, with which Novak was intimately involved, accused the bishops of overlooking.

Nearing the publication of the final version of the pastoral letter, Novak complained that the bishops did not include in the conversation the more market-friendly perspective expressed by the commission, a perspective he asserted was shared by millions of other American Catholics.[81] This objection helps to explain why, following the publication of the commission's second statement in 1986, both Novak and Simon were so bold, if not presumptuous, as to request that the bishops append *Liberty and Justice for All* to their final pastoral letter. Doing so would presumably help to soften the bishops' conclusions and partly relativize these conclusions by pointing out to the public that there were multiple "Catholic" approaches to the economic questions being addressed. Needless to say, the bishops conference declined.[82]

The neoconservative Catholics clearly took the theological and political implications of the bishops' pastoral letters seriously. They extensively commented on these statements and their implications for policy formation, particularly in the context of Cold War concerns. How Catholic leadership understood the Soviet threat and communist influence had implications in other areas. One area in particular was Latin America, because of both the political and the cultural turmoil that was taking place throughout the region and the rising influence of liberation theology in the church there. Examining how these debates played out will help to clarify differences within American Catholicism and further define neoconservative Catholic identity.

81. Robert Di Veroli, "Catholic Bishops, Laity Debate Role of Capitalism; Documents Illustrate Two Approaches to Economic System," *San Diego Union Tribune,* March 2, 1985, A12.

82. Ari Goldman, "Catholic Bishops Criticized on Poor," *New York Times,* November 5, 1986, http://www.nytimes.com/1986/11/05/us/catholic-bishops-criticized-on-poor.html.

6 ❖ LATIN AMERICA, LIBERATION THEOLOGY, AND THE CATHOLIC CHURCH

INSPIRED IN PART by the example of Fidel Castro and the Cuban revolution, the Sandinista National Liberation Front (FSLN) was formed in 1961 with the express purpose of overthrowing the authoritarian Somoza-led government in Nicaragua. Within two decades the group evolved from a guerrilla organization based in northern Nicaragua to the country's ruling party following the overthrow of the Somoza government in July 1979. Many conservative organizations and intellectuals, including the neoconservative Catholics, interpreted the Sandinista revolution as reflecting poorly on American foreign policy decision making during the post-Vietnam era. There was an abiding concern that after Vietnam, America had lost its political will and had become too passive in the face of an aggressive Soviet-style Marxism. With Castro firmly ensconced in Cuba and revolutionary movements emerging in Nicaragua, El Salvador, and elsewhere, the threat from the Soviet Union was no longer overseas but had arrived at America's back door.

In the months leading up to the 1980 election a group of conservative intellectuals, under the designation Committee of Santa Fe, published a report titled *A New Inter-American Policy for the Eight-*

ies, which argued that the Carter administration had abandoned the American commitment to the Monroe Doctrine and offered confused leadership in foreign policy, particularly in the face of Soviet aggression.[1] With the influx of communist influence in Central America, the United States was faced with a direct challenge to the Western way of life. America's failure to make this a central component of its foreign policy during the Carter presidency signified a moment of great peril that harkened to the possible arrival of a *Pax Sovietica,* absent a more aggressive presence in the region by the United States. The Committee of Santa Fe contended in their broadside that "U.S. foreign policy is in disarray; that the norms of conflict and social change adopted by the Carter administration are those of the Soviet Union; that the area in contention is the sovereign territory of U.S. allies and Third World trading partners; [and] that the sphere of the Soviet Union and its surrogates is expanding."[2]

While sometimes criticized and "discredited" as a "right-wing" manifesto even by proponents of a strong military presence in the Caribbean and Latin America, this document expressed foreign policy themes consistent with the wider conservative critique of President Carter's administration.[3] In addition to their assessment of Carter's human rights policy, the political neoconservatives echoed the committee's concerns that the Carter administration had abandoned the Monroe Doctrine as a guiding principle in American foreign policy.[4] The 1980 Republican platform endorsed a foreign policy similar to that propounded by the Committee of Santa Fe and expressed a comparable criticism of Carter.[5] In a section that

1. The Committee of Santa Fe, *A New Inter-American Policy for the Eighties,* republished in *Vital Interests: The Soviet Issue in U.S. Central American Policy,* ed. Bruce Larkin (London: Lynne Rienner, 1988), 16–19. The authors of this report included L. Francis Bouchey, Roger W. Fontaine, David C. Jordan, Gordon Sumner, and Lewis Tambs, some of whom were appointed to positions in the Reagan administration. Lewis Tambs, for example, was named the U.S. ambassador to Colombia in the early years of the administration.

2. Ibid., 19.

3. Bruce Larkin, "Forward," *Vital Interests,* 3.

4. Jeane Kirkpatrick, "U.S. Security and Latin America," in *Vital Interests,* ed. Larkin, 51.

5. Glenn P. Hastedt and Anthony Ekserowicz, "Perils of Presidential Transition," *Seton Hall Journal of Diplomacy and International Relations* (Winter/Spring 2001): 75.

focused on Central and South America, the platform declared that "the Carter Administration stands by while Castro's totalitarian Cuba, financed, directed, and supplied by the Soviet Union, aggressively trains, arms, and supports forces of warfare and revolution throughout the Western hemisphere," and called for a policy that directly counteracted all Soviet and Marxist activity in the region.[6]

This objective became established in American foreign policy with the election of Ronald Reagan. Reflecting on the shift to a more aggressive and confrontational style under Reagan, Robert Pastor, the national security advisor on Latin America and the Caribbean under Carter, remarked that while the Carter administration saw in the Sandinista regime a potential ally, Ronald Reagan saw a Marxist threat. Whereas Carter tended to approach the problems in Nicaragua with an eye toward diplomacy and economic aid as a way to ease tensions, Reagan took a more hard-line approach, eventually cutting off all economic assistance to the country and providing military support to the FSLN's opponents.[7] Reagan channeled money to the Contra movements, regularly referred to as "freedom fighters" in the White House, even after such activity was explicitly prohibited by Congress. Economic, military, and political support was also given to authoritarian regimes in the region who found themselves in their own fight against what the Reagan administration understood to be Marxist-inspired revolutionaries.[8] The birth of the Reagan doctrine, which called for the support of anti-Marxist guerrillas aimed at bringing about democratic reform, informed Reagan's support of such guerrilla movements in Latin America.[9]

Parallel to the criticisms aimed at America's secular political

6. Republican Party Platforms: "Republican Party Platform of 1980," July 15, 1980, online at Gerhard Peters and John T. Woolley, The American Presidency Project, http://www.presidency.ucsb.edu/ws/?pid=25844..

7. Robert Pastor, *Condemned to Repetition: The United States and Nicaragua* (Princeton, N.J.: Princeton University Press, 1987), 230–31.

8. Sean Wilentz, *The Age of Reagan: A History, 1974–2008* (New York: HarperCollins, 2008), 165–67.

9. Kagan, *A Twilight Struggle: American Power and Nicaragua, 1977–1990* (New York: Free Press, 1996), 209–12.

leadership, criticisms with which they sympathized, the neoconservative Catholics worried that a significant portion of the Catholic hierarchy, leading Catholic intellectuals, and influential Catholic media outlets underestimated the Soviet threat in Latin America and in doing so misconstrued the problems confronting the region. The emergence of Latin American liberation theology and its influence in the region further highlighted the religious dimension of these debates. Often critical of American involvement in the developing world, liberation theologians provided a religious framework that could be used to channel the revolutionary impulse at work in countries like Nicaragua and El Salvador. Strongly opposed to this framework, the neoconservative Catholics sought to undermine liberation theology's legitimacy, both domestically and abroad. As with other contentious political issues of the day, the neoconservative Catholics found themselves fighting a two-front war, one against the more secular liberal political wing in American politics, and the other against what they considered to be a more liberal wing within the church itself.

The differences between the neoconservative Catholics and the American Catholic bishops on the political debates surrounding Central America are stark. The framework each used to interpret the underlying issues confronting the region differed, as did the solutions promoted to counter these problems. By the mid-seventies opposition to the Somoza regime, which was partly motivated by the autocratic tendencies of Nicaragua's ruling elite, had become well established. Radical and moderate forces inside the country began to cooperate in their opposition to the Somoza family and began to work together for its downfall. Simultaneously, segments of the Nicaraguan Catholic church, traditionally of a conservative political bent, began to voice discontent with existing conditions and at times cooperated with these revolutionary movements.[10] By the late 1970s the Catholic bishops of the United States had begun to condemn

10. Manzar Fooroohar, *The Catholic Church and Social Change in Nicaragua* (New York: State University of New York Press, 1989), 211–14.

the human rights abuses perpetrated by the Somoza regime against its people. In a June 12, 1979, statement Bishop John Quinn, then president of the United States Catholic Conference, condemned with "utter disgust and horror ... the ruthless terror being visited upon the people of Nicaragua."[11] One month later the Somoza regime fell and soon thereafter the Sandinistas solidified control over the country.

The first major statement issued by the American Catholic bishops on Nicaragua in the aftermath of the Sandinista revolution was a product of their 1981 annual meeting. Here the bishops laid out a framework for understanding the problems in the region, which in turn informed future statements on the topic. The core rationale that guided them was that, while geopolitics are a contributing factor in regional conflicts, "the dominant challenge is the internal conditions of poverty and the denial of basic human rights which characterize many of these societies. These conditions, if unattended, become an invitation for interventions."[12] Rather than interpreting the conflicts plaguing the region as primarily a product of the Cold War and a sign of communist aggression in Latin America, the bishops asserted an economic and humanitarian basis to the problem. While not denying the presence of foreign influences, they believed that these influences took advantage of underlying revolutionary impulses that emerged in reaction to economic and social injustices already present. From the time of Bishop Quinn's letter cited above to at least the mid-eighties the bishops' position remained consistent in this conviction.[13]

---

11. Bishop John Quinn, "U.S. Policy and the Conflict in Nicaragua," *Origins* 9, no. 6 (June 28, 1979).

12. National Conference of Catholic Bishops, "U.S. Bishops' Statement on Central America," *Origins* 1, no. 25 (December, 3, 1981): 3.

13. For examples of this reiteration see Archbishop James Hickey, Archbishop Patrick Flores, and Archbishop Peter Gerety, "Fact Finding Mission to Central America," Origins 12, no. 38 (March 3, 1983); Archbishop John Roach, "Toward a Diplomatic, Non-Military Solution in Central America," *Origins* 13, no. 10 (August 4, 1983); Father Bryan Hehir, "Testimony on Central America," *Origins* 13, no. 43 (April 5, 1984).

By the early 1980s the neoconservative Catholics had developed a competing analysis: they argued that in Latin America Soviet-Marxist aggression, and not economic injustice, was the core problem. Throughout his writings, Novak emphasized the influence that Marxist-inspired and Soviet-funded revolutionaries have had on the political and economic turmoil in Nicaragua. Philosophically, Novak argued, the Sandinista government in Nicaragua and the revolutionaries throughout Central America who looked to them as an example are little different from any Marxists of the Soviet bloc.[14] As Novak did, George Weigel rejected the bishops' conclusion that endemic poverty was the primary disruptive force in Latin America. While socioeconomic conditions were a contributing factor in the present turmoil, it was not a sufficient condition to explain the emergent conflicts affecting Nicaragua, El Salvador, and elsewhere. A crucial element that had not existed in years past was Marxist influence, which was often fed through Cuban, and thus Soviet, activity.[15]

Given their different starting points, the American bishops and the neoconservative Catholics promoted different solutions. Generally opposing President Reagan's policy positions on Nicaragua, in one statement after another the bishops criticized his perceived dependence on a military solution. They argued that the funding of counter-revolutionaries could easily prove destabilizing to the entire region and, in contrast, supported a two-part plan to deal with the problem. First, the administration ought to resume carefully monitored economic aid that would address the underlying problem of underdevelopment. Following the resumption of economic aid, the United States should abandon any attempts at unilaterally solving these difficulties and rely on a regional approach to negotiations that would include participation of countries throughout Central America. A unilateral approach, the bishops argued, would likely fail because the United States was seen as a partisan in the debate

14. Michael Novak, "On Nicaragua," *Catholicism in Crisis* 1, no. 8 (July 1983): 1–3.
15. Weigel, *Tranquillitas Ordinis,* 307–8.

and would thus be unduly biased in any negotiations. While many of these ideas can be found in a range of bishops' documents, the most systematic explanation of this position was provided in the Catholic conference's testimony before the Kissinger commission.

The National Commission on U.S. Policy in Central America, more popularly known as the Kissinger commission, was established to investigate the problems in Central America and report to the president and to Congress on possible solutions.[16] On October 21, 1983, Archbishop James Hickey of Washington gave testimony on behalf of the U.S. Catholic Conference. At the core of his testimony was his assertion that "because the conflicts in Central America are fundamentally rooted in questions of social injustice and the persistent denial of basic human rights for large sectors of the population, the USCC has always opposed interpretations of the Salvadoran and Central American conflict which place primary emphasis on the superpower or East-West rivalry." Any policy that relies primarily on an appeal to a military solution will fail and could lead to a regional conflict that will only serve to promote more damage and suffering to the region. For this reason Hickey rejected current administration policies that "give the appearance of encouraging war in Nicaragua," and one in El Salvador that "continues primarily in a military direction." In its place, Hickey called for a strategy that was multilateral and included other countries in Latin America, thus downplaying any sense of imperialistic overreach by the United States; emphasized the need for ceasefire in both Nicaragua and El Salvador; and recommended the initiation of strategies that would bring about political and economic change to promote the protection of human rights.[17]

In a later round of testimony Father Bryan Hehir, also speaking on behalf of the conference, commented on the findings of the

16. National Bipartisan Commission on Central America, *The Report of the President's National Bipartisan Commission on Central America* (New York, 1984).

17. Archbishop James Hickey, "U.S. Catholic Conference Testimony on Central America," *Origins* 12, no. 41 (March 24, 1983).

Kissinger commission and noted that while the "report's style of stressing the complexity of the region's multiple crises—political, economic, military—rather than reducing the problem immediately to its geopolitical element, is a welcome shift of official statement.... The inner logic of the report reaffirms and intensifies the basic direction of a policy which stands in need of fundamental redirection."[18] The primary failure of the report was the commission's continued support of a policy that would emphasize a military strategy at the expense of a diplomatic and economic solution.

Although the neoconservative Catholics disagreed with the bishops that socioeconomic conditions were the fundamental cause of conflict in Nicaragua and El Salvador, they supported efforts to promote economic development in the developing world. In fact, the importance of development was repeatedly emphasized by them as a component in American foreign policy both in the case of Nicaragua specifically and in international affairs more generally. In one instance, George Weigel wrote that "America should help facilitate the emergence of economically viable societies in Central America whose leadership respected basic human rights."[19] This would help the leadership in these countries to provide for the basic needs of the people there and simultaneously reinforce institutional structures that enable human rights to thrive. While it was just one component in the neoconservatives' thought, they emphasized the importance of American power and of geopolitical concerns when confronting Soviet communism much more so than did the American Catholic hierarchy.

Given their conviction that the root problem in Central America was Soviet activity and influence, the neoconservative Catholics consequently supported, at least in principle, the usefulness of a military threat and the importance of military support for allies in the region. Worried that Marxists were seeking to make a home for themselves in parts of Latin America, Novak was skeptical of

18. Hehir, "Testimony on Central America," 3–4.
19. Weigel, *Tranquillitas Ordinis,* 310.

the value of negotiation and argued that an over-reliance on such a tactic misunderstood the Soviet threat.[20] By its very nature Marxism was inherently imperialistic and would inevitably use whatever means necessary to spread its "gospel" message. Given the aggressive nature of communism, conflict of some sort was a likely consequence eventually, either directly or indirectly through some sort of proxy war. It might someday be necessary to confront the Soviet threat head on with military power since the communist leadership of Moscow, Havana, and Managua will "pay attention, alas, only to power. It is our moral and Christian responsibility to 'dialogue' with them in the only language they understand."[21]

Weigel also toyed with the idea that armed force might be a legitimate option under certain circumstances.[22] The bishops' resistance to the possible use of the military or military aid to allies betrayed, according to Weigel, a form of "soft neo-isolationism" that, if popularized, would undercut Reagan's ability to exert American influence in the region and simultaneously undermine the influence of Moscow.[23] He further accused the bishops of failing to develop a nuanced understanding of the situation and of merely mouthing the talking points of certain segments within secular politics. Weigel argued that the bishops failed to "create a new spectrum of morally sensitive public debate capable of leading to a more humane future in Central America.... Rather than being creators of a new debate, [the bishops] had simply become partisans at one pole of the debate already underway in American political culture."[24]

In other words, rather than promoting a distinctive Catholic understanding of the problems in Latin America, the bishops had capitulated to a left-wing politics. Michael Novak extended this critique when in a 1981 article for the *National Review* he accused the NCCB

20. Michael Novak, "To Fight or to Appease," *National Review,* July 22, 1983, 878.

21. Ibid.

22. George Weigel, "How the U.S. Catholic Bishops Missed Their Chance to Be a Force for Peace," *This World,* no. 13 (1986): 8–10.

23. Ibid., 22.

24. Weigel, *Tranquillitas Ordinis,* 312.

Latin American expert Thomas Quigley, and by extension the conference in general, of functioning as a mouthpiece for a left-wing political perspective on Latin America.[25] Both Novak and Weigel argued that this signified the abandonment of a distinctive Catholic voice and a capitulation to a pre-established, secular political perspective. More problematic still, the National Catholic Conference was not the only Catholic group guilty of doing this; large segments of the Catholic intellectual class and Catholic press did the same.

In his book examining the Catholic press's coverage of Central America in the seventies and eighties, Edward Brett wrote that "throughout the 1980s, publications such as the *National Catholic Reporter, America, Commonweal, Our Sunday Visitor,* and the *Catholic Worker* held firm to their primary focus, that is, to demonstrate their belief that U.S. policy toward Nicaragua was illegal and immoral and therefore needed to be changed."[26] In contrast, more conservative magazines tended to present an outlook largely favorable to these same policies. These magazines included *The Wanderer,* the *National Catholic Register,* and Michael Novak's very own *Catholicism in Crisis.*[27]

Both in the pages of the journal he co-founded, *Catholicism in Crisis,* and in his essays written for magazines like the *National Review,* Novak was particularly critical of the *National Catholic Reporter (NCR),* which emerged as one of the more vocal Catholic critics of Reagan and the most sympathetic supporter of left-wing governments like the Sandinistas.[28] He criticized the *NCR* for being full of inaccuracies and misrepresentations of the situation in Central America and argued that Catholic intellectuals sympathetic to the *NCR* embraced a leftist secular worldview that was at odds with American interests and Catholic thought.

25. Michael Novak, "The Moral Minority and the Savior," *National Review,* March 6, 1981, 228.

26. Edward Brett, *The U.S. Catholic Press on Central America* (Notre Dame, Ind.: University of Notre Dame Press, 2003), 109.

27. See in particular Brett, *The U.S. Catholic Press on Central America,* 123–57.

28. Ibid., 116.

In a cover story written in mid-1983, *NCR* editor Arthur Jones accused the Reagan administration of engaging in outright deception regarding the relationship between Nicaragua and the Soviet Union. Contrary to presidential rhetoric, argued Jones, Nicaragua was not a Marxist totalitarian regime. The administration was also in error regarding the relationship between Nicaragua and El Salvadoran revolutionary movements—Nicaragua had stopped the flow of arms across its borders to these movements when Reagan threatened to cut off aid early in his administration. Finally, he accused Reagan of distorting the facts to provide an excuse to use military action, covert or otherwise, against an unfriendly regime.[29]

In return Novak accused Jones, along with others who shared his perspective, for relying too much on Sandinista-friendly interpretations of the conflict and ideas promoted by left-wing think tanks like the Council on Hemispheric Affairs (COHA).[30] Founded in 1975, COHA was a self-declared independent research organization in Washington with a focus on inter-American affairs.[31] While avowedly non-partisan, it took a consistently antagonistic approach to the Reagan administration's Latin American policy. At one point COHA claimed that such policies amounted to an act of international terrorism and that the Reagan administration had solidified itself as the leading exporter of terrorism worldwide.[32]

Elsewhere, COHA accused the administration of engaging in a campaign of deception that would allow the administration to continue its "classified, undeclared war against Nicaraguan innocents and the civilian Nicaraguan economy."[33] COHA showed a great

29. Arthur Jones, "U.S. Policies Built on Deception," *National Catholic Reporter,* May 27, 1983.

30. Michael Novak, "On Nicaragua," *Crisis,* July 1, 1983, 1–3.

31. Council on Hemispheric Affairs website, http://www.coha.org/about-coha/.

32. Council on Hemispheric Affairs, press release, "Administration Engages in International Terrorism," April 13, 1984, http://www.coha.org/Press%20Release%20Archives/archives_index.htm (accessed March 10, 2009).

33. Council on Hemispheric Affairs, press release, "Senate to Vote on Funding Today for Interdiction of Non-Existent Sandinista Weapons Shipments to Salvadoran Guerrillas," June 25, 1984, http://www.coha.org/Press%20Release%20Archives/archives_index.htm.

deal more sympathy for the Reagan administration's foreign opposition, including the Sandinista government. At various times they rebutted and rejected conservative accusations that the Sandinistas were running arms to El Salvador in support of revolutionaries, that the Sandinistas had aggressive intentions toward their other neighbors, that the Soviet Union was providing military assistance to the Sandinistas, and that the latter were engaging in widespread human rights abuses.[34]

Similar to Novak, George Weigel criticized the left-wing Catholic intellectual class, particularly as found in magazines like *Commonweal* and *America*. He claimed that these Catholic journals all too often singled out the United States' activities and its allied leadership in the region as the primary culprits that motivated a rise in revolutionary sentiment throughout Central America.[35] These commentators often failed to give a balanced account of the problems confronting the region, had too easily capitulated to left-wing interpretations of the situation, and had become unmoored from the established Catholic moral tradition. Such a tradition affirmed "economic development coupled with political reform aimed at the creation of stable, democratic, peaceful societies capable of providing freedom, bread, and nonviolent means to settle claims of injustice."[36]

A debate over how well Weigel's understanding represented the Catholic moral tradition can remain open for the time being. What it did reflect was the post–World War II emphasis on economic aid programs in American foreign policy. During the 1950s, the Eisenhower administration began to take seriously the importance of

34. Council on Hemispheric Affairs, press releases, "State Department's 1982 Latin American Human Rights Report," February 11, 1983, http://www.coha.org/Press%20Release%20Archives/archives_index.htm; "House Vote Well Intentioned by Misguided," July 29, 1983, http://www.coha.org/Press%20Release%20Archives/archives_index.htm; "Commensurate with Its Security Needs," February 28, 1985, http://www.coha.org/Press%20Release%20Archives/ archives_index.htm.

35. Weigel, *Tranquillitas Ordinis*, 297–98.

36. Ibid., 293.

providing development assistance to Latin American countries, primarily as a way to inhibit the spread of communism into the Western hemisphere.[37] Near the end of his term, Eisenhower was able to secure passage of the Social Progress Trust Fund, the intended purpose of which was to increase aid to Latin America and, in doing so, to promote economic reform and development in the region. While the fund proved largely unsuccessful, it did establish a framework that was further developed by the Kennedy administration.[38] Following Eisenhower's initial push, President Kennedy promoted the Alliance for Progress, a $20 billion aid package that was to be distributed over a ten-year period. As with the Social Progress Trust Fund, the Alliance for Progress was motivated primarily by the desire to counteract Soviet expansion in the region.

George Weigel remarked that the implementation of the Alliance for Progress provided an important counter to Castro, who often used Latin American poverty as a rhetorical tool to build resentment against the United States.[39] It also lined up with the interests of the Catholic church of the day. With the exception of certain activists, in the early 1960s most of the American Catholic community took for granted that "America had a responsibility to actively intervene in the world.... The necessity of engagement was accepted as a first principle."[40] While military intervention might at times be necessary, a program such as the Alliance for Progress was a peaceful form of economic intervention aimed at helping Latin American reformers.[41]

While hopes were high at the launch of the program, the Alliance for Progress is largely deemed to have been a failure. Compet-

37. Michael Adamson, "'The Most Important Single Aspect of Our Foreign Policy'? The Eisenhower Administration, Foreign Aid, and the Third World," in *The Eisenhower Administration, the Third World, and the Globalization of the Cold War,* ed. Kathryn Statler et al., 48–59 (Lanham, Md.: Rowman and Littlefield, 2006).

38. Jeffrey Taffet, *Foreign Aid as Foreign Policy: The Alliance for Progress in Latin America* (New York: Routledge, 2007), 19–20.

39. Weigel, *Tranquillitas Ordinis,* 292.   40. Ibid., 190.

41. Ibid.

ing political interests, bureaucratic infighting, cultural differences, and growing distrust between Latin American governments and the United States undermined the long-term objectives of the program.[42] As the 1960s progressed, disillusionment with American intervention became more pronounced. Part of the shift against American intervention overseas had to do with the fallout from Vietnam and a growing disenchantment with America's role in the post–World War II world. In light of these changing perceptions of American life, the Alliance for Progress at times took on the cast of imperial overstretch rather than a sign of well-meaning developmental aid as it was initially intended.[43]

At the core of this critique was a model of underdevelopment that asserted that "peripheral" countries of the world would remain economically stagnant so long as they remained dependent on the economic and political power of the first world. Dependency theorists, as they came to be known, often argued that developed nations took advantage of the developing world's natural resources, labor force, and other economic assets for their own benefit. Radical versions of this theory held that capitalist activity thus consigned the developing world to a permanent state of underdevelopment and total dependency. Milder versions held that the benefits accrued by economic growth would be dramatically weighted toward the developed world at the expense of the developing ones, thus relegating them to a state of relative dependency.

Dependency theory was not only of interest to secular intellectuals but was also embraced in some Catholic and non-Catholic Christian intellectual circles, both domestically and abroad. In this context, dependency theory provided the foundation for a moral worldview as much as an economic one that generally ended with a critical account of America's role in this process. Critical of this

42. Piki Ish-Shalom, "Theory Gets Really Real and the Case for a Normative Ethic: Rostow, Modernization Theory, and the Alliance for Progress," *International Studies Quarterly* 50 (2006): 302–5.

43. See in particular ch. 8 in Taffet, *Foreign Aid as Foreign Policy.*

pessimistic strain in Catholic thought, Weigel isolated for criticism two essays that signified this shift. Both were published in the magazine *America* and each provided a skeptical assessment of the American presence in Latin America.

The first essay expressed a sharp critique of Western involvement in Latin America, throughout which the author, Denis Goulet, argued that, while programs like the Alliance for Progress preached the virtues of democracy, economic development, and national self-reliance, in reality they did little more than export a crass materialism that benefited already established right-wing governments and corporations.[44] Programs of this sort supported American foreign policy positions that are unfriendly toward anything leftist and downright disdainful of anything smelling of communism or socialism.[45] For the developing world to flourish, it was important that American policy shift its sights away from immediate, self-interested political goals and enter into a relationship of true solidarity with foreign powers. America must undergo a moral conversion that rejects an economy based solely on self-interested acquisitiveness and excessive wealth. Failure to do so will only reinforce a system that is beneficial to those in the developed world at the expense of those in the developing one.[46]

Following the logic of the first essay, the second essay cited by Weigel traced out the ways in which American political and economic power can be expressed and reinforced through cultural and religious institutions.[47] Ivan Illich, the essay's author, argued that while done in good faith, missionary movements from the United States and other Western countries to Latin America come at a cost. Although beneficial in some respects, missionaries necessarily bring with them a political culture "that colors the public image of the

---

44. For the reference in Weigel's work, see *Tranquillitas Ordinis*, 202. For the article citation, see Denis Goulet, "A Missing Revolution," *America,* April 2, 1966, 438–40.

45. Goulet, "A Missing Revolution," 438–39.

46. Ibid., 439–40.

47. For Weigel's citation see *Tranquillitas Ordinis*, 292. For the article, see Ivan Illich, "The Seamy Side of Charity," *America,* January 21, 1967, 88–91.

Church.... The Alliance [for Progress] appears directed by Christian justice and is not seen for what it is: a deception designed to maintain the status quo."[48] In doing so, Illich argued, church leadership had married itself to a political regime and an economic program that distorted the Gospel and reinforced American political power in the region. While the American political regime expressed an interest in the life of the average Latin American, it had a more abiding interest in its own short-term political goals: namely, its struggle against communism.[49] Taken together, both essays reveal a deep skepticism regarding American power expressed internationally and an American church that provides an all too willing defense of that power. Laying out both authors' viewpoint so as to reject it, Weigel argued that they are representative of an increasingly large segment of the Catholic church that claimed that "the fundamental problems were not in Latin America, but in North America. Latin American poverty was caused by North American greed and acquisitiveness. Foreign aid was a sop to guilty consciences at best, and an imperial instrument of control at worst. A radical transformation of the economic system of the North was the precondition to any genuine progress."[50]

Growing skepticism of American foreign policy aimed at the developing world was not restricted to domestic academic debates that took place in the pages of highbrow journals and magazines. A sharp reaction also occurred, and was in some respects born, in the developing world itself. In the Latin American Catholic community the reaction to U.S. foreign policy was perhaps most visible in liberation theology. While indebted to dependency theorists, liberation theology was not merely a product of an economic or political worldview but emerged following the Second Vatican Council and applied an interpretation of the council to a distinctly Latin American milieu.[51]

48. Illich, "The Seamy Side of Charity," 90.
49. Ibid., 91.
50. Weigel, *Tranquillitas Ordinis,* 202.
51. Philip Berryman, *Liberation Theology: Essential Facts about the Revolutionary Movement in Latin America and Beyond* (Oak Park, Ill.: Pantheon Books, 1987), 64–68.

Liberation Theology and the Latin American Church

Pope John XXIII's invocation of the Second Vatican Council marked an important turning point in the life of the Catholic church that renewed engagement with the world, a world with which the church had often been at odds since at least the onset of the French Revolution. While at times the process was halting, throughout the twentieth century the church began slowly to reconcile herself to the modern world and, during the post–World War II period, began to hesitatingly support certain philosophical principles that she had until recently deemed irreconcilable with the faith. The council signified not only a renewed engagement with the modern world but also recognized that the world with which the church was engaged extended beyond a European context.

While modern Catholic social teaching is often said to have begun with Leo XIII's encyclical *Rerum Novarum,* his focus was largely centered on European concerns; the non-European world was of peripheral interest. Throughout the encyclical he primarily addressed issues related to labor/employer relations, capitalism and socialism, and other concerns that, while applicable to a broad audience, were primarily focused on a European one.[52] By the 1960s the situation had changed dramatically. In an essay on the Vatican II document *Gaudium et Spes,* the theologian David Hollenbach wrote that at the council "the presence of Asian, African, and Latin American participants highlighted the need to avoid viewing Christianity as a European religion to be exported to the rest of the world along with European culture. The challenge now was to relate Christianity to the diverse cultures of the world in ways that respected their differences and avoided domination or manipulation in the name of the gospel."[53]

52. Pope Leo XIII, *Rerum Novarum, http://www.vatican.va/holy_father/leo_xiii/encyclicals/documents/hf_l-xiii_enc_15051891_rerum-novarum_en.html.*

53. David Hollenbach, SJ, "Commentary on Gaudium et Spes," in *Modern Catholic Social Teaching: Commentaries and Interpretations,* ed. Kenneth Himes et al., 285 (Washington, D.C.: Georgetown University Press, 2005).

Following the close of the council many of the non-European Catholic bishops and intellectuals interpreted the council in light of their own political, economic, and cultural contexts. This tendency was evident with the Latin American bishops during their 1968 conference at Medellin. In contrast to the traditional theological approach, which highlighted the church's moral principles or theological concepts and then applied them to a given set of social conditions, the bishops at Medellin began with the political, economic, and social conditions in Latin America and attempted to understand the faith in light of these conditions. This approach rejected a deductive theology and instead emphasized the distinctive circumstances confronting a historically situated society. Within the context of the Catholic church in Latin America, this approach contributed to criticisms of unjust economic and political structures that oppressed large segments of the population.[54] The Medellin conference, along with the critical perspective on modern society that it provided, helped lay the groundwork for the emergence of liberation theology.[55]

Liberation theology was influenced not only by developments in the church that were taking place in a Latin American context; developments in Europe also had an important influence. Given the intellectual framework that contributed to it, liberation theology is in important respects a European invention. In the post-war years, most of the leading liberation theologians studied in one or more of the major academic centers in Europe and thus had training similar to that of their contemporary European counterparts. Gustavo Gutierrez, for example, studied philosophy at Louvain and, following that, theology in Lyons, France.[56] The liberation theologians' education in Europe exposed them to the social sciences and various

54. Phillip Berryman, *The Religious Roots of Rebellion: Christians in Central American Revolutions* (Maryknoll, N.Y.: Orbis Books, 1984), 27.

55. Hollenbach, "Commentary on Gaudium et Spes," 286–88.

56. Jeffrey Klaiber, "Prophets and Populists: Liberation Theology, 1968–1988," *The Americas* 46, no. 1 (July 1989), 4–5. It was during his studies in Louvain that Gutierrez did his licentiate on Freud.

theories related to Marxism and evolution. Theologically, it would also not have been unusual for the liberation theologians to become familiar with and influenced by European theologians, including Jurgen Moltmann and Johannes Baptist Metz, "both of whose theological theories intended to relate theology more directly and critically to the problems of the modern secular world."[57] The liberation theologian Jose Ignacio Gonzalez Faus at one pointed admitted that "Metz deserves undeniable credit for having opened our eyes to ... 'bourgeois religion,'" which emphasized an individualistic spirituality that undermines and weakens the communal nature of the faith.[58]

Although liberation theology as a theological perspective is multifaceted and contested, Gustavo Gutierrez's views exhibit a general framework, particularly as expressed in his seminal work, *A Theology of Liberation*.[59] Three interrelated elements in Gutierrez's writings will be briefly addressed: his methodological outlook, his economic worldview, and his theological perspective, which links his political worldview to his ecclesiology. Gutierrez's interest in issues related to the economy and political theory, both of which are themes prominent in his work, should be understood in the context of his larger theological vision.

From the very first page of the introduction to *A Theology of Liberation,* Gutierrez rejected a theological method that relies on deduction. Instead, he engaged in a theological approach that begins from the shared experiences of his people and uses this perspective as a springboard to develop a theological framework to make sense of these experiences. In particular, his central focus on the poor of the underdeveloped world—the preferential option for the poor— was central to his vision. This concern for the poor and his central

57. Paul E. Sigmund, *Liberation Theology at the Crossroads: Democracy or Revolution* (New York: Oxford University Press, 1990), 32.

58. Jose Ignacio Gonzales Faus, "Anthropology: The Person and the Community," in *Mysterium Liberationis: Fundamental Concepts of Liberation Theology,* ed. Ignacio Ellacuria et al., 506–9 (Maryknoll, N.Y.: Orbis Books, 1993).

59. Gustavo Gutierrez, *A Theology of Liberation* (Maryknoll, N.Y.: Orbis Books, 1988).

conviction that their plight was largely due to conditions outside their control led him to call for a reconstitution of the international economic system, one that he claimed had only served to maintain the influence of those already in power and further oppress those who are already powerless.[60] Rejecting the prevailing international capitalist structures already in place, Gutierrez called for the implementation of a socialist economy that would assist in lifting up the poor and the downtrodden.[61] He wrote that the poor are beginning to realize that "their own development will come about only with a struggle to break the domination of the rich countries.... Only a radical break from the status quo, that is, a profound transformation of the private property system ... that would break this dependence would allow for a change to a new society."[62] In this radical reworking of the world's economic system, the church ought to step forward and play a leading role.[63]

The work of the church in this task cannot be understood from the context of a secular political and economic ethic garbed in religious clothing, but instead reflects a theological imperative rooted in the mission of the church. This theological outlook rejects the "separation of planes" distinction that tends to remove the church from having an active role in political life. Abandoned is a passive church that lies prostrate in the face of political powers, or which functions as an apologist for the prevailing political system. Affirmed is the recognition that while the Kingdom is not of this world it can partially be realized in this world and the church should be at the forefront of this disclosure.[64] The religious activity of the church and the question of social justice cannot be separated so complete-

---

60. Gustavo Gutierrez, "Renewing the Option for the Poor," in *Liberation Theologies, Postmodernity and the Americas,* ed. David Batstone, 69 (New York: Routledge, 1997).

61. Gutierrez, *A Theology of Liberation,* 13–26.

62. Ibid., 17.

63. For a well-developed outline of liberation theology ecclesiology, see T. Howland Sanks and Brian Smith, "Liberation Theology: Praxis, Theory, Praxis," *Theological Studies* 38, no. 1 (March 1977).

64. Phillip Berryman, *The Religious Roots of Rebellion: Christians in Central American Revolutions* (Maryknoll, N.Y.: Orbis Books, 1984), 28–29.

ly that it inhibits the church and its members, both lay and clergy alike, from working for a more just world.[65] It is its responsibility as a religious institution to "take a stand against the established order and publicly and continually denounce specific forms of economic exploitation and violation of the rights and dignity of the poor."[66]

Gutierrez's claim that the construction of a more just society is a central task of the church in the world grounded his economic position in the context of a theological vision. It is through "liberation" from injustice of every sort that God is encountered.[67] By recognizing its own cooperation with unjust systems in the past, repenting for that cooperation, and becoming politically involved so as to overcome any modern-day injustices, the church will live out her mission more completely.[68]

While not opposed to every feature promoted by Gutierrez, the neoconservative Catholics disagreed with much of his vision. Disagreements include a politico-economic critique that focused on both the sociological underpinnings of liberation theology, opposition to the theoretical political philosophy proposed, and a rejection of their ecclesiological assumptions. Each of these critiques will be spelled out below.

Neoconservative Catholics on Liberation Theology

The Politico-Economic Critique

Although critical of liberation theology on many points, one area of agreement consisted in the neoconservative Catholics' and liberation theology's shared support for the "preferential option for the poor" as a fundamental moral principle that ought to guide the Catholic church's social teaching and action.[69] Given that they ex-

65. Gutierrez, *A Theology of Liberation*, 41–46.
66. Sanks and Smith, "Liberation Theology," 16.
67. Berryman, *Liberation Theology*, 26.
68. Gutierrez, *A Theology of Liberation*, 63–65.
69. Michael Novak, *Catholic Social Thought and Liberal Institutions: Freedom with Justice*, 2nd ed. (New Brunswick, N.J.: Transaction, 1989), 192.

pressed agreement on this option, the question that emerged centered on the most effective mechanisms that will benefit the poor and lift them out of poverty. On the answer to this question, the neoconservative Catholics and liberation theologians differed dramatically.

Liberation theologians tended to place much of the blame for third world poverty on the international capitalist system that they claimed created systems of dependence that benefitted rich nations at the expense of poor ones. The neoconservative Catholics disagreed and argued that capitalism properly understood and applied would in the long run benefit the poor more than the vision laid out by the liberation theologians. In his book *Will It Liberate?*, Novak notes that his objections to liberation theology were not primarily theological but rooted in what he believed were flaws in their political economy.[70] His ideas on this point are developed in a series of books that he has since referred to as his trilogy on political life, which include his *The Spirit of Democratic Capitalism, Catholic Social Thought and Liberal Institutions,* and the aforementioned *Will It Liberate?*[71]

In these books Novak provides a practical, theoretical, and sociological critique. The first line of argument he used against liberation theology was a practical one, namely, that liberation theology's economic theory will not benefit the poor. Novak argued that socialism had failed to be a reliable source for economic development. The criticisms that Novak levied against socialism and its impotence in driving development was explored in the previous chapter of this volume, as were his claims related to the benefits of democratic capitalism in this regard. The case of liberation theology merely provides an instance of this critique.

A second related criticism was of a more theoretical nature. In its early formulations, liberation theology placed a great deal of

---

70. Michael Novak, *Will It Liberate? Questions about Liberation Theology* (Mahwah, N.J.: Paulist Press: 1986), 30.

71. Novak, *Catholic Social Thought and Liberal Institutions,* xvii.

emphasis on dependency theory. To reiterate, this theory held that through the international capitalist system developed nations, the "center," create systems of dependence that ensnare the underdeveloped world, the "periphery," in a cycle of poverty. While keeping the developing world in a cycle of dependence, rich nations benefit from cheap resources that will fuel their own economic growth. Thus, the poverty of Latin America has less to do with Latin America and more to do with the rich Western world's economic imperialism.

Novak rejected dependency theory as a reliable guide to understanding the economy. While recognizing the underdeveloped state of much of Latin America, he argued that the problem with this region is not too much capitalism but too little. For centuries, both church and state in Latin America have tended to resist capitalist enterprise, and in doing so resisted the economic system that has shown successes in bringing about development.[72] The failure of the Latin American economy is thus not dependence on the developed world but the failure to nurture an economic system that would help bring about development.

To buttress his point, Novak turned to the example of Japan, which at the end of World War II was in shambles. Given its lack of natural resources and reliance on the United States in the decades following World War II for its economic recovery, one would imagine that its condition would today be similar to that of Latin America, if not worse. In contrast, Novak noted, many countries of the Asian rim have in fifty years' time been demonstrably more successful at overcoming poverty than Latin American countries, and he proceeded to ask how this apparent discrepancy could be explained in light of the assumptions built into dependency theory.[73]

A final criticism of liberation theology was sociological. Novak claimed that, while liberation theology expresses a kind of prophetic condemnation of capitalism and injustice that brings with it a revo-

72. Novak, *The Spirit of Democratic Capitalism*, 276–80.

73. Michael Novak, "The Case against Liberation Theology," *New York Times Magazine*, October 21, 1984, 86; Novak, *Catholic Social Thought and Liberal Institutions*, 189.

lutionary excitement, liberation theologians too often speak in generalities and vague propositions.[74] Socialism functions as an exciting symbol to encapsulate what liberation theologians envision after the collapse of international capitalism, but without further development or some concrete demonstration as to what socialism entails institutionally, it remains an empty concept. At its core liberation theology "has no concrete vision of political economy. It refuses to describe the institutions of human rights, economic development, and personal liberties that will be put in place after the revolution."[75]

Underlying Novak's critique of liberation theology is the affirmation that when discussing economics and political theory, specificity matters. While one can speak of social justice and the evils of international capitalism, if there is not a clear conception of how the proposed solution will be institutionalized, one is left with very little on which to proceed. The move from "social justice" to "political economy" is crucial because "the principles of social justice represent a very high degree of abstraction ... but the principles of political economy move decisively toward concretion. To choose a political economy is to choose a fundamental *ordo* or ordering of basic institutions."[76]

Liberation theologians, according to Novak, continually failed to lay out a clearly defined institutional framework that grounded their broader theological and philosophical worldview. At one point Novak claimed of liberation theologians that "one finds in them minimal concrete descriptions of persons, events and institutions. Their tone is inspirational and hortatory.... Liberation theology is remarkably abstract."[77] At another point he wrote that "one of the most striking things about the writing of liberation theologians is its abstractness. Far from being descriptive, concrete and practical, it is intricately speculative, ideological, and academic."[78]

For the neoconservative Catholics the failure of liberation theolo-

74. Novak, *The Spirit of Democratic Capitalism*, 113.
75. Novak, *Will It Liberate?* 31.
76. Novak, *Catholic Social Thought and Liberal Institutions*, 35.
77. Novak, *The Spirit of Democratic Capitalism*, 293.
78. Novak, *Catholic Social Thought and Liberal Institutions*, 186.

gians to properly address the importance of institutional structures is not a problem strictly relegated to the political and economic spheres. They further argued that liberation theologians misunderstood how the church ought to be institutionalized in the world. Turning to this problem the neoconservatives provide an ecclesiological critique of liberation theology, claiming that liberation theology promoted a distorted vision of the church by relegating it to the role of a partisan actor with a mission that is all too much of the world.

The Ecclesiological Critique

In a review of Gutierrez's *A Theology of Liberation,* Richard Neuhaus noted the importance of the work and the stature of Gutierrez the theologian, but provided a critique of the dangers that his theology entails.[79] Neuhaus granted what is in effect an inevitable consequence of theology, that there is a tendency to compartmentalize the Christian message in the context of a given culture or historical period. There is always "a degree of inevitability in our tendency to take the gospel culturally captive."[80] In this respect, at least, Gustavo Gutierrez's theology is not exceptional. What is problematic, Neuhaus insisted, was Gutierrez's tendency to become so mired in the parochial conditions in Latin America that he distorted the universal claims of Christianity that would otherwise function as a counterbalance to these "captivities of Jesus." Gutierrez's struggle against what he sees to be imperialist capitalism and his application of the Christian faith to that struggle led him to an identification of the church's mission with this revolutionary struggle.[81] This identification leads Gutierrez to a vision of the church that is no longer "a meeting place where understanding can be sought, ideas shared and communion celebrated among those on opposite sides of the barracks. The church must decide, must make an unambiguously

79. Richard John Neuhaus, "Liberation Theology and the Captivities of Jesus," *Worldview* (June 1973): 41–48.
80. Ibid., 42.
81. Ibid., 46–47.

partisan commitment."[82] In claiming this, Neuhaus argued that such a vision radically distorted the role of the church in the world and the mission she is called to live out.

Some fifteen years after the publication of this review essay, Neuhaus expanded on many of the same themes in part 4 of his book *The Catholic Moment*. At the core of his critique is his assertion that liberation theologians lay the groundwork for an overly partisan church. On this point George Weigel was in agreement, declaring that "liberation ecclesiology was self-consciously at the service of a partisan church. The church must be a partisan in the creation of a this-worldly utopia, the Kingdom of justice that would result in peace."[83] In this respect, Neuhaus argued, liberation theology is straightforward. He wrote that for liberation theologians "the Christian Gospel is a message of social justice; social justice is measured and established by the role of the poor; identification with the poor means identification with their struggle for justice, which is a struggle for socialism."[84] Connecting liberation theology to a political agenda is not an inherently misguided venture. Where it becomes problematic is when the long view of history, where the Kingdom, which is still to come, becomes lost in light of a secular political vision.[85]

A second problem is that the identification of the church with a political agenda runs the risk of losing the church's spiritual identity to a political one. This is, Neuhaus claimed, what happened with liberation theology. In the pre–Vatican II era, the church often flirted with right-wing political entities that resisted the revolutionary fervor sometimes found in places like post-revolutionary France and pre-unified Italy. Something similar was happening in the case of Latin America, except that the reemergence of Christendom is reflected not in the marriage of the church to right-wing authoritarians, such as Franco in Spain, but to left-wing ones such as Marxists in Nicaragua.[86] Rejecting a "distinction of planes" model

82. Ibid., 48.   83. Weigel, *Tranquillitas Ordinis*, 289.
84. Neuhaus, *The Catholic Moment*, 176.   85. Ibid., 184–85.
86. Ibid.

that would enable the "church to liberate itself from its misalliance with the regimes of the earthly," Neuhaus argued that adherents of liberation theology had too often aligned themselves with left-wing movements that distorted the proper relationship between church and state.[87] In his *The Spirit of Democratic Capitalism*, Michael Novak expressed the concern that the path marked out by liberation theology is one that "is ill-defended against state tyranny, is vulnerable to a new union of church and state (this time on the left), and is likely to lead to economic decline."[88]

The allegedly improper church/world relationship that emerged was little different from the right-wing Constantinianism prevalent in earlier decades; both are inherently monistic.[89] One of the political and social principles reiterated and reaffirmed time and again by the neoconservative Catholics is the inevitable fact of pluralism in the world. The promotion of a monistic view of the world, intentionally or otherwise, inevitably leads to a distorted view of the church and political life. Pluralism is not merely an accidental condition of our time but is part of the providential purpose of God. Consequently, a monistic vision of the church and the world, which Neuhaus contended liberation theologians risked propounding, affirmed a theological vision that was contrary to this providential purpose.[90]

While the neoconservative Catholics provided a potent criticism of liberation theology on the basis of the latter's political and economic theories, at the core of their criticism is the contention that the liberation theologians posit a flawed ecclesiology. In doing so they opened the door for a political activism that is inconsistent with the proper role for the church in the world. In short, if the liberation theologians properly situated the church in the world and understood the relationship that the church was called to have with

---

87. Ibid., 192.
88. Novak, *The Spirit of Democratic Capitalism*, 314.
89. Neuhaus, *The Catholic Moment*, 192.
90. Ibid., 193.

the world, it would be much more difficult to promote the political theology that the liberation theologians promoted. In this way, the neoconservative Catholics' ecclesiological critique is prior to their political and economic ones. Their emphasis on the primacy of ecclesiological issues is not restricted to the liberation theologians. A parallel critique was levied against the Catholic hierarchy of the United States.

7 ❖ WHEN SHEPHERDS BECOME SHEEP

At the Intersection of Politics and Ecclesiology

IN HIS REVIEW of Thomas Reese's book *A Flock of Shepherds: The National Conference of Catholic Bishops,* George Weigel closed with a question. Playing on its title he stated that shepherds lead flocks, but "when shepherds become flocks, is something in the nature of being a shepherd irreparably damaged?"[1] One of the purposes of Reese's book is to explore the workings of the National Conference of Catholic Bishops (NCCB), from its general structure to the component parts that give it life. Central to Weigel's concern is the size of this infrastructure and the extent to which it has given birth to a bureaucracy that works against the charism unique to the office of the bishop.

With the growth of the NCCB following Vatican II, the bishops committed themselves to a wide range of activities, both political and pastoral. Some activities were long practiced, while others were an expansion of their traditional activities. As had always been the case on the diocesan level, the bishops were entrusted with responding to the religious needs of local parishes, priests, and laity. On the national level they became enmeshed in a wide range of policy ques-

1. George Weigel, "When Shepherds Are Sheep," review of *Flock of Shepherds: The National Conference of Catholic Bishops* by Thomas Reese, *First Things* (February 1993): 40.

tions that included international poverty and trade policies, war, and immigration. While some of these political activities had roots in the pre–Vatican II National Welfare Conference, the extent to which the bishops engaged these issues after the council expanded significantly.

The increasing responsibilities made it difficult for individual hierarchs to respond to the myriad demands on their time. In one essay, Richard Neuhaus recounted a comment made to him by an unnamed bishop, who noted that "early on I decided that I would either have to be bishop of this diocese or try to take a hand in re-shaping the Washington bureaucracy. I can't do both, and neither can the other bishops."[2] If the bishops hoped to remain influential in both arenas, it meant that they would have to develop a national infrastructure that could focus on the many areas of interest to the church. This meant staffing the infrastructure, bestowing on respective staff the responsibility to run the day-to-day affairs of the conference, and, in doing so, endowing them with significant influence in the policy-related decisions made on behalf of the bishops. For this reason, Weigel lamented, it was "simply preposterous to suggest that the NCCB/USCC is not an agency in which the staff is very, and perhaps determinatively, influential."[3]

The extent of this influence was so pronounced, Novak believed, that in the contemporary American church, "when the 'church' speaks, it is the staff of the conference of bishops that speaks," and their "views are invariably partisan."[4] Such partisanship, argued Richard Neuhaus, promoted a process of accommodation to the modern world that tailored Christian teaching to "serve the civil religion of liberal democracy, or to gain respectability in the eyes of secularized academe, or to advance the revolutionary struggle."[5] Put

2. Neuhaus, *The Catholic Moment*, 266.
3. Weigel, "When Shepherds Are Sheep," 39.
4. Michael Novak, "Liberal Catholicism Will Rise Again," *National Review*, June 11, 1982, 694.
5. Neuhaus, *The Catholic Moment*, 102.

another way, accommodationalists sought to "forge a new Christianity more consonant with the spirit of the age ... [and] attempt to sustain Christianity's midcentury reconciliation with Western liberalism by adapting itself to the changing cultural circumstances."[6]

While exemplified in the worldview of the conference staff this political and philosophical bias was a pervasive problem manifest in diverse sectors of Catholic life, including influential elements within Catholic leadership and the hierarchy. Throughout the eighties the neoconservative Catholics criticized the bishops for embodying a "liberal" Catholicism run amok, alongside Catholic leadership found within wide swaths of higher education, an array of men's and women's religious orders, and prominent sectors of Catholic media.[7] If the influence of these ideologies was negligible among the Catholic faithful, there might be little reason for concern. But, given that they were often expressed by those in established positions of power, their personal judgments on policy questions were often confused with the official church teaching. As Richard Neuhaus put it, "Today—in national and diocesan offices, in universities and colleges, in networks of activist collaboration—the leaders are a 'minority of articulate prophets challenging accepted beliefs.'" In the process, these "articulate prophets" have effectively "seized control of key institutions," and presented their views "as representing *the* Roman Catholic position on myriad issues in public debate."[8] By the early eighties it was a commonplace for neoconservative Catholics to criticize liberal Catholics, which often included many of the American bishops, as being quasi-socialist, soft on communism, supportive of liberation movements, and beholden to a social justice agenda that was disconnected from a proper understanding of Catholic thought and not rooted in a realistic understanding of political life.

George Weigel argued that this divergence marked a departure

6. Ross Douthat, *Bad Religion: How We Became a Nation of Heretics* (New York: Free Press, 2012), 97.

7. Novak, "Liberal Catholicism Will Rise Again," 694.

8. Neuhaus, *The Catholic Moment*, 267.

from traditional Catholic teaching and signified an abandonment of the unique perspective that such teaching provided on matters of public importance. Having lost sight of this tradition, Catholic leaders had lost the rudder that had for a long time helped guide the church in the midst of difficult choices. In its place, this same leadership had all too often opted, often unwittingly, for secular alternatives and, in doing so, allowed the world to guide the mission of the church. In light of this, Weigel stated that while "neoconservative American Catholicism welcomes Pope John XXIII's call for the church to open its windows to a dialogue with the modern world, … it wants the dialogue to be that, a dialogue, and not a monologue in which the *ecclesia docens* simply collapses into the *ecclesia discerns*."[9] The implication is that, content to remain a "learning church," its leadership had strayed from their authentic calling and in doing so risked playing the role of sheep in the midst of the shepherds of American secular political life.

Novak hinted at this disconnect from tradition when he wrote that it sometimes seemed that for progressive Catholics the nearly two-thousand-year history of the Christian church never happened and the great theologians Augustine, Aquinas, Maritain, among others, were forgotten; "it was as if the world somehow started fresh yesterday, or in any case about 1965."[10] While an exaggeration, the decade following Vatican II signified a period in which experimentation and a reevaluation of church teaching occurred. Following the civil rights movement, black power, the feminist movement, the fallout from Vietnam, and other cultural upheavals that brought into question long-standing authority structures, not to mention dramatic changes that were brought about through the council's teachings, such a reevaluation should not come as a great surprise. Nevertheless, they did mark a stark departure from the vision that guided the thought of the neoconservative Catholics.

Given the extent to which the post–Vatican II liberal Catholic

9. Weigel, "The Neoconservative Difference," 149.
10. Michael Novak, *Confession of a Catholic,* 46.

worldview was understood to have intersected with a progressive secular one, the neoconservative Catholics found themselves in the position of fighting a two-front war. They were trying to counter left-wing elements in the secular political sphere that they believed were acting in ways detrimental to the American political tradition, while simultaneously attempting to root out radical and inauthentic elements in the church that had been influenced by these secular ideas. One way to guard against these influences was to take steps to de-politicize the church, or at least properly situate politics and politicking in its proper place within it.

In a speech given to the American Bar Association in 1984, Cardinal Joseph Bernardin expanded on his vision as it pertained to the role of religion in the development of public policy.[11] More precisely, what in particular was the bishops' role in policy making and how proactive should they be in the debates and discussions surrounding secular political life? His insights in this regard are useful because they highlight similarities to and differences from those of the neoconservative Catholics and provide a springboard to understand neoconservative Catholic concerns about the ecclesiological crisis in the American church.

Cardinal Bernardin highlighted three fundamental points. First, he argued that religion ought to have a formative influence on society and, consequently, in the formation of public policy. Second, and a related point, Bernardin addressed and affirmed the long-standing society/state distinction, claiming that while the church should maintain a distinct presence in relation to the state, it could not remain entirely separate from the former and still live out her mission to the world. One of the fundamental roles of the church was in the formation of society and, through that formation, influencing the contours within which political debate took place.[12] There is very little divergence between the neoconservative Catholics and

11. Joseph Cardinal Bernardin, "Role of the Religious Leader in the Development of Public Policy," *Journal of Law and Religion* 2, no. 2 (1984): 369–79.

12. Ibid., 369–74.

Cardinal Bernardin on these first two points. Where disagreement becomes evident is in relation to his third.

Assuming that the church's moral vision ought to at least inform public policy decisions, either through direct engagement or more indirectly through the formation of a culture conducive to "Catholic-friendly" legislation, Cardinal Bernardin laid out the case for an overt public role of the hierarchy in this process. In doing so he argued that "the Catholic bishop's role in the development of public policy is an extension of his teaching role in the Church."[13] While the neoconservative Catholics never contended that the hierarchy ought to remain mute on questions of public policy, they were increasingly uncomfortable when the clergy played a prominent role in the development of policy. Novak highlighted this concern when he wrote that "not for nothing ... did Maritain warn us about the danger of the clergyman's judgment in politics. True, the priest is a citizen like any other. But the Church is not the world, the cleric is not the layman, the laws of politics are not yet, at any rate, not by a long shot those of the Gospels."[14] One can trace in the writings of the neoconservative Catholics a line of thought that argues that the excessive involvement in public policy questions by the clergy was indicative of a much deeper problem in the church. In effect, the clerical class had become seduced by the temptations of political relevancy and in the process put at risk the credibility of the church, turning it into one interest group among many. This led to the downgrading of their ministerial and sacramental role in society.

The critique was grounded in what they took to be three important shifts that occurred in the two decades following the council, each of which shaped the bishops' political activities and perspective on public policy. First, the neoconservative Catholics were deeply concerned that in the aftermath of Vatican II the institu-

---

13. Ibid., 376.

14. Novak, "Blue Bleak Embers ... Fall, Gall Themselves ... Cash Gold-Vermillion," in *Conspiracy; The Implications of the Harrisburg Trial for the Democratic Tradition,* ed. John Raines, 65 (New York: Harper and Row, 1974).

tional Catholic church had become preoccupied with political issues, a tendency that they claimed was the direct result of the "loss
of the sense of the transcendent" among many of the leadership in
the church. While an obvious generalization, this problem was not
specific to the Catholic church but widespread in the American
Christian churches and rooted in important sociological changes
that occurred in the post-World War II world. It was in reaction
to these changes that Richard Neuhaus helped to pen *The Hartford
Appeal for Theological Affirmation* in 1977, an ecumenical document
that expressed distress regarding the loss of the transcendent in religious life and a growing obsession with secular affairs on the part
of the churches.

Second, having become enmeshed in secular political affairs,
the Catholic church had allegedly begun to form a clergy that was
preoccupied with secular politics, which led to a confusion of the
roles and responsibilities of the clergy with those of the laity. These
concerns had gained popularity as early as the mid-seventies in
some Catholic circles and found voice in publications like the *Chicago Declaration of Christian Concern*. While the neoconservative
Catholics were not directly involved in the production of this document, the *Declaration* expressed some of the central themes in their
thought and will thus provide a useful segue into this discussion.

Finally, following their interest in political activism, the clergy
had succumbed to what might be called the Constantinian temptation, in which they took sides and embraced a politically partisan
perspective. More distressing still for the neoconservative Catholics was that the position with which much of the leadership in
the Catholic church expressed agreement tended to line up with the
political perspective of progressive secular politics. Concerns over
this left-leaning Constantinianism inspired the founding of the
magazine *Catholicism in Crisis,* which was co-founded by Novak.

The Loss of the Transcendent

The Hartford Appeal for Theological Affirmation was a joint project initiated by Richard Neuhaus and Peter Berger and issued in Hartford, Connecticut, in January 1975. It was an ecumenical document that, while written by two Lutherans, was eventually signed by some twenty individuals from eighteen different Christian denominations. Given its ecumenical nature, the principles that it developed avoided doctrinally contentious topics and instead focused on what the signers understood to be broad, and generally destructive, trends currently affecting the Christian churches in the modern world. Avery Dulles, one of its co-signers, noted that the general tone of the *Appeal* was "clearly negative and admonitory. It may be described as a common attempt by Christians of various traditions to identify certain widely pervasive assumptions that are in fact undermining the vigor and integrity of Christian faith, witness, life and action."[15]

Its critical tone functioned as a call to renewal and a plea for the churches to return to some of the fundamental principles that they had slowly abandoned over the course of the twentieth century. Given its ecumenical approach, the statement was clearly intended to appeal to a large swath of the Christian community, but its implications clearly applied to the Roman Catholic Church in America. Reflecting on the importance of this document for the church, George Weigel claimed that the *Hartford Appeal* "marked one of the points at which Catholic theology in America began to reground itself in the Church's ancient and ongoing tradition, rather than imagining that theology (and everything else, for that matter), had started all over again with the Second Vatican Council."[16]

The sentiment expressed by Weigel was one that emerged with some frequency in the writings of the neoconservative Catholics:

15. Avery Dulles, *The Resilient Church: The Necessity and Limits of Adaptation* (Garden City, N.Y.: Doubleday, 1977), 73.
16. George Weigel, "Remembering Avery Dulles, S.J." *Denver Catholic Register,* January 28, 2009.

following Vatican II, the American Catholic church had veered away from traditional teaching, not because the teachings of the Second Vatican Council were misguided, but because they were misinterpreted or misunderstood and poorly applied by church leadership to contemporary events. This tendency was made easier once influential segments of church leadership had lost sight of their primary calling, which was sacramental in nature and directed toward the Kingdom of God. Those advocating on behalf of the *Appeal* argued that the marginalization of this calling had occurred because leadership in the Christian churches had begun to lose a sense of the transcendent and had abandoned the distinctive voice that brought clarity to the tasks to which God has called them.

Peter Berger sought to understand some of the sociological causes for this loss of the transcendent and, in doing so, made a pair of distinct yet complementary arguments. First, he attempted to make the case that this loss in the churches was "a direct result of the increasing tendency toward secularization in the West."[17] Secularization theorists held that as society moved into modernity, religious beliefs would become increasingly untenable as socially binding agents and would eventually be displaced by the functional rationality of modern capitalism, the proliferation of the modern sciences, or some other modernizing tendency. This would, in turn, consign religion to the private sphere of the individual and undermine its social power. Berger had been for some time a strong proponent of classical secularization theory and, while his acceptance of it softened notably over time, it still held some sway in the late seventies.[18]

17. Peter Berger, "For a World Without Windows: Hartford in a Sociocultural Context," in *Against the World, For the World: The Hartford Appeal and the Future of American Religion* (New York: The Seabury Press, 1977).

18. For Berger's early take on secularization theory, see *The Sacred Canopy: Elements of a Sociological Theory of Religion* (Garden City, N.Y.: Doubleday, 1967). For his more recent take, in which he expresses a far more nuanced understanding of the effects of secularization, see "Reflections on the Sociology of Religion Today," *Sociology of Religion* 62, no. 4 (Winter 2001): 443–54. For a useful overview of secularization theory, see Olivier Tschannen, "The Secularization Paradigm: A Systematization," *Journal for the Scientific Study of Religion* 30, no. 4 (December 1991): 395–415.

While promoting secularization theory as a possible explanation, his growing discomfort with it by this time led him to back away from it as an explanatory factor, going so far as to admitting that the apparent trend toward secularization may just be a momentary trend and not a final destination.[19]

While downplaying secularization theory to explain the apparent loss of the transcendent, Berger continued to maintain that secularism was a potent force in this process. He asserted that since the end of the Second World War there had emerged the "new class," which had an important influence on the direction of American political culture.[20] He maintained that the intellectual milieu of academia, media, governmental institutions, and similar forums tended to be far more secular than the rest of society. While a minority compared to the general population, these social segments had an influence out of proportion to their size because their position in society put them "in control of many of the institutions that produce and disseminate cultural symbols, notably in the educational system and the communication media."[21] In other words, their influence was enhanced due to their institutional capacity to tap into and take advantage of channels that are linked to the "knowledge industry," which was in contemporary life a central force in the creation of culture.[22] As a consequence, secular ideas permeated social life more rapidly than if the new class did not have the reach that they in fact possessed.

Berger contended that because this class of intellectuals and bureaucrats had become so powerful in the construction of Western society and culture, they had an undue ability to construct the intellectual framework through which everyone within this culture understood and interpreted everyday experience. Their influence had become so prevalent that even those who espoused a religious

19. Berger, "For a World Without Windows," 11–12.

20. For a useful early exploration into his understanding of the new class, see Peter Berger, "Ethics and the Present Class Struggle," *Worldview* (April 1978): 6–11.

21. Peter Berger, "Reflections of an Ecclesiastical Expatriate," *The Christian Century,* October 24, 1990, 966.

22. Berger, "Ethics and the Present Class Struggle," 12.

worldview had embraced a secular bias in which religious ideas had become reinterpreted in light of normative standards that were alien to a religious outlook. Consequently, "the transcendent elements of the tradition are de-emphasized or put aside completely: transcendence is translated into immanence."[23] One consequence was that the churches tended to focus more on secular political, social, and personal activities.

The vision promoted by Berger was one component of a larger interpretive framework that was popular during the seventies. While he advanced a sociological explanation for the "de-transcendentalization" of American life, this framework also had, according to some, a psychological counterpart. Christopher Lasch, for example, argued that in contemporary religious life the "climate is therapeutic, not religious. People today hunger not for personal salvation ... but for the feeling, the momentary illusion, of personal well-being, health and psychic security."[24] In other words, there was in modern Western experience a tendency to experience religion not according to its traditional framework, but in the context of personal fulfillment. This dynamic was thus a pervasive force that had institutional and psychological consequences.

The neoconservative Catholics touched on both aspects of this dynamic, although less so on its psychological expression. George Weigel wrote some years later that the precipitous decline in Catholic participation in sacramental life and particularly confession signified an unhealthy embrace of the therapeutic society at the expense of religious experience.[25] While providing a nod to some of the psychological consequences of the therapeutic society, the neoconservative Catholics were more interested in its sociological underpinnings and, as a result, generally focused on Berger's concerns surrounding the idea of the new class.

23. Berger, "For a World Without Windows," 12–13.

24. Christopher Lasch, *The Culture of Narcissism* (New York: W.W. Norton, 1979), 7.

25. George Weigel, *The Truth of Catholicism: Ten Controversies Explored* (New York: HarperCollins, 2001), 89.

In one of his earliest commentaries on democratic capitalism, Novak echoed Berger's contention that since the Second World War the new class had grown in power and strength, largely due to the emergence of social instruments and media that are perfectly suited to its needs. He asserted that members of the new class tended toward their own aggrandizement often to the greater harm of the political, economic, and cultural systems of the American tradition. As the knowledge industry became increasingly important in modern society, academic institutions, government bureaucracy, and the media became central to the proliferation of ideas, it was in the interest of the new class to ensure that these institutions remained a dominant force in everyday life. This could mean, for example, taking the necessary steps to ensure the continued influence of government power in the economy and cultural affairs. To maintain their influence, elites needed to ensure that their positions of power were maintained. For Novak this risked unduly strengthening certain segments of society (that is, government institutions) at the expense of others (for example, religious institutions and other economic and political associations) and, in doing so, throwing off the careful balance of power that ought to exist between various segments of society.[26]

Although concerned about the new class's influence on political life broadly understood, they were particularly worried that the new class represented a corrupting force within the Catholic church. George Weigel, for instance, asserted that "the rise of a new social elite whose power base is the knowledge industry is a fact of life in contemporary American Catholicism."[27] The Catholic new class was evident in the expansive church bureaucracy that had emerged in recent decades, and particularly in the proliferation of justice and peace networks that focused primarily on social justice issues. Grounded in a particular reading of church documents, the Catholic new class had become preoccupied with, or at least sympathetic

26. Novak, *The American Vision*, 29–34.
27. Weigel, *Catholicism and the Renewal of American Democracy*, 48–49.

to, a variety of activist and liberationist movements. In recent decades, according to the neoconservative Catholics, this new class of intellectuals had proliferated throughout the church, particularly in academia, in the teachings of some bishops, and in the bosom of many of its religious orders.[28] This disproportionate interest in peace and justice issues was an important marker of the politicization of the church that undermined its ability to remain an independent exemplar of the Gospel values that was not tied to one political faction or another. The overly politicized approach, embraced by many American Catholic activists and archbishops alike, resulted in the weakening of a distinctive Catholic identity and gave the impression that the church was little more than a "pathetic appendage to partisanships already well established."[29]

While the neoconservative Catholics recognized that the hierarchy had long been engaged in questions of public policy, it was in the aftermath of Vatican II that this engagement became pronounced.[30] The bishops' extensive engagement on issues as diverse and technical as farm policy, Latin American affairs, economic policy, and nuclear weapons risked making the church little more than a lobbyist or political interest group. Weigel wrote that "the official Church in the United States, and most of its vocal elites, did not help shape a more intelligent, less demagogic, morally sensitive public debate capable of advancing peace and freedom. Rather, the official Church, following many of its intellectual and journalistic elites, became a protagonist at one pole of public argument already underway."[31] This approach hampered the bishops' realization of one of the central missions of the church: to shape society according to a Catholic moral worldview.[32]

This concern was shared by Richard Neuhaus. In an essay titled

28. Ibid., 51–62.
29. Michael Novak, "No Fault Prophecy," *National Review*, April 10, 1987, 44.
30. Weigel, *Catholicism and the Renewal of American Democracy*, 139.
31. Weigel, *Tranquillitas Ordinis*, 329–30.
32. Ibid., 349–50.

"Let the Church Be the Church," Neuhaus claimed that the institutional churches in the United States too often abandoned their religious calling in favor of a predominately political one. At its core, this represented a "crisis of faith," in which the church capitulated too easily and too often to an agenda set by the world, rather than an agenda of its own making.[33] Neuhaus reiterated his concern that the church leadership was undergoing a crisis of faith in an article written specifically on the importance of the *Hartford Appeal*. Here he wrote that "the crisis in Christian social ethics today is, far more than anything else, a crisis of faith. We must indeed find better, more careful, more credible ways to articulate religiously-grounded truth in the political realm, but our most important contribution as believers is to relativize the realm of the political. Our engagement in the provisional politics of the present must be informed by our commitment to the radically 'new politics' of the promised Kingdom."[34]

Neuhaus's point was not that the Christian churches ought to disengage from the world, but instead that the church maintain its distinct voice when discussing questions related to the world. The fundamental problem was not so much that the church was involved in secular politics, but rather that church leadership too often did so according to the standards of secular society. Neuhaus held that the "abandonment of Christian particularism ... was a collapse of faith in the face of what was thought to be the superior weight of modern thought and its dogmas of secularism."[35] Under such conditions, religion would be stripped from decisions of political and social importance.

Although an important vocation in Christian life, secular politics ought to be subservient to a much broader agenda, including proclamation of the Gospel and a seriousness about devotional life,

---

33. Richard Neuhaus, "Let the Church Be the Church" *Center Journal* (Fall 1983): 35–38.

34. Richard Neuhaus, "Speaking for the Church to the World," *The Cresset* 46, no. 8 (September 1983): 4.

35. Richard Neuhaus, "Calling a Halt to Retreat," in *Against the World, For the World: The Hartford Appeal and the Future of American Religion*, ed. Peter Berger et al., 138–64 (New York: The Seabury Press, 1976).

prayer, and contemplation. It was Neuhaus's contention that taking seriously these non-secular activities would, in fact, further the political message of the church more effectively than if Christians were to focus primarily on a social justice agenda.[36] In a presentation given at the Rockford Institute, whose president at the time was Richard Neuhaus, Avery Dulles echoed this point, saying that he deplored "the politicization of the Gospel and the tendency to equate the Kingdom of God with the results of human efforts to build a just society." Dulles insisted "on the utter transcendence of the kingdom and on the primary duty of the church to proclaim the Gospel of eternal life."[37] On a similar note, Novak noted how unfortunate it was that "the church we Catholics experience in 1982 is also far more clerical than it was before Vatican II. These days 'the church' is often a lobbying agent on Capitol Hill. It issues more and more statements on foreign policy in Central America, military budgets, nuclear weapons, specific policies on jobs and welfare."[38]

The above quote links the first moment in the neoconservative Catholic argument regarding what they understand to be the church's ecclesiological crisis to the second one. When the bishops become immersed in questions of policy, not only do they risk becoming entangled in the ambiguities of mundane politics, giving the impression that the church is simply one more interest group among many, they also threaten the proper distinction of roles between the laity and the clergy.

A Confusion of Roles

In December 1977, a group of Chicago Catholics came together and signed the *Chicago Declaration of Christian Concern* in an act of defiance against what they understood to be the clericalization of the Catholic church in the United States. While the neoconservative Catholics were not active participants in the development of

36. Ibid., 152–61.
37. Avery Dulles, "The Gospel, The Church, and Politics," *Origins* (February 19, 1987).
38. Novak, "Liberal Catholicism Will Rise Again," 694.

the *Chicago Declaration,* the document highlighted ideas that the neoconservative Catholics wrestled with well into the eighties. Of particular concern was their conviction that the roles of the laity and the clergy had become blurred in the aftermath of Vatican II. This blurring had taken place in two related ways. First, according to the signers of the *Declaration,* in the decade following the council excessive lay involvement in church activities, including pastoral ministry, religious education, and liturgy, had distracted them from secular pursuits that more properly defined their vocation.[39]

Complementing this shift, the signers contended, while the laity was spending more time working in the churches, the clergy and the church hierarchy were spending more time working in the world and, in doing so, co-opting the responsibilities of their lay counterparts. On this point, the *Declaration* expressed concern that "during the last decade especially, many priests have acted as if the primary responsibility in the church was uprooting injustice, ending wars and defending human rights rested with them as ordained ministers. As a result they bypassed the laity to pursue social causes on their own rather than enabling lay Christians to shoulder their own responsibilities. These priests and religious have sought to impose their own agendas for the world upon the laity."[40]

One consequence of the *Declaration* was the founding of the National Center for the Laity the following year, which was eventually housed at Mundelein College. Its primary responsibility was to keep alive the message of the *Declaration* by highlighting the central role that the laity is to have in the world on issues of secular importance. This was in turn followed by the convening of a national conference called the National Assembly of the Laity, which was held at the Center for Pastoral and Social Ministry at Notre Dame in 1979. The conference convened to discuss the "larger tasks, both theoretical and practical, which will have to be accomplished in order to devel-

39. *The Chicago Declaration of Christian Concern,* in *Challenge to the Laity,* ed. Russell Barta, 21–22 (Huntington, Ind.: Our Sunday Visitor, 1980), 21–22.

40. Ibid., 22.

op and sustain the vision of the laity as articulated by the *Chicago Declaration*."[41] At its close, the "Report of the National Assembly of the Laity" was adopted, the findings of the *Chicago Declaration* were reaffirmed, and the central role that the laity was called to play in secular life reemphasized.[42]

One of the presenters at the Notre Dame conference was Michael Novak. His paper reiterated and reaffirmed many of the themes expressed in the *Declaration*. He began by reflecting on the Lay Catholic Congress of 1889, and argued that the American laity of the late twentieth century were bearers of a confidence expressed nearly a hundred years earlier. Although embodying a vision similar to that expressed in the lay Catholic congresses, the lay members of the Catholic church in the post-World War II world, although their demographics were changing, had posed new challenges while offering new possibilities.[43] Particularly following Vatican II the laity was given an opportunity to fill a prominent leadership role in American affairs that reflected their true vocation in the world. This vocation was expressed in their "special responsibilities for evolving, through trial and error, institutional expressions of Catholic witness in the development of humane, social, economic, and political institutions."[44] While the laity was finally able to fulfill this important function, Novak expressed concern that this opportunity was slipping by before it fully became a reality. Threatening the lay vocation was a "confusion of roles" that occurs when the clergy attempt to usurp that which properly belongs to the laity, leading once again to an expansion of clericalism in the church.[45] A few years following the close of the conference, Novak argued that "it used to be thought that laymen and laywomen had a special vocation in the church, a vocation to make Christian conscience present

41. Russell Barta, "Introduction," *Challenge to the Laity*, 12.

42. "Report of the National Assembly of the Laity," in *Challenge to the Laity*, ed. Barta, 125.

43. Michael Novak, "What the Laity Can Teach the Church," in *Challenge to the Laity*, ed. Barta, 45–50.

44. Ibid., 56.   45. Ibid., 52–57.

in the world, in temporal matters. According to this view, the clergy are not to be confined to the pulpit or the sacristy, but they do have a special sacred role, crucial in nourishing the laity. The laity, however, in all their splendid variety, are expected to be the primary dealers with the contingencies and fruitful polemics of the temporal order. This was, for quite a long time, the liberal Catholic view."[46]

Although Novak noted that the role distinction between the clergy and the laity had for "quite a long time" been the liberal Catholic view of things, it is important to note that the liberal Catholic view of things was itself of relatively recent vintage. While extolling the virtues of this distinction, Novak failed to point out that it did not emerge in full force until the mid-twentieth century. For a very long time the laity was generally relegated to a status that was subservient to clerical leadership. In his study of the development of authority in the church, Yves Congar noted that since at least the reforms of Leo IX in the early eleventh century, the pope began to claim sovereign rights not only over the church but also over that of the kings and their kingdoms throughout Europe. While risking an unnecessary oversimplification, there was from that point on a tendency to subjugate the laity under the authority of the hierarchy and in doing so, identify the "church" with the hierarchy, thus making it in many respects a juridical institution.[47]

Throughout American history the hierarchy exerted its control over the activities of the laity. This is not to say that lay Catholics did not play an important role in the development of the American Catholic church. One can look to the early American church, when large segments of the Catholic population were compelled to keep the faith without the benefit of the clergy. In the early nineteenth century when lay trusteeism was widespread, members of the laity often held leadership roles in the church. Historically, the import-

46. Novak, "Liberal Catholicism Will Rise Again," 694.

47. Yves Congar, O.P., "The Historical Development of Authority in the Church: Points for Christian Reflection," in *Problems of Authority,* ed. John M. Todd, 136–44 (Baltimore: Helicon Press, 1961).

ant role of the laity in political and secular affairs was also evident in charismatic lay leaders like Terence Powderly, Mother Jones, Orestes Brownson, and his son Henry, the last of whom helped to organize the lay congresses in 1889 and 1894.[48]

However important these lay leaders' contributions were, they were to a large extent dependent on ecclesiastical support. The Knights of Labor, founded by Powderly, depended on Cardinal James Gibbons's intercession at the Vatican in order to avoid the organization's suppression.[49] The lay congresses, to provide another example, dissolved after 1894, in large part because of a lack of hierarchical backing. Support for lay independence was lacking because some bishops feared that the laity would develop a power structure that was independent of their own, thus instilling among some resistance to the rising tide of lay consciousness.[50]

The hierarchy's attempt to assert control over the lay Catholic population, and in particular its political activities, continued into the early decades of the twentieth century. In his book discussing the first decade of the National Catholic Welfare Conference (NCWC), Douglas Slawson highlighted some of the conflicts that arose between the church hierarchy and lay organizations at this time. One of the major impetuses for the foundation of the conference was the concern some bishops had in relation to the growing independence of the Knights of Columbus, a group that had been very active during World War I and sought to continue its social activities independent of clerical oversight and control. Many within the church hierarchy, and particularly those in leadership positions in the NCWC, thought it important to rein in the Knights of Columbus and guide their activities according to the interests of the institutional church.[51]

48. Patrick Carey, "Lay Catholic Leadership in the United States," *U.S. Catholic Historian* 8, no. 3 (Summer 1990): 224–25.

49. Thomas Shelley, "Biography and Autobiography: James Cardinal Gibbons and John Tracy Ellis," *U.S. Catholic Historian* 21, no. 2 (Spring 2003): 40–41.

50. Carey, "Lay Catholic Leadership," 233.

51. Douglas Slawson, *The Foundation and First Decade of the National Catholic Welfare Council* (Washington, D.C.: The Catholic University of America Press, 1992), 53.

Another example of the bishops' attempt to control lay activity in the secular sphere becomes evident with the establishment of the Department of Lay Activities in the NCWC. In 1901 the American Federation of Catholic Societies (AFCS) was established with the aim of defining and asserting a Catholic viewpoint on important political questions of the day, particularly in the defense of church rights and the pursuit of social justice issues. By 1917, its leadership sought to enroll every Catholic layman in a local diocesan association.[52] One of the primary goals of the Department of Lay Activities, which was established in 1920 as part of the NCWC, was to subsume the AFCS within the NCWC, thus ensuring that activities of the federation would have direct clerical oversight. This attempt eventually resulted in the emergence of the National Council of Catholic Men and the National Council of Catholic Women, both of which helped to coordinate lay activities on the diocesan level under the direct leadership of the local bishop.[53] Writing on the establishment of these two lay organizations, the church historian Patrick Carey noted that "both groups represented lay activity under the supervision of the hierarchy—a precursor to Pope Pius XI's Catholic Action."[54]

Following on the Americanist crisis of the early twentieth century the hierarchy came to believe that "what was needed was lay action that would not undermine the subordinate role of the laity within the church.... The mission of spreading the message of the gospel and 'restoring all things in Christ' had been given by Jesus to the apostles and their successors, the bishops and priests. Only under their direction was lay action officially Catholic."[55] In 1937 the Archbishop of Milwaukee, Samuel Stritch, called together a conference that focused on Catholic Action and its continued importance in the life of the church. Mrs. George Fell, a member of the Toledo Council of Catholic Women and a speaker at the closing banquet,

52. Ibid., 13.
53. Ibid.; see in particular ch. 5 and pp. 76–81.
54. Carey, "Lay Catholic Leadership," 234.
55. David J. O'Brien, *Public Catholicism* (New York: Orbis Books, 1996), 208.

expressed sentiments that were fairly common among the laity of the day. In her speech she emphasized the leadership role that the clergy embodied and, in like fashion, the role of the laity as devoted followers of this leadership. Members of the laity were called to be soldiers of Christ and to dutifully follow the course of action outlined by church leadership.[56]

During this pre-Vatican II period the laity tended to espouse a cultic view of the clergy in which the former looked to the latter as a group set apart, in both their spiritual and their administrative authority. Members of the laity were, in somewhat simplified terms, called to "pray, pay, and obey."[57] While an appeal to hierarchical control of lay action was a dominant theme in the first half of the twentieth century, it was neither lasting nor the only one. This became particularly apparent in the period between 1920 and 1950 through, for example, the launch of *Commonweal* magazine, the emergence of the Catholic Worker Movement, the establishment of Friendship Houses and the Christian Family Movement. By the fifties the growing self-awareness among the laity contributed to a growing sense of autonomy from direct clerical oversight. This was in part due to changing demographics of the church that included a more highly educated, economically independent, and confident laity when it came to secular affairs.[58] One commentator writing in the early sixties claimed that whereas the laity once looked to the priest "for wisdom on the whole gamut of life's problems, he is now expected only to provide guidance on the more narrowly 'spiritual' problems. In Church, the priest is indispensable, outside of Church, he is simply one more person with one more opinion."[59]

56. Mary Irene Zotti, "The Young Christian Workers," *U.S. Catholic Historian* 9, no. 4 (Fall 1990): 391.

57. James Davidson and Dean Hoge, "Mind the Gap: The Return of the Lay/Clerical Divide," *Commonweal*, November 23, 2007, 18–19.

58. Yves Congar, OP, "The Historical Development of Authority in the Church: Points for Christian Reflection," in *Problems of Authority*, ed. John M. Todd (Baltimore, 1961), 238.

59. Daniel Callahan, *The Mind of the Catholic Layman* (New York: Charles Scribner's Sons, 1963), 127.

The Second Vatican Council had an indispensable role in this process, particularly through the publication of *The Decree on the Apostolate of the Laity (Apostolicam Actuositatem)* and *Lumen Gentium*. In contrast to earlier constructions, which often subjugated the laity to clerical oversight, these documents partially liberated the laity from this authority and recognized an intrinsic integrity in secular matters for such Catholics. In this regard, the council fathers remarked in *Lumen Gentium* that "the laity, by their very vocation, seek the kingdom of God by engaging in temporal affairs and by ordering them according to the plan of God.... Since they are tightly bound up in all types of temporal affairs it is their special task to order and to throw light upon these affairs in such a way that they may come into being and then continually increase according to Christ to the praise of the Creator and the Redeemer."[60]

Within years of the council's end, the distinction between the clerical and lay roles was, to the chagrin of the neoconservative Catholics, being increasingly ignored and overlooked. The clergy and the bishops in particular were becoming vocal on issues of political importance. The excessive attention given to political affairs by the clergy was a distraction from their primary responsibilities, which related directly to the preaching of the Gospel and the sacramental character of the priesthood. Failing to maintain this proper division of labor within the church was thus a betrayal of the council's vision for the church. George Weigel was explicit on this point when he wrote that "the clear teaching of the Second Vatican Council is that the laity, by reason of baptism has a special ministry 'in the world.' ... A reclericalized Church, in which priestly and Episcopal prescriptors are the primary fashioners and chief public exponents of the official Church's prudential judgments ... would not be a church in accord with the vision of Vatican II."[61]

60. Dogmatic Constitution on the Church, *Lumen Gentium,* Vatican II, November 21, 1964, no. 31, http://www.vatican.va/archive/hist_councils/ii_vatican_council/documents/vat-ii_const_19641121_lumen-gentium_en.html.

61. Weigel, *Tranquillitas Ordinis,* 352.

The neoconservative Catholics took this vision to heart but did not comment on the fact that, in the life of the church, this sort of lay independence was in fact a novel phenomenon. Their embrace of lay independence has important historical precursors, but it is a vision that in practice was marginal well into the twentieth century. Michael Novak advanced this perspective in an essay for the *National Review,* where he wrote that "it used to be thought that laymen and laywomen had a special vocation in the church, a vocation to make Christian conscience present in the world, in temporal political matters. According to this view, the clergy are not to be confined to the pulpit or the sacristy, but they do have a special sacred role, crucial in nourishing the laity. The laity, however, in all their splendid variety, are expected to be the primary dealers with the contingencies and fruitful polemics of the temporal order."[62]

The neoconservative Catholics never went so far as to argue that the clergy had no role in political affairs. Such a position would be untenable, if for no other reason than that, after his conversion, Neuhaus himself remained very outspoken on political affairs and yet remained a priest. Nevertheless, one of the central criticisms that the neoconservative Catholics made of the American hierarchy in the decades following the council pertained to the overt political activity that the bishops and clergy engaged in and the way in which this behavior usurped the proper role of the laity and also distorted the proper role to be played by the clergy.

At this point the first two shifts in the neoconservative Catholic ecclesiological critique of the clergy had come to a head. First, they argued that there was among the clergy a growing obsession with secular political affairs, which had taken their eye off of the transcendent character that defines their primary responsibility in the world. This led to a blurring of the roles of the laity and the clergy. As political issues became an increasingly important priority for church leadership, the activities of the clergy adjusted accordingly.

62. Novak, "Liberal Catholicism Will Rise Again," 694.

With their growing involvement in secular political affairs, the clergy became actively engaged in concrete questions of public policy. It is on this point that the third shift under discussion became a factor in the neoconservative Catholic critique of church leadership.

In November 1982 Michael Novak, in cooperation with Ralph McInerny, published the first issue of a new magazine called *Catholicism in Crisis,* which was some years later renamed simply *Crisis.* It looked to the popular journal *Christianity in Crisis* as its model, but restricted the focus primarily to the Catholic church. Novak wrote the lead editorial, which spelled out the rationale behind the magazine, and titled it "The Present Crisis."[63] The present crisis to which he alluded focused on the public role that the American Catholic clergy took in respect to secular political affairs. More specifically, it is a crisis of power, wherein clerics overstep their authority and engage far too much in the affairs of the world. This reflects the content of the previous shift, although here Novak extended the argument when he wrote that "the church seems in danger of losing its true, original, and profound identity, in order to become what it is not, an instrument of temporal power. Nearly always today, this temporal assertion of the church is leftward in force, as in former times it was often rightward. Yet whether tilting to the left or to the right, the fundamental theological error is the same."[64] In the post-Vatican II world, according to Novak, not only has the clergy tried to assert temporal power far too often in the pursuit of political ends but, worse still, the political ends for which this power is being used are almost always in favor of left-wing causes. This is a tendency which might best be referred to as the Constantinian temptation.

---

63. Michael Novak, "The Present Crisis," *Catholicism in Crisis,* November 1982, 1–2. The founding of this journal, if not the initial editorial itself, is clearly of lasting importance to Novak. As of 2009, in his office at the American Enterprise Institute, a copy of the editorial was blown up to poster size and hung on the wall behind his assistant's desk.

64. Ibid., 2.

The Constantinian Temptation

The politicization of the church had brought with it, according to Neuhaus, an unfortunate consequence: religious identity in modern America was less about the Gospel and more about a person's political affiliation. As he put it, "there is, in sociological jargon, an elective affinity among Christians who address public affairs. As often as not, the affinity is based more on one's politics than on one's Christianity.... We have arrived at the sorry state where innumerable Americans choose their church by their choice of politics. This makes a mockery of the notion that the church should inform the political decision-making of its members. It also makes ludicrous the notion that the church has anything of significance to say to the public order. To that notion, the obvious question is, 'Which church?'"[65] Taken as a whole, the Christian churches presented a plurality of positions on any given issue; with strictly theological and denominational differences no longer defining loyalties, political commitments became an increasingly important marker for religious identity. As Catholics became increasingly divided by political differences, there emerged a tendency for the laity and leadership alike to align themselves with institutional structures that would more effectively realize their political objectives. It was for the neoconservatives what one might refer to as the "Constantinian temptation," a temptation to which they feared the American bishops had fallen prey.

The temptation to cooperate closely with political interests and institutions was not something that was unique to the post-Vatican II church. In the pre-conciliar era it was not abnormal for the European church to align itself closely with governments and related institutions that showed favor to the church and its interests. During the early modern period the church associated herself with monarchical governments, particularly through the use of "concor-

65. Neuhaus, "Let the Church Be the Church," 40.

dats that guaranteed the rights of the church, including religious uniformity and financial support, and special rights in the areas of education and marriage."[66]

Typically conservative in orientation, many of the popes during the nineteenth century were interested in maintaining or regaining their moral influence in political decision making and in resisting the inroads that liberal-oriented governments were making on this authority. The example par excellence of this tendency was Pius IX, whose *Syllabus of Errors* and other writings rejected liberalism as an erroneous political theory.[67] As late as 1953, Cardinal Alfredo Ottaviani, secretary of the Holy Office in the Roman Curia during Vatican II, expressed support for a policy in Spain that respected non-Catholic worship only in the private sphere.[68] Well into the twentieth century the Latin American bishops tended to defend a more traditionalist style of government that protected church interests.

The neoconservative Catholics showed little sympathy in their writings for these closely guarded alliances between church and state, whether of the right or the left. Having assumed that such alliances had been finally overcome with Vatican II, the neoconservative Catholics were troubled by the fact that they had reemerged shortly thereafter. In an editorial written for *Commonweal,* Michael Novak criticized the bishops for embracing an overly politicized and noticeably left-wing political style.[69] While they had abandoned their commitment to conservative political institutions such as the monarchy during the previous two decades, he claimed, the "'progressives' had seized nearly all places of authority in seminaries and chanceries, church agencies and publications. The old authoritarian style, however, has not much changed."[70]

66. Paul Sigmund, "The Catholic Tradition and Modern Democracy," *The Review of Politics* 49, no. 4 (Autumn 1987): 534.

67. Michael Novak, *Catholic Social Thought and Liberal Institutions,* 19–24.

68. Sigmund, "Catholic Tradition and Modern Democracy," 545.

69. Michael Novak, "A Closed Church, Again," *Commonweal,* February 5, 1982, 113.

70. Ibid.

The neoconservative Catholic claim that the Catholic bishops had lurched to the left on policy issues became apparent in a letter to the editor that Neuhaus wrote in defense of Pope John Paul II. In the winter of 1979, the *New York Times* published an editorial critical of John Paul II for comments that he made related to the involvement of the clergy in political life. Here the editors commented on a recent speech given by the pope to the Latin American bishops in Puebla, in which he spoke out against liberation theology and reiterated that the church's mission is "religious and not social or political."[71] The editorial proceeded to declare the speech "disappointing" and instead held that it was the clergy's role to stand out as a voice against political oppression and to lay claim to a more aggressive political activism.[72]

Neuhaus's response highlighted the issue of clerical involvement in political affairs by pointing to Pope John Paul I's refusal to be crowned with the papal tiara as a demonstration that the pope himself had rejected such identification. This refusal officially marked an end to the Constantinian tendency, which sought to establish through political intervention what the church believed to be representative of a just and Christian social order. The church having moved beyond the Constantinian temptation, at least in an official capacity, the appeal of liberation theology in Latin America and the call for a politically active clergy ought to be disconcerting. It would be a shame, he further stated, to be witness to the Catholic church's rightful abandonment of "its alliance with the Constantines and Francos of history to resume its old habits now in partnership with Marx."[73]

71. Editorial, "A Voice against 'Liberation Theology,'" *New York Times,* January 30, 1979, A18.

72. Ibid.

73. Richard John Neuhaus, "Letter to the Editor," *New York Times,* February 12, 1979, A16.

❖ CONCLUSION

THERE IS AN INTERESTING TENSION at play in neoconservative Catholic thought as it pertains to public perception, Catholic identity, and the role that both the clergy and the laity ought to play in the world. While the neoconservative Catholics insisted on the importance of lay activity in political life, they maintained a high regard for the clergy and the role of the bishops. While intent on protecting lay prerogatives, the neoconservative Catholics were also concerned that excessive involvement by the hierarchy in political affairs would damage the long-term integrity of the church. By sullying themselves in ongoing political debates, the clergy ran the risk of diminishing the stature of the church in the eyes of others; political activity by the bishops carried with it the possibility of contributing to the construction of a public perception that the church is just one more interest group among many. Nowhere do the neoconservative Catholics express the concern that an aggressive lay Catholic presence in political life would result in the same. Quite the opposite: it is expected by them that in light of Vatican II teaching the laity will be more involved in secular political affairs while the clergy ought to remain more aloof from such matters. It is difficult to get beyond the impression that the hierarchy, and the clergy more generally, represent the church in the world in a more fundamental way than do the laity.

Such a vision contributes to the impression that for the neoconservative Catholics the hierarchy both embodies and reflects the sacred character of the church in ways that the laity does not. To the extent that this is the case, the neoconservative Catholics embrace a traditional view of the clergy that envisions them as occupying an exalted position in the church, while at the same time the neoconservatives manifest a very post–Vatican II view of the laity that stresses their relative independence, particularly in political affairs, from clerical interference.

The neoconservative Catholic concern about the dangers of hierarchical and clerical involvement in political affairs is not without merit, particularly when understood through the broader ecclesiological paradigm that contributes to their worldview. Appealing to Avery Dulles's "models of the church" framework, George Weigel asserted that "because the Church is a sacrament of Christ's presence to the world, the Church is witness to the divine intention for humanity revealed in the Incarnation and the Resurrection."[1] The "church as sacrament" model advanced by Dulles promotes the idea that at the most fundamental level the church is a visible embodiment of God's grace that is in the process of coming to fulfillment. Dulles wrote that "the Church becomes an actual event of grace when it appears most concretely as a sacrament—that is, in the actions of the Church as such whereby men are bound together in grace by a visible expression."[2] In the context of such a model, the church's primary responsibility is to further enable those within the church to better articulate and live their lives in the light of their faith. They live their lives in such a way as to evangelize the culture and shape society so that it is more consistent with a Catholic ethic. The political mission of the church is of secondary importance; it is not the primary role of the church to erect a just and prosperous society.[3] The church is called on to be a public witness to God's grace that is revealed in the incarnation and resurrection.[4]

---

1. Weigel, *Tranquillitas Ordinis*, 354.
2. Avery Dulles, *Models of the Church* (New York: Image Books, 1974), 69.
3. Neuhaus, *The Catholic Moment*, 189–91.
4. Ibid., 142.

Thus, the primary role that the institutional church ought to play in secular life happens in an arena that precedes policy making. Rather than getting trapped in the weeds of policy formation, the hierarchy ought to engage in the "culture-forming task of constructing a religiously informed public philosophy for the American experiment in ordered liberty."[5] In taking this approach, Neuhaus and his neoconservative Catholic allies held, the church will in fact be more effective than their opponents in shaping political debate because the church will help shape the culture within which such debate occurs. George Weigel made this point when he wrote that "the gravest temptation in contemporary American Catholicism is to reduce the church's role to that of lobbyist for particular policies." The notion that "society comes before polity is not an abstract affirmation of political theory," he writes; "it is a fundamental fact of life in American political culture."[6] In short, for the neoconservative Catholics, leadership within the American church had misplaced priorities. They too often looked to directly shape policy in Washington, rather than shaping the culture to which Congress responds, and in doing so succeeded in making the institutional church one political interest group among many others.

5. Ibid., 283.
6. Weigel, *Tranquillitas Ordinis,* 349.

BIBLIOGRAPHY

"Abortion Reform." Editorial, *New York Times.* February 14, 1967, 42.

Adamson, Michael. "The Most Important Single Aspect of Our Foreign Policy?: The Eisenhower Administration, Foreign Aid, and the Third World." In *The Eisenhower Administration, the Third World, and The Globalization of the Cold War,* 47–74. Lanham, Md.: Rowman and Littlefield, 2006.

Addington, Larry. *America's War in Vietnam: A Short Narrative History.* Bloomington: Indiana University Press, 2000.

Allen, John. "Fr. Richard John Neuhaus, Dead at 72." *National Catholic Reporter,* January 8, 2009. ncronline.org/news/people/fr-richard-john-neuhaus-dead-age-72.

Allitt, Patrick. *Catholic Intellectuals and Conservative Politics in America, 1950–1985.* Ithaca, N.Y.: Cornell University Press, 1993.

American Enterprise Institute. *A Conversation with Michael Novak and Robert Schifter.* Washington, D.C.: American Enterprise Institute, 1981.

Anderson, David. "No More Vietnams: Historians Debate the Policy Lessons of the Vietnam War." In *The War that Never Ends: New Perspectives on the Vietnam War,* edited by David Anderson and Jonathan Ernst. Lexington: University Press of Kentucky, 2007.

Appleby, R. Scott. "Triumph of Americanism: Common Ground for U.S. Catholics." In *Being Right: Conservative Catholics in America,* edited by Mary Jo Weaver and R. Scott Appleby, 37–62. Bloomington: University of Indiana Press, 1995.

———. "Catholics and the Christian Right: An Uneasy Alliance." In *Sojourners in the Wilderness: The Christian Right in Comparative Perspective,* edited by Corwin Smidt and James Penning, 93–113. Lanham, Md.: Rowman and Littlefield, 1997.

Au, William. *The Cross, the Flag, and the Bomb: American Catholics Debate War and Peace, 1960–1983.* Westport, Conn.: Greenwood Press, 1985.

Austin, Charles. "Protestant Leaders Debate the Role of Religion in Public Affairs." *New York Times,* March 25, 1982, A16.

Barbieri, William. "Beyond the Nations: The Expansion of the Common Good in Catholic Social Thought." *The Review of Politics* 63, no. 4 (Autumn 2001): 723–54.

Bell, Daniel. *The Cultural Contradictions of Capitalism.* New York: Basic Books, 1976.

Bellah, Robert. "Civil Religion in America." *Daedalus* 96, no. 1 (Winter 1967): 1–21.

Berger, Peter. *The Sacred Canopy: Elements of a Sociological Theory of Religion.* Garden City, N.Y.: Doubleday, 1967.

———. "For a World Without Windows: Hartford in a Sociocultural Context." In *Against the World, For the World: The Hartford Appeal and the Future of American Religion,* edited by Peter Berger and Richard John Neuhaus. New York: Seabury Press, 1977.

———. "Reflections of an Ecclesiastical Expatriate." *The Christian Century,* October 24, 1990, 964–69.

———. "Reflection on the Sociology of Religion Today." *Sociology of Religion* 62, no. 4, "Religion and Globalization at the Turn of the Millennium" (Winter 2001): 443–54.

Berger, Peter, and Richard John Neuhaus. *Movement and Revolution.* Garden City, NY: Doubleday and Company, 1970.

———. "To Empower People." In *To Empower People: From State to Civil Society,* edited by Michael Novak, 157–214. Washington, D.C.: American Enterprise Institute, 1996.

Bernardin, Archbishop Joseph. "Comments of Archbishop Bernardin Regarding Jimmy Carter's Views on Abortion." *Origins,* September 2, 1976.

Bernardin, Joseph Cardinal. "Role of the Religious Leader in the Development of Public Policy." *Journal of Law and Religion* 2, no. 2 (1984): 369–79.

Berryman, Philip. *The Religious Roots of Rebellion: Christians in Central American Revolutions.* New York: Orbis Books, 1984.

———. *Liberation Theology: Essential Facts about the Revolutionary Movement in Latin America and Beyond.* Oak Park, Ill.: Pantheon Books, 1987.

Bianchi, Eugene, and Rosemary Radford Ruether. "Introduction," *A Democratic Catholic Church: The Reconstruction of Roman Catholicism* (New York: Crossroad, 1992), 7.

Bivins, Michael. *The Fracture of Good Order: Christian Anti-Liberalism and the Challenge to American Politics.* Chapel Hill: University of North Carolina Press, 2003.

Blanshard, Paul. *American Freedom and Catholic Power.* Boston: Beacon Press, 1949.

Bloch, Ruth. "Religion and Ideological Change in the American Revolution." In *Religion and American Politics: From the Colonial Period to the Present,* edited by Mark Noll and Luke Harlow, 47–64. New York: Oxford University Press, 2007.

Boot, Max. "Myths about Neoconservatism." In *The Neocon Reader,* edited by Irwin Stelzer, 45–52. New York: Grove Press, 2003.

Brett, Edward. *The U.S. Catholic Press on Central America.* Notre Dame, Ind.: University of Notre Dame, 2003.

Briggs, Kenneth, "Bishops, Gratified, Prepare to Teach Letter on Peace," *New York Times,* May 5, 1983. http://www.nytimes.com/1983/05/05/us/bishops-gratified-prepare-to-teach-letter-on-peace.html

Brown, Cynthia. "The Right's Religious Red Alert." *The Christian Century,* March 12, 1983, 302–6.

Brown, Robert McAfee. "One Sided Terms for Dialogue." *The Christian Century,* May 25, 1983, 530–31.

Buckley, Willliam. "Introduction." In *Moral Clarity in the Nuclear Age,* by Michael Novak. New York: Thomas Nelson, 1983.

Burnham, James. "The Protracted Conflict." *National Review,* May 23, 1975, 549.

Burt, Richard. "Presidential Candidates Stake Out Divergent Ground on Foreign Policy." *New York Times,* October 19, 1980, 1.

Cadegan, Una. "The Queen of Peace in the Shadow of War: Fatima and U.S. Catholic Anticommunism." *U.S. Catholic Historian* 22, no. 4 (2004): 7–16.

Callahan, Daniel. *The Mind of the Catholic Layman.* New York: Charles Scribner's Sons, 1963.

Carey, Patrick. "American Catholic Religious Thought: An Historical Overview." *U.S. Catholic Historian* 4, no. 2 (1985): 123–42.

———. "Lay Catholic Leadership in the United States." *U.S. Catholic Historian* 8, no. 3 (Summer 1990): 223–47.

Carmines, Edward G., and Edward W. Stanley. "The Transformation of the New Deal Party System: Social Groups, Political Ideology, and Changing Partisanship among Northern Whites, 1972–1988." *Political Behavior* 14, no. 3, "Special Issue on Party Identification" (September 1992): 213–37.

Casanova, Jose. "Roman and Catholic and American: The Transformation of Catholicism in the United States." *International Journal of Politics* 6, no. 1 (1992): 75–111.

Castelli, Jim. *The Bishops and the Bomb.* Garden City, N.Y.: Image Books, 1983.

Cavanaugh, William. *The Theopolitical Imagination: Christian Practices of Space and Time.* New York: T&T Clark, 2002.

Chan, Sewell. "Is Anti-Catholicism Dead?" *New York Times,* January 13, 2010. http://cityroom.blogs.nytimes.com/2008/07/23/is-anti-catholicism-dead/.

The Chicago Declaration of Christian Concern. In *Challenge to the Laity,* edited by Ed Marciniak. Huntington, Ind.: Our Sunday Visitor, 1980.

Clermont, Betty. *The Neo-Catholics: Implementing Christian Nationalism in America.* Atlanta: Clarity Press, 2009.

Coleman, John. "Vision and Praxis in American Theology: Orestes Brownson, Jhn A. Ryan, and John Courtney Murray." *Theological Studies* (March 1976): 3–40.

————. "A Limited State and a Vibrant Society." In *Christian Political Ethics,* edited by John Coleman, 22–53. Princeton, N.J.: Princeton University Press, 2008.

Committee of Santa Fe. *A New Inter-American Policy for the Eighties.* In *Vital Interests: The Soviet Issue in U.S. Central American Policy,* edited by Bruce Larkin. London: Lynne Rienner, 1988.

Congar, Yves. "The Historical Deveopment of Authority in the Church: Points for Christian Reflection." In *Problems of Authority,* edited by John M. Todd. Baltimore, Md.: Helicon Press, 1961.

Cornell, George. "Catholic Group Praises U.S. Economy Prior to Bishops' Critique." Associated Press, November 7, 1984.

Council on Hemishpheric Affairs. "State Departments 1982 Latin American Human Rights Report." Press Release, February 11, 1983, www.coha.org/press%20 release%20archives/archives_indext.htm.

————. "Administration Engages in International Terrorism." Press Release, April 13 1984, www.coha.org/press%20release%20archives/archives_indext. htm.

————. "Senate to Vote on Funding Today for Interdiction of Non-Existent Sandinista Weapons Shipments to Salvadoran Guerrillas." Press Release, June 25, 1984, www.coha.org/press%20release%20archives/archives_indext.htm.

————. "Commensurate with its Security Needs." Press Release, February 28, 1985, www.coha.org/press%20release%20archives/archives_indext.htm.

————. "House Vote Well Intentioned but Misguided." Press Release, July 29, 1983, www.coha.org/press%20release%20archives/archives_indext.htm.

Cuervo, Robert. "John Courtney Murray and the Public Philosophy." In *John Courtney Murray and the Civil Conversation,* edited by Robert P. Hunt and Kenneth Grasso, 67–88. Grand Rapids, Mich.: Eerdmans, 1992.

Cuneo, Michael. *The Smoke of Satan.* Oxford: Oxford University Press, 1997.

Cuneo, Michael W. "Life Battles: The Rise of Catholic Militancy within the American Pro-Life Movement." In *Being Right: Conservative Catholics in America,* edited by Mary Jo Weaver and R. Scott Appleby. Bloomington: Indiana University Press., 1995.

"Current Comment: Storm Over Father Berrigan." *America,* December 1965, 736.

Davidson, James, and Dean Hoge. "Mind the Gap: The Return of the Lay/Clerical Divide." *Commonweal,* November 23, 2007, 18–19.

DeBenedetti, Charles, and Charles Chatfield. *An American Ordeal: The Antiwar Movement of the Vietnam War.* Syracuse, N.Y.: Syracuse University Press, 1990.

Deedy, John. *Seven American Catholics.* Chicago, Ill.: Thomas Moore Press, 1978.

Dinges, William. "Roman Catholic Traditionalism in the United States." In *Being Right: Conservative Catholics in America,* edited by Mary Jo Weaver and R. Scott Appleby. Bloomington: Indiana University Press, 1995.

Dogmatic Constitution of the Church, Lumen Gentium. Vatican II, November 21, 1964. http://www.vatican.va/archive/hist_councils/ii_vatican_council/documents/vat-ii_const_19641121_lumen-gentium_en.html.

Dolan, Jay. *The Immigrant Church: New York's Irish and German Catholics, 1815–1865.* Baltimore, Md.: Johns Hopkins University Press, 1975.

Dorrien, Gary. *The Neoconservative Mind.* Philadephia: Temple University Press, 1993.

———. *Neoconservatism and the Pax Americana.* New York: Routledge, 2004.

Dougherty, James. *The Bishops and Nuclear Weapons: The Catholic Pastoral Letter on War and Peace.* Hamden, Conn.: Archon, 1984.

Douthat, Ross. *Bad Religion: How We Became a Nation of Heretics.* New York: Free Press, 2012.

Dulles, Avery. *The Resilient Church: The Necessity and Limits of Adaptation.* Garden City, N.Y.: Doubleday, 1977.

———. "The Gospel, the Church, and Politics." *Origins,* February 19, 1987.

Durkheim, Emile. *The Elementary Forms of Religious Life.* Translated by Karen Fields. New York: Free Press, 1995.

Ehrman, John. *The Rise of Neoconservatism: Intellectuals and Foreign Affairs, 1945–1994.* New Haven, Conn.: Yale University Press, 1994.

"End Support for Controversial Church Councils? Yes." Editorial, *New York Times.* October 31, 1983, 55.

Evangelicals and Catholics Together. "Evangelicals and Catholics Together: The Christian Mission in the Third Millennium." *First Things,* May 1, 1994, 15–22.

———. "The Gift of Salvation." *First Things,* January 1, 1998, 20–23.

———. "Your Word Is Truth." *First Things,* August 1, 2002, 38–42.

———. "The Communion of Saints." *First Things,* March 1, 2003, 26–33.

———. "The Call to Holiness." *First Things,* March 1, 2005, 23–26.

———. "That They May Have Life." *First Things,* October 1, 2006, 18–25.

———. "That They May Have Life." *First Things,* October 1, 2006, 18–25.

———. "Do Whatever He Tells You: The Blessed Virgin Mary in Christian Faith and Life." *First Things,* November 1, 2009, 49–59.

"Ex-Treasury Chief Simon Named Foundation Head." Editorial, *New York Times.* March 2, 1977, 22.

Fassett, Thom White Wolf. "Purveyors of False Memory: Unmasking the Institute on Religion and Democracy." In *Hard Ball on Holy Ground,* 40–47. North Berwick, Me.: Boston Wesleyan, 2005.

Finke, Roger, and Roger Starke. *The Churching of America, 1776–1990: Winners and Losers in Our Religious Economy.* New Brunswick, N.J.: Rutgers University Press, 1992.

Flippens, J. Brook. *Jimmy Carter, the Politics of Family, and the Rise of the Religious Right.* Athens: University of Georgia Press, 2011.

Fooroohar, Manzar. *The Catholic Church and Social Change in Latin America.* New York: State University of New York Press, 1989.

Fowler, Robert Booth. *Believing Skeptics: American Political Intellectuals, 1945–1964.* Westport, Conn.: Greenwood Press, 1978.

Friedman, Murray. *The Neoconservative Revolution: Jewish Intellectuals and the Shaping of Public Policy.* New York: New York University Press, 2005.

Gannon, Thomas, ed. *The Catholic Challenge to the American Economy: Reflections on the U.S. Bishops' Pastoral Letter on Catholic Social Teaching and the U.S. Economy.* New York: Macmillan, 1987.

Garfinkle, Adam. *Telltale Hearts: The Origins and Impact of the Vietnam Antiwar Movement.* New York: St. Martin's Press, 1995.

Gaudium et Spes, December 7, 1965. http://www.vatican.va/archive/hist_councils/ii_vatican_council/documents/vat-ii_cons_19651207_gaudium-et-spes_en.html.

Glazer, Nathan. "The Limits of Social Policy." *Commentary,* September 1988, 51–58.

Gleason, Philip. "Catholicism and Cultural Change in the 1960s." *The Review of Politics* 34, no. 4, America in Change: Reflections on the 60's and 70's (October 1972): 91–107.

Goldman, Ari. "Catholic Bishops Criticized on Poor." *New York Times,* November 5, 1986. http://www.nytimes.com/1986/11/05/us/catholic-bishops-criticized-on-poor.html.

Goulet, Denis. "A Missing Revolution." *America,* April 22, 1966, 438–40.

Grace, J. Peter. "Facts, Credibility and the Bishops' Economic Pastoral." In *Private Virtue and Public Policy,* edited by James Finn, 59–68. New Brunswick, N.J.: Transaction Publishing, 1990.

Grubisich, Thomas. "Norman Podhoretz: New Left's Enemy from Within." *Washington Post,* April 11, 1971, G1.

Guild, William. "John Paul and the Catholic Moment." *Washington Post,* September 6, 1987, B2.

Gutierrez, Gustavo. *A Theology of Liberation.* 2nd ed. Maryknoll, N.Y.: Orbis Books, 1988.

———. "Renewing the Option for the Poor." In *Liberation Theologies, Postmodernity and the Americas,* edited by David Batstone, 69–82. New York: Routledge, 1997.

Hall, Mitchell. *Because of Their Faith: CALCAV and Religious Opposition to the Vietnam War.* New York: Columbia University Press, 1990.

Halsey, William. *The Survival of American Innocence: Catholicism in an Era of Disillusionment, 1920–1940.* Notre Dame, Ind.: University of Notre Dame Press, 1980.

Harrington, Michael. "The Welfare State and Its Neoconservative Critics." *Dissent,* Fall 1973, 435–54.

Hartmann, Hauke. "US Human Rights and Policy under Carter and Reagan, 1977–1981." *Human Rights Quarterly* 23 (2001): 402–30.

Hartz, Louis. *The Liberal Tradition in America.* New York: Harcourt, Brace and World, 1955.

Hastedt, Glenn P., and Anthony Ekserowicz. "Perils of Presidential Transition." *Seton Hall Journal of Diplomacy and International Relations* (Winter/Spring 2001): 67–85.

Hatch, Nathan. *Democratization of American Christianity.* New Haven, Conn.: Yale University Press, 1989.

———. "The Democratization of Christianity and the Character of American Politics." In *Religion and American Politics: From the Colonial Period to the Present,* edited by Mark Noll and Luke Harlow. New York: Oxford University Press, 2007.

Hehir, Bryan. "Testimony on Central America." *Origins,* April 5, 1984.

Herbutt, Paul. "Church Council Policies 'Leftist,' Institute Charges in Booklet." *Washington Post,* February 13, 1983, B6.

Herring, George. "The War that Never Seems to Go Away." In *The War that Never Ends: New Perspectives on the Vietnam War.* Lexington: University of Kentucky Press, , 2007.

Hickey, Archbishop James. "U.S. Catholic Conference Testimony on Central America." *Origins,* March 24, 1983.

———. "Steps Toward New U.S. Policy in Central America." *Origins,* November 10, 1983.

Hickey, Archbishop James, Archbishop Patrick Flores, and Archbishop Peter Gerety. "Fact Finding Mission to Central America." *Origins,* March 3, 1983.

Higham, John. *Strangers in the Land: Patterns of American Nativism, 1860–1925.* New Brunswick, N.J.: Rutgers University Press, 2002.

Hollenbach, David. "Public Theology in America: Some Questions for Catholicism after John Courtney Murray." *Theological Studies* 37, no. 2 (June 1976): 290–303.

———. *Claims in Conflict: Retrieving and Renewing the Human Rights Tradition.* New York: Paulist Press, 1979.

———. "War and Peace in American Catholic Thought: A Heritage Abandoned?" *Theological Studies* (December 1987): 711–26.

———. "Commentary on *Gaudium et Spes.*" In *Modern Catholic Social Teaching: Commentary and Interpretations,* edited by Kenneth Himes, 266–91. Washington, D.C.: Georgetown University Press, 2005.

———. "Human Rights in Catholic Thought." *America,* October 31, 2005, 16–18.

Illich, Ivan. "The Seamy Side of Charity." *America,* January 21, 1967, 88–91.

"IRD Denies Charge." *The Christian Century,* January 22, 1986, 64.

Ish-Shalom, Piki. "Theory Gets Real and the Case for a Normative Ethic: Rostow, Modernization Theory, and the Alliance for Progress." *International Studies Quarterly* 50, no. 2 (June 2006): 287–311.

Pope John XXIII. *Pacem in Terris.* April 11, 1963. http://www.vatican.va/holy_father/john_xxiii/encyclicals/documents/hf_j-xxiii_enc_11041963_pacem_en.html.

Johnson, Robert David. "The Origins of Dissent: Senate Liberals and Vietnam, 1959–1964." *The Pacific Historical Review* 65, no. 2 (1996): 249–75.

Kagan, Robert. *A Twilight Struggle: American Power and Nicaragua, 1977–1990.* New York: Free Press, 1996.

Kari, Camilla. *Public Witness.* Collegeville, Minn.: Liturgical Press, 2004.

Kelly, James. "Catholicism and Modern Memory: Sociological Reflections on Symbolic Foundations of Rhetorical Force of the Challenge of Peace." *Sociological Analysis* 45, no. 3 (Summer 1984): 131–44.

Kennedy, Eugene. *Re-Imagining Catholicism: The American Bishops and Their Pastoral Letters.* New York: Vintage Books, 1985.

Kirkpatrick, Jeane. "Dictatorships and Double Standards." *Commentary,* November 1979, 34–45.

———. "U.S. Security & Latin America." In *Vital Interests: The Soviet Issue in U.S. Central American Power,* edited by Bruce Larkin, 49–72. London: Lynne Rienner, n.d.

Komonchak, Joseph. "Interpreting the Council: Catholic Attitudes Toward Vatican II." In *Being Right: Conservative Catholics in America,* edited by R. Scott Appleby and Mary Jo Weaver, 18–35. Bloomington: Indiana University Press, 1995.

Krauthammer, Charles. "The Unipolar Moment." *Foreign Affairs* 70, no. 1 (1990/1991): 23–33.

Kristol, Irving. "Welfare: The Best of Intentions, The Worst of Results." *Atlantic Monthly,* August 1971, 45–47.

———. "American Conservatism: 1945–1995." *The Public Interest,* Fall 1995, 80–91.

———. "The Neoconservative Persuasion." *The Weekly Standard,* August 25, 2003, 23–25.

Larkin, Bruce. Foreword to *Vital Interests: The Soviet Issue in U.S. Central American Policy,* edited by Bruce Larkin. London: Lynne Rienner, 1988.

Lasch, Christopher. *The Culture of Narcissism.* New York: W. W. Norton, 1979.

Lay Commission on Catholic Social Teaching and the U.S. Economy. *Toward the Future: Catholic Social Thought and the U.S. Economy.* New York: American Catholic Committee, 1984.

———. "Liberty and Justice for All." In *Private Virtue and Public Policy,* edited by James Finn, 1–28. New Brunswick, N.J.: Transaction, 1990.

Lease, Gary. "Vatican Foreign Policy and the Origins of Modernism." In *Catholicism Contending with Modernity,* edited by Darryl Jodock, 31–55. Cambridge: Cambridge University Press, 2000.

"Lest We Forget." Editorial. *National Review,* July 18, 1975.

Linker, Damon. *The Theocons: Secular America under Siege.* New York: Doubleday, 2006.

Longley, Kyle. *Congress and the Vietnam War: Senate Doves and Their Impact on the War,* edited by David Anderson and John Ernst. Lexington: University of Kentucky Press, 2007.

Luckey, William. "The Contribution of John Courtney Murray, S.J.: A Catholic

Perspective." In *John Courtney Murray and the American Civil Conversation,* edited by Robert Hunt and Kenneth Grasson. Grand Rapids, Mich.: Eerdmans, 1992.

Luckmann, Thomas, and Peter Berger. *The Social Construction of Reality.* New York: Doubleday Books, 1966.

MacIntyre, Alasdair. *After Virtue: A Study in Moral Theory.* Notre Dame, Ind.: University of Notre Dame Press, 1984.

———. *Whose Justice? Which Rationality?* Notre Dame, Ind.: University of Notre Dame Press, 1988.

Mahoney, Daniel. *Aleksandr Solzhenitsyn: Ascent from Ideology.* Lanham, Md.: Rowman and Littlefield, 2001.

Mann, James. "Neoconservatives Aim at Liberals." *The Christian Century,* November 4, 1981, 1115–17.

———. "More 'Red' Controversy for Church Council." *U.S. News and World Report,* February 13, 1983, 36.

Maritain, Jacques. *Man and the State.* Washington, D.C.: The Catholic University of America Press, 2004.

Mathisen, James. "Twenty Years after Bellah: Whatever Happened to American Civil Religion?" *Sociological Analysis* 50, no. 2 (Summer 1989): 129–46.

McCartan, M. "American Catholic Reception of the Bishops' Program of Social Reconstruction 1919–1986: The Continuing Conflict between Catholic Social Teaching and Economic Rights and the American Way." Ph.D. diss.: Marquette University, 1994.

McCarthy, Colman. "The Council of Churches and an Attack from the Right." *Washington Post,* February 27, 1983,: H5.

McCarthy, George, and Royal Rhodes. *Eclipse of Justice: Ethics, Economics and the Lost Traditions of American Catholicism.* Eugene, Ore.: Wipf and Stock, 1992.

McElroy, Robert. *The Search for an American Public Theology: The Contribution of John Courtney Murray.* New York, N.Y.: Paulist Press, 1989.

———. "Catholicism and the American Polity: John Courtney Murray as Interlocutor." In *John Courtney Murray and the Growth of Tradition,* 1–23. Kansas City: Sheed and Ward, 1996.

McGreevey, John. "Catholics, Democrats, and the GOP in Contemporary America." *American Quarterly* 59, no. 3 (2007): 669–81.

McGrory, Mary. "Solzhenitsyn Doesn't Love Us." In *Solzhenitsyn at Harvard,* 60–62. Washington, D.C.: Ethics and Public Policy Center, 1980.

McInerney, D.Q. "The Social Thought of Jacques Maritain." *The Catholic Social Science Review* 12 (2007): 155–72.

McKenna, George. "Criss-Cross: Democrats, Republicans, and Abortion." *The Human Life Review* (Summer/Fall 2006): 57–79.

McKim, Robert. "An Examination of a Moral Argument Against Deterrence." *Journal of Religious Ethics* (Fall 1985): 279–97.

McNamara, Patrick. *A Catholic Cold War: Edmund A. Walsh, S.J., and the Politics of American Anticommunism.* New York: Fordham University Press, 2005.

Miller, John. "Foundation's End." *National Review Online,* April 6, 2005. http://www.nationalreview.com/articles/214092/foundations-end/john-j-miller (accessed October 4, 2010).

Montgomery, Paul. "Priest Lays Shift to His Peace Role." *New York Times,* December 12, 1965, 5.

Morgan, Iwan. *Beyond the Liberal Consensus: A Political History of the United States since 1965.* New York: St. Martin's Press, 1994.

"Mr. Solzhenitsyn as Witness." *Washington Post,* June 18, 1978, C6.

Muravchik, Joshua. *The Uncertain Crusade: Jimmy Carter and the Dilemmas of Human Rights.* New York: Hamilton Press, 1986.

———. *Exporting Democracy.* Washington, D.C.: American Enterprise Institute, 1992.

———. "The Neoconservative Cabal." In *The Neocons Reader,* edited by Irwin Stelzer, 241–58. New York: Grove Press, 2003.

Murray, John Courtney. "Contemporary Orientations of Catholic Social Thought on Church and State in the Light of History." *Theological Studies* 10 (June 1949): 177–234.

———. *We Hold These Truths: Catholic Reflections on the American Proposition.* New York: Rowman and Littlefield, 2005.

Nash, J. "Economic Rights: The Status of the Debate in the United States." PhD. diss.: The Catholic University of America, 1990.

National Conference of Catholic Bishops. *Human Life in Our Day.* Washington, D.C.: United States Catholic Conference, 1968.

———. *To Live in Christ Jesus.* Washington, D.C.: United States Catholic Conference, 1976.

———. "U.S. Bishops' Statement on Central America." *Origins,* December 3, 1981.

———. *Economic Justice for All.* Washington, D.C.: United States Catholic Conference, 1986.

Neuhaus, Richard John. "American Religion and the War." *Worldview,* October 1967, 9–13.

———. "Christianity Against the Democratic Experiment." *Cross Currents,* Spring 1969, 133–48.

———. "The War, the Churches, and Civil Religion." *Annals of the American Academy of Political and Social Science* 387, "The Sixties: Radical Change in American Religion" (January 1970): 128–40.

———. "American Ethos and the Revolutionary Option." *Worldview,* December 1970, 5–9.

———. "Going Home Again: America after Vietnam." *Worldview,* May 1971, 30–36.

————. "Loneliness of the Long Distance Runner." *The Christian Century,* April 26, 1972, 477–81.

————. "Sense and Nonsense about Victimless Crimes." *The Christian Century,* March 7, 1973, 281–85.

————. "Liberation Theology and the Captivities of Jesus." *Worldview,* June 1973, 41–48.

————. "A Radical Witness." *The Christian Century,* November 13, 1974, 1071–72.

————. "The Politics of Hunger." *Commonweal,* February 8, 1974, 460–63.

————. *Time Toward Home: The American Experiment as Revelation.* New York: Seabury Press, 1975.

————. "Calling a Halt to Retreat." In *Against the World, For the World: The Hartford Appeal and the Future of American Religion,* edited by Peter Berger and Richard John Neuhaus, 138–64. New York: Seabury Press, 1976.

————. "Why I Am for Carter." *Commonweal,* October 22, 1976, 683–86.

————. *Christian Faith and Public Policy.* Minneapolis: Augsburg Publishing House, 1977.

————. "Two Views on the Human Rights Amendment." *U.S. Catholic,* April 1977, 28–31.

————. "What We Mean By Human Rights and Why." *The Christian Century,* December 6, 1978, 1177–80.

————. Letter to the Editor. *New York Times,* February 12, 1979.

————. "Hyde and Hysteria." *The Christian Century,* September 10–17, 1980, 849–82.

————. "The IRD and Church Dialogue." *The Christian Century,* April 6, 1983, 317–20.

————. "Speaking for the Church to the World." *The Cresset,* August 1983, 4–10.

————. "Let the Church Be the Church." *Center Journal* (Fall 1983): 31–47.

————. *The Naked Public Square.* Grand Rapids, Mich.: Eerdmans, 1984.

————. *The Catholic Moment: The Paradox of the Church in the Postmodern World.* New York: Harper and Row, 1987.

————. "No-Fault Prophecy." *National Review,* April 10, 1987, 44.

————. "Economic Justice Requires More than Economic Justice." *Journal of Ecumenical Studies* 24, no. 3 (Summer 1987): 371–81.

————. "Christianity and Democracy." *First Things,* October 1996, 30–36.

————. "The Public Square." *First Things,* November 1998. http://www.firstthings.com/article/2009/03/a-world-of-our-own-making-50.

————. "Reflections on IRD." Address to the Board of the Institute on Religion and Democracy, October 2005. Unpublished.

————. "American Religion and the War." *Worldview,* October 10, 1967, 9–13.

Neuhaus, Richard John, and George Weigel. "Could Glasnost Make a Difference in Human Rights?" *The Wall Street Journal,* January 28, 1988, 22.

"Nicaragua Defended." *The Christian Century,* November 7, 1984, 1031–32.

Nisbet, Robert. *Community and Power.* New York: Oxford University Press, 1962.

———. *The Sociology of Emile Durkheim.* New York: Oxford University Press, 1974.

Noll, Mark. *The Scandal of the Evangelical Mind.* Grand Rapids, Mich.: Eerdmans, 1994.

———. *America's God: From Jonathan Edwards to Abraham Lincoln.* New York: Oxford University Press, 2002.

Novak, Michael. *The Open Church: Vatican II, Act II.* New York: Macmillan, 1964.

———. "Moral Society and Immoral Man." In *A Time to Build,* edited by Michael Novak, 354–69. New York: Macmillan, 1964.

———. *Belief and Unbelief: A Study of Self Knowledge.* New York: Macmillan, 1965.

———. "Stumbling Into War and Stumbling Out." In *Vietnam: Crisis of Conscience,* edited by Robert McAfee Brown, 11–47. New York: National Board of Young Men's Christian Association, 1967.

———. *A Theology for Radical Politics.* New York: Herder and Herder, 1969.

———. "Power, Disruption, and Revolution." *Cross Currents,* Winter 1969.

———. "Blue Bleak Embers ... Fall, Gall Themselves ... Cash Gold-Vermillion." In *Conspiracy: The Implications of the Harrisburg Trial for the Democratic Tradition,* edited by John Raines. New York: Harper and Row, 1974.

———. "'Family Democrats' Elected Carter." *The News and Courier,* November 11, 1976, 10A.

———. "The Closet Socialists." *The Christian Century,* February 23, 1977, 171–74.

———. "An Underpraised and Undervalued System." *Worldview,* July/August 1977, 9–12.

———. "Seven Theological Facts." In *Capitalism and Socialism: A Theological Inquiry,* edited by Michael Novak, 109–23. Washington, D.C.: American Enterprise Institute, 1979.

———. "Choosing Our King." *The News and Courier,* March 19, 1979, 10A.

———. "Changing the Paradigms: The Cultural Deficiencies of Capitalism." In *Democracy and Mediating Structures: A Theological Inquiry,* edited by John Cooper and Michael Novak, 180–200. Washington, D.C.: American Enterprise Institute, 1980.

———. "On God and Man." In *Solzhenitsyn at Harvard,* edited by Ronald Berman,131–43. Washington, D.C.: Ethics and Public Policy Center, 1980.

———. "What the Laity Can Teach the Church." In *Challenge to the Laity,* edited by Ed Marciniak. Huntington, Ind.: Our Sunday Visitor, 1980.

———. "Democracy Takes Sin Seriously." In *Solzhenitsyn and American Democracy,* 9–15. Washington, D.C.: Ethics and Public Policy Center, 1981.

———. "A Theology of the Corporation." In *The Corporation: A Theological*

Inquiry, edited by John Cooper and Michael Novak, 203–24. Washington, D.C.: American Enterprise Institute for Public Policy Research, 1981.

———. "The Moral Minority and the Savior." *National Review,* March 6, 1981, 228.

———. "Why I Am Not a Conservative." *National Review,* June 26, 1981, 726.

———. "Alasdair MacIntyre Takes Flight." *National Review,* November 13, 1981, 1349.

———. "The Snoop Report." *National Review,* December 11, 1981, 1488.

———. "Human Rights and White Sepulchres." In *Human Rights and U.S. Human Rights Policy: Theoretical Approaches and Some Perspectives on Latin America,* edited by Howard Wiarda, 79–83. Washington, D.C.: American Enterprise Institute, 1982.

———. "A Closed Church, Again." *National Review,* February 5, 1982, 113.

———. "Liberal Catholicism Will Rise Again." *National Review,* June 11, 1982, 694.

———. "Mahonyism." *National Review,* July 9, 1982, 838.

———. "The Fourteen Families." *National Review,* October 1, 1982, 1222.

———. "Making Deterrence Work." *Catholicism in Crisis,* November 1982, 4–5.

———. "The Present Crisis." *Catholicism in Crisis,* November 1982, 1–2.

———. *Confession of a Catholic.* San Francisco: Harper and Row, 1983.

———. "Rescued from Disaster: The Bishops Speak Out." In *Moral Clarity in the Nuclear Age,* edited by Michael Novak. Nashville, Tenn.: Thomas Nelson, 1983.

———. "Moral Clarity in the Nuclear Age." *Catholicism in Crisis,* March 1983. Reprinted in *National Review,* April 1, 1983.

———. "On Nicaragua." *Catholicism in Crisis,* July 1983, 1–3.

———. "To Fight or to Appease." *National Review,* July 22, 1983, 878.

———. "Democracy and Development." *Catholicism in Crisis,* September 1983, 41–46.

———. "Reflections on War and Peace." *U.S. Catholic Historian* 4, no. 1, "American Catholics: Patriotism and Dissent in War and Peace" (1984): 90–99.

———. "Reconciliation and the Russians." *National Review,* July 27, 1984.

———. "The Case against Liberation Theology." *New York Times Magazine,* October 21, 1984, 86.

———. "The Bishops and the Poor." *Washington Post,* November 13, 1984.

———. "The Two Catholic Lay Letters on the U.S. Economy." In *Challenge and Response: Critiques of the Catholic Bishops' Draft Letter on the U.S. Economy,* edited by Robert Royal, 30–32. Washington, D.C.: Ethics and Public Policy Center, 1985.

———. "Red Hats and Hinges." *National Review,* May 31, 1985, 37.

———. "With Rousseau in Latin America." *National Review,* August 23, 1985.

———. *Human Rights and the New Realism: Strategic Thinking in a New Age.* New York: Freedom House, 1986.

————. *Will It Liberate: Questions about Liberation Theology.* Manwah, N.J.: Paulist Press, 1986.

————. "Three Porcupines of Pluralism." *This World,* no. 19 (1987): 27–51.

————. "No Fault Prophecy." *National Review,* April 10, 1987.

————. "A Theology of Peace." *New York Times Book Review,* June 7, 1987: 35.

————. "The Future of Economic Rights." In *Private Virtue and Public Virtue: Catholic Thought and National Life,* edited by James Finn, 69–83. New Brunswick, N.J.: Transaction, 1990.

————. *The Spirit of Democratic Capitalism.* 2nd ed. New York Madison Books, 1991.

————. "Introduction." In *To Empower People: From State to Civil Society,* edited by Michael Novak. 2nd ed. Washington, D.C.: American Enterprise Institute, 1996.

————. *Unmeltable Ethnics: Politics and Culture in American Life.* 2nd. New Brunswick, N.J.: Transaction, 1996.

————. "Errand into the Wilderness." In *On Cultivating Liberty,* edited by Michael Novak, 259–303. Lanham, Md.: Rowman and Littlefield, 1999.

————. "Controversial Engagements." *First Things* 92 (April 1999): 21–29.

————. *Writing from Left to Right: My Journey from Liberal to Conservative.* New York: Crown Publishing, 2013.

Novak, Michael, and Robert Schifter. *Rethinking Human Rights: Speeches by the United States Delegation to the 37th Session of the United States Commission on Human Rights.* Washington, D.C.: Foundation for Democratic Education, 1981.

O'Brien, David. "Public Catholicism." *U.S. Catholic Historian* 8, no. 4, Bicentennial Symposium, "Historians and Bishops" (1989): 89–99.

————. *Public Catholicism.* New York: Orbis Books, 1996.

————. "What Happened to the Catholic Left." In *What's Left? Liberal American Catholics,* edited by Mary Joe Weaver, 255–82. Bloomington: Indiana University Press, 1999.

————. "Catholics and American Politics." *Journal of Religion and Society, Supplementary Series* 4 (2008): 20–26.

"The Obsession of Solzhenitsyn." *New York Times,* June 13, 1978, A18.

Olson, James. *Catholic Immigrants in America.* Chicago: Nelson Hall, 1987.

Pals, Daniel. *Seven Theories of Religion.* New York: Oxford University Press, 1996.

Pastor, Robert. *Condemned to Repetition: The United States and Nicaragua.* Princeton, N.J.: Princeton University Press, 1987.

Pelotte, Donald. *John Courtney Murray: Theologian in Conflict.* New York: Paulist Press, 1975.

Pickus, Robert. "Full Turn Toward Peace." *MANAS* 15, no. 6 (February 1962): 1–12.

Pickus, Robert, and Robert Woito. *To End War.* 3rd ed.. Berkeley, Calif.: World Without War Council, 1974.

Podhoretz, Norman. "A Note on Vietnamization." *Commentary* 51, no. 5 (May 1971): 6–9.

————. *The Present Danger.* New York: Simon and Schuster, 1980.

Powers, Richard Gid. "American Catholics and Catholic Americans: The Rise and Fall of Catholic Anticommunism." *U.S. Catholic Historian* 22, no. 4 (2004): 17–35.

Quinn, Bishop John. "U.S. Policy and the Conflict in Nicaragua." *Origins,* June 28, 1979.

Ramirez, Bishop Ricardo. "The U.S. Bishops' Pastoral Letter 'Economic Justice for All' Twenty Years Later." Third Annual University of St. Thomas Summer Institute, June 6, 2006. http://www.dioceseoflascruces.org/assets/bp_sp_16.pdf.

"Religion: The Little Institute Facing Goliath." *Time,* March 28, 1983, http://www.time.com/time/magazine/article/0,9171,923428-1,00.html.

"Report of the National Assembly of the Laity." In *Challenge to the Laity,* edited by Russell Barta. Huntington, Ind.: Our Sunday Visitor, 1980.

The Report of the President's National Bipartisan Commission on Central America. New York: Macmillan, 1984.

Republican Party Platforms: "Republican Party Platform of 1980," July 15, 1980. Online at Gerhard Peters and John T. Woolley, *The American Presidency Project.* http://www.presidency.ucsb.edu/ws/?pid=25844.

Ribuffo, Leo. "Jimmy Carter: Beyond the Current Myths." *Magazine of History* (Summer/Fall 1988): 19–24.

Roach, Archbishop John. "Toward a Diplomatic, Non-Military Solution in Central America." *Origins,* August 4, 1983.

Robinson, Douglas. "Catholics Picket Spellman's Office." *New York Times,* December 6, 1965, 1.

Ross, Susan. "Catholic Women Theologians of the Left." In *What's Left? Liberal American Catholics,* edited by Mary Jo Weaver and R. Scott Appleby, 19–45. Indianapolis: Indiana University Press, 1999.

Rourke, Thomas. *A Conscience as Large as the World: Yves R. Simon versus the Neoconservative Catholics.* Lanham, Md.: Rowman and Littlefield, 1997.

Rovere, Richard. "Liberal Anti-Communism Revisited." *Commentary,* September 1967.

Sanks, T. Howland, and Brian Smith. "Liberation Ecclesiology: Praxis, Theory, Praxis." *Theological Studies* 38, no. 1 (1977): 163–68.

Schindler, David. *Heart of the World, Center of the Church: Communio Ecclesiology, Liberalism and Liberation.* Grand Rapids, Mich.: Eerdmans, 1996.

Schlesinger, Arthur. "The Solzhenitsyn We Refuse to See." In *Solzhenitsyn at Harvard,* edited by Robert Berman, 63–74. Washington, D.C.: Ethics and Public Policy Center, 1980.

Schmitz, David, and Natalie Fousekis. "Frank Church, the Senate, and the Emergence of Dissent on the Vietnam War." *The Pacific Historical Review* 63, no. 4 (November 1994).

Settje, David. "Dueling Catholic Periodicals: America's and Commonweal's Perceptions of the Cold and Vietnam Wars, 1964–1975." www.catholicsocial

scientists.org. 2004. www.catholicsocialscientists.org/cssrix/article—settje .pdf (accessed October 1, 2007).

Shanberg, Sydney. "State's Eight Catholic Bishops." *New York Times,* February 13, 1967, 1.

Shelley, Thomas. "Slouching Toward the Center: Cardinal Francis Spellman, Archbishop Paul. J. Halliman and American Catholicism in the 1960s." *U.S. Catholic Historian* 17, no. 4, "Episcopal Leadership in the 1960s: Some Historical and Comparative Studies" (1999): 23–49.

———. "Biography and Autobiography: James Cardinal Gibbons and John Tracy Ellis." *U.S. Catholic Historian* 21, no. 2, "Memory and History" (Spring 2003): 31–46.

Sigmund, Paul. "The Catholic Tradition and Modern Democracy." *The Review of Politics* 49, no. 4 (1987): 530–48.

Slawson, Douglas. *The Foundations and First Decade of the National Catholic Welfare Council.* Washington, D.C.: The Catholic University of America Press, 1992.

Solzhenitsyn, Alexsandr. "A World Split Apart." In *Solzhenitsyn at Harvard,* edited by Robert Berman, 3–22. Washington, D.C.: Ethics and Public Policy Center, 1980.

———. "Men Have Forgotten God." *National Review,* May 10, 1983, 872–76.

Steinfels, Peter. *The Neoconservatives: The Men Who Are Changing American Politics.* New York: Simon and Schuster, 1979.

Stricherz, Mark. "Goodbye, Catholics." *Commonweal,* November 5, 2005, 9–13.

———. *Why the Democrats Are Blue.* New York: Encounter Books, 2007.

Strong, Robert A. *Working in the World: Jimmy Carter and the Making of American Foreign Policy.* Baton Rouge: Louisiana State University Press, 2000.

Taffet, Jeffrey. *Foreign Aid and Foreign Policy: The Alliance for Progress in Latin America.* New York: Routledge, 2007.

Taylor, Andrew. "The Ideological Development of the Parties in Washington, 1947–1994." *Polity* 29, no. 2 (Winter 1996): 273–92.

"Theology and Philosophy in Public: A Symposium on John Courtney Murray's Unfinished Agenda." *Theological Studies* 40, no. 4 (1979).

"They Come to Listen in Cherry Blossom Time." *The Christian Century,* May 1, 1985, 439–40.

Tomes, Robert. *Apocalypse Then: American Intellectuals and the Vietnam War, 1954–1975.* New York: New York University Press, 1998.

Tschannen, Olivier. "The Secularization Paradigm: A Systematization." *Journal for the Scientific Study of Religion* 30, no. 4 (1991): 395–415.

"Vatican Communique on the Informal Consultation on the War and Peace Pastoral." *Origins,* February 3, 1983.

Veroli, Robert Di. "Catholic Bishops, Laity Debate Role of Capitalism: Documents Illustrate Two Approaches to Economic System." *San Diego Union Tribune,* March 2, 1985.

Wall, James. "Neoconservatives Aim at Liberals." *The Christian Century*, November 4, 1981, 1115–17.

———. "Reds: A Timely Film on Political Religion." *The Christian Century*, December 23, 1981, 1331–32.

———. "Anticommunism Binds IRD to White House." *The Christian Century*, November 28, 1984, 1115–16.

———. "They Come to Listen in Cherry Blossom Time." *The Christian Century*, May 1, 1985, 440.

———. "Playing for Peace on the World Stage." *The Christian Century*, December 4, 1985, 1107–08.

Walsh, James. *The Thirteenth: Greatest of Centuries*. New York: Catholic Summer School Press, 1912.

Wattenberg, Ben. *Fighting Words: A Tale of How Liberals Created Neoconservatism*. New York: St. Martin's Press, 2008.

Weaver, Mary Jo. "Introduction: Who Are Conservative Catholics?" In *Being Right: Conservative Catholics in America*, edited by R. Scott Appleby and Mary Jo Weaver, 1–16. Bloomington: Indiana University Press, 1995.

———. "Introduction." In *What's Left? Liberal American Catholics*, edited by Mary Jo Weaver. Bloomington: Indiana University Press, 1999.

Weigel, George. "The Common Covenant: Catholic Theology and American Civil Religion." *Chicago Studies* 15 (Summer 1976): 209–21.

———. "Hard-Nosed Idealism: A Model for Disarmament." *America*, October 1, 1977, 186–88.

———. "The Catholics and the Arms Race: A Primer for the Perplexed." *Chicago Studies* 18 (Summer 1979): 169–95.

———. *The Peace Bishops and the Arms Race: Can Religious Leadership Help in Preventing War?* Chicago: World Without War Council, 1982.

———. Untitled essay. *Center Journal* 1, no. 3 (Summer 1982): 73–83.

———. *Peace and Freedom: Christian Faith, Democracy, and the Problem of War*. New York: Institute on Religion and Democracy, 1983.

———. "Beyond the Challenge of Peace: Quaestiones Disputatae." *Center Journal* 2 (Winter 1983): 101–21.

———. "Making Deterrence Work." *Catholicism in Crisis*, January 1983, 13–17.

———. "Christian Century Foundation Colloquium." *Catholicism in Crisis*, May 1983, 23–26.

———. "Public Nudity?" *This World* 9 (1984): 117–19.

———. Review of Joshua Muravchik's *The Uncertain Crusade: Jimmy Carter and the Dilemmas of Human Rights Policy*. *World Affairs* 148, no. 2 (Fall 1985): 131–34.

———. "John Courtney Murray and the American Proposition." *Catholicism in Crisis*, November 1985, 8–13.

———. "The Margin Makes the Difference: John Courtney Murray on Morality and Foreign Policy." *Catholicism in Crisis*, December 1985, 6–9.

———. "How the U.S. Catholic Bishops Missed Their Chance to Be a Force for Peace." *This World, 13* (1986): 8–26.

———. *Tranquillitas Ordinis: The Present Failure and Future Promise of American Catholic Thought on War and Peace.* Oxford: Oxford University Press, 1987.

———. "The National Interest and the National Purpose: From Policy Debate to Moral Argument." *This World* 19 (1987): 80–101.

———. "Exorcising Wilson's Ghost: Morality and Foreign Policy in America's Third Century." *Washington Quarterly,* Autumn 1987, 31–40.

———. *Catholicism and the Renewal of American Democracy.* Mahwah, N.J.: Paulist Press, 1989.

———. "When Shepherds Are Sheep." *First Things,* February 1993, 33–40.

———. "The Neoconservative Difference: A Proposal for the Renewal of Church and Society." In *Being Right: Conservative Catholics in America,* edited by Mary Jo Weaver and R. Scott Appleby, 138–62. Bloomington: Indiana University Press, 1995.

———. *Soul of the World: Notes on the Future of Public Catholicism.* Washington, D.C.: Ethics and Public Policy Center, 1996.

———. *The Truth of Catholicism: Ten Controversies Explored.* New York: HarperCollins, 2001.

———. *Witness to Hope: The Biography of Pope John Paul II.* New York: HarperCollins, 2001.

———. "Robert Pickus: A Life Lived Vocationally." *The Catholic Difference,* November 2003. www.eppc.org/publications/pubID.1926/pub_detail.asp.

———. *Letters to a Young Catholic.* New York: Basic Books, 2004.

———. "Remembering Avery Dulles, S.J." *Denver Catholic Register,* January 28, 2009.

Whitmore, Todd David. "The Growing End: John Courtney Murray and the Shape of Murray Studies." In *John Courtney Murray and the Growth of Tradition,* edited by J. Leon Hooper and Todd David Whitmore, v–xxvii. Kansas City, Kan.: Sheed and Ward, 1996.

Wientraub, Bernard. "On the Right: Long Wait for Foreign Policy Hero." *New York Times,* July 22, 1985, A12.

Wilentz, Sean. *The Age of Reagan: A History, 1974–2008.* New York: HarperCollins, 2008.

Will, George. "Solzhenitsyn's Critics." *Washington Post,* June 18, 1978, B7.

Winik, Jay. "The Neoconservative Construction." *Foreign Policy* 73 (Winter 1988–1989): 135–52.

Woodward, Kenneth, and David Gates. "Ideology under the Alms." *Newsweek,* February 13, 1983, 61.

Wuthnow, Robert. *The Restructuring of American Religion.* Princeton, N.J.: Princeton University Press, 1988.

Zotti, Mary Irene. "The Young Christian Workers." *U.S. Catholic Historian* 9, no. 4, "Labor and Lay Movements: Part Two" (1990): 387–400.

INDEX

abortion: abortion mentality, 85; Blumenthal Bill, 76, 78; Catholic Church, 73–78; human life amendment, 77, 85; *Roe v. Wade*, 7, 76–77, 85–86; socioeconomic causes, 79–80, 83–84. *See also* Catholic Church in America; *and individuals by name*

Alliance for Progress, 177; criticism of, 179–80. *See also* economic development

American Catholic Committee, 150–51

American Enterprise Institute, 20

American political thought: conservatism, 2; institutional pluralism, 19; liberalism, 86, 105–6; religious foundations, 11–13, 20, 25–26, 28–31, 36–38, 43–54, 60–62, 116

American religious thought: colonial period, 43–44; decline of denominationalism, 4; post–World War II, vii, 3–5, 29–30; secular enlightenment, 91

anti-Catholicism, 3, 51, 55

anticommunism: in American Catholicism, 138–40, 145–46; decline of, 139–42; in Vatican, 137–38, 140–42

Apostolicam Actuositatem, 214

Appleby, R. Scott: on neoconservative Catholics 11–12

Aquinas, Thomas: natural law, 64; political community, 132

Augustine: political community, 132. *See also tranquilitas ordinis*

Bell, Daniel: democratic capitalism, 24; public philosophy, 34–35. *See also tranquilitas ordinis*

Berger, Peter: mediating institutions, 17, 19; secularization, 201–3. *See also* mediating institutions

Bernardin, Joseph, Cardinal: liberalism, 9; religion and politics, 197–98

Berrigan, Daniel, viii

Blue Army of Our Lady of Fatima, 138

Boot, Max, 131

Booth, Robert: *Believing Skeptics,* 34–35

Cardinal Midsentzy Foundation, 138

Carroll, John, Bishop, 12

Carter, Jimmy: abortion, 87–88; election of *1976,* viii, 88–91; election of *1980,* 95–96; foreign policy, 96, 99–100, 166; human rights, 97–98; Notre Dame commencement, 97. *See also* White House Conference on the American Family

Castro, Fidel, 165

Catholic Church in America: abortion, 73–76; American experiment, 50–53, 55; anticommunism, 145–46; clergy/ lay roles, 208–13; integration of, 3–4, 52; liberalism, 194–95; polarization, 1–2; socialism, 160–61; trusteeism, 210; Vietnam, 133–36. *See also individual bishops by name*